INFORM

Germany, Garbage, and the Green Dot

Challenging the Throwaway Society

Bette K. Fishbein

Editor: Sharene L. Azimi

INFORM, Inc.
381 Park Avenue South
New York, NY 10016-8806
Tel (212) 689-4040
Fax (212) 447-0689

Library of Congress Cataloging-in-Publication Data

Fishbein, Bette K.
   Germany, garbage, and the green dot : challenging the throwaway society /
Bette K. Fishbein.
      p.   cm.
   Includes bibliographical references and index.
   ISBN: 0-918780-61-6
   1. Recycling (Waste, etc.)--Law and legislation--Germany. 2. Recycling
(Waste, etc.)--Government policy--Germany. 3. Packaging--Law and legisla-
tion--Germany. 4. Refuse and refuse disposal--Law and legislation--Ger-
many. 5. Recycling (Waste, etc.)-- Government policy--United States.
   6. Refuse and refuse disposal--Law and legislation--United States   I. Title.
KK6254.F57   1994
344.43'0462--dc20
[344.304462]   93-41060
                                            CIP

INFORM, Inc., is a nonprofit environmental research organization that identifies
solutions to problems related to chemical hazards, municipal solid waste, and
air quality and alternative fuels. Founded in 1974, INFORM publishes its research in books, reports, articles and a quarterly newsletter. INFORM is supported by individual, foundation, government, and corporate contributions.

Table of Contents

Tables

Figures

Acknowledgments

Preparing a report on German legislation and public policy presented IN-FORM with the challenge of understanding programs in a foreign country and, particularly, with the difficulty of getting accurate English translations of technical information. INFORM is indebted to the many people in Germany, Brussels, and the United States who helped bring this project to fruition.

First, I wish to thank each of those people listed in Appendix C who took the time to meet with me in Germany and to provide information. They include: Olaf Bandt, Jan C. Bongaerts, Bernd Buckenhofer, Bernd Franke, Rolf Friedel, Renate Fries, Hubert Gehring, Wigand Kahl, Sibille Kohler, Eberhard Kraft, Petra Löcker, Marlene Mühe, Jürgen Maas, Hans-Jürgen Oels, Helmut Paschlau, Anja Raffalsky, Maria Rieping, Erwin Rothgang, Frieder Rubik, Hans-Dieter Schulz, Rafaella Schuster, Wolfgang Schutt, Michael O. E. Scriba, Cynthia Pollock Shea, Karl-Heinz Striegel, Clemens Stroetmann, Matthias Wellmer.

Special thanks to Markus Hesse, and Marianne Guinsburg for identifying those in Germany knowledgeable about waste policy and arranging many of these appointments. Also thanks to Maggie Heller, who provided a consumer perspective, and to Carla Schulz-Hoffman, Rainer Lucas, and Uta von Winterfeld for their hospitality.

I was able to keep informed on changing developments through those in Europe who were willing to answer my many questions and provide current information and documents. Special thanks to Ines Siegler at Duales System Deutschland GmbH for her help and the voluminous statistics and press releases she provided. Also to Ursula Schliessner and Timothy Feighery in Brussels for keeping me up-to-date on developments in the European Community (EC). Very special thanks to William D'Alessandro who provided invaluable judgment and guidance in understanding the complexities of EC environmental regulations as well the new German waste policies.

I am very grateful to Sigrun Wolff Saphire for her excellent translations of the technical materials that were essential to this work.

Many reviewers offered helpful suggestions and I especially thank James McCarthy, Reid Lifset, Jack Azar, Karl-Heinz Ziwica, Bruce Smart, and Gerhärd Stark for their comments.

At INFORM I wish to thank Joanna D. Underwood, president, for her support and guidance, and Warren Muir, INFORM's science director, for contributing his technical expertise. Thanks to Sharene Azimi, editor of this report, for her incisive analysis and her major role in bringing clarity and style to the final manuscript, and to Elisa Last, production coordinator, for creative design and for assistance before and during production. Thanks also to the INFORM staff who reviewed the manuscript: Mimi Bluestone, David Saphire, John Winter, Carolyn Nunley, and Joseph Mohbat, and to Rona Hampton for her assistance in communication with Germany. Thanks to Illy Valyi and Emery Valyi for additional translations and technical advice.

I would also like to thank my husband, Peter Fishbein, for his support and patience throughout the duration of this project.

Finally, INFORM thanks the Risk Reduction Engineering Laboratory of the Office of Research and Development of the US Environmental Protection Agency for support for this research and the American Council on Germany for support for the travel in Germany. Although the information in this document has been funded almost wholly by the United States Environmental Protection Agency, it does not necessarily reflect the views of the Agency and no official endorsement should be inferred.

While this report benefitted from the help of these and many other individuals, the contents and analysis expressed are the sole responsibility of INFORM.

Preface

For US policymakers and citizens who are grappling with the question of how to handle this country's mounting municipal garbage and commercial wastes, this new INFORM report offers exciting news. *Germany, Garbage, and the Green Dot: Challenging the Throwaway Society* looks at the revolutionary approach taken by Germany to promote both recycling and source reduction — an approach that is producing results.

The sweeping new German legislation is stimulating industry efforts to reduce packaging and product waste. How is it doing this? Simply by requiring that the businesses producing packages and products be financially responsible for taking back their used materials and recycling, reusing, or disposing of them.

The Germans call the concept underlying their legislation, "making the polluter pay." Their approach is especially intriguing because it so directly rewards business innovation. Businesses that move most rapidly and effectively to cut back packaging wastes and to make products that last longer and are more easily repaired and recycled will incur the lowest recycling and disposal costs in the long run.

Over the last decade, US citizens and public and private sector leaders have worried about many aspects of the waste problem: about the fact that 252 million Americans produce more than 4 pounds of garbage per person per day — a rate that is projected to increase; about how to manage the 196 million tons of municipal solid waste generated each year — a figure that may rise to 222 million tons by the end of the century; about the costs of and political resistance to new landfills and incinerators for waste disposal; and about the complex and expensive processes required to advance recycling. Clearly, as a society we must take significant measures to reduce wastes at source.

Germany, Garbage and the Green Dot describes not only what the Germans have done in their solid waste policies, but also what difficulties they are confronting, and what impact on wastes is visible to date. INFORM has also outlined a series of questions that we believe US policymakers will need to address in considering whether and how the German concept might contribute to waste-reduction progress in our own country.

This report, like the more than 60 others that INFORM has published in the last 18 years, seeks not just to discuss the environmental problems that the United States and other industrialized countries face, but to identify practical solutions: programs and policies that work to conserve our valuable air, land, water, and natural resources and enable us to live and do business less wastefully. We hope that *Germany, Garbage and the Green Dot: Challenging the Throwaway Society* will contribute to the thinking of those government, business and environmental leaders who must chart this country's environmental course ahead.

Joanna D. Underwood
President
INFORM

Notes to the Reader

Reporting on such a dynamic subject as Germany's packaging legislation has entailed dealing with rapidly changing events. The main text of this report includes information gathered up to mid-1993, when the editorial and production processes began. The Epilogue highlights three major developments between mid-1993 and the end of that year, when the report went to press. These are:

1. The resolution of Duales System Deutschland GmbH's financial crisis of September 1993.
2. The German Federal Environment Ministry's proposed amendments to the 1991 Packaging Ordinance.
3. The political agreement reached in December 1993 on the European Community Packaging Directive.

The fact that changes are being proposed to the Packaging Ordinance makes it even more important to understand the original ordinance and why the need for change developed. Germany has not altered its goals or the principles upon which its legislation is based; rather, it is proposing a slight reduction in the mandated recycling rates and a delay in the dates by which they must be achieved.

■

Technical Notes

German unification: East and West Germany became unified on October 3, 1990, to form the Federal Republic of Germany. All national data in this report refer to the unified country unless otherwise specified.

Units of Measure: The metric system is used in Germany and throughout the European Community. This text refers to both "metric tons" and "tons" — the latter being the measurement used in the United States. The conversion table on the next page illustrates how to convert from commonly used metric measurements to US figures.

Currency: The basic unit of German currency is the Deutsche Mark, abbreviated DM. All monetary conversions in this report are based on average exchange rates from January 1992 through the first quarter of 1993. During this period the relationship between the Deutsche Mark and the dollar hovered about 1.6:1. However, when interpreting cost data, the reader is reminded that international monetary values fluctuate.

Conversion Tables

Units of Measure

To Convert:

From	To	Multiply by
Kilograms	Pounds	2.2
Metric Tons	US tons (short)	1.1
Liters	Ounces (beverages)	33.8
Liters	US gallons (garbage)	0.26
Meters	Feet	3.3

Currency

To Convert to Dollars:

From	Multiply by
Deutsche Marks (DM)	0.6
European Currency Units (ECU)	1.3
British Pounds (£)	1.7
French Francs	0.2

■

Terminology: Translating from German to English has posed difficulties for this study because a single word in German may have a number of different English translations. INFORM has tried to make the terminology in this report consistent and clear for the US reader.

Translations of packaging materials categories presented a particular challenge. In German, packaging made of mixed materials is called *"Verbunde,"* which was translated in source materials as "composite," "compound," or "laminate." This report refers to *"Verbunde"* as "composite." The literal translation of the German packaging material category called *"Feinblech"* is "thinsheet," which is not meaningful to the non-technical reader. This category will be called "steel," as it consists of steel barrels, drums, transport containers, pallets, and straps. In the case of paper-based packaging materials, categorized as *"Papier/Pappe/ Karton"* in German, INFORM will call the category "paper/paperboard." This is consistent with terminology used by the United States Environmental Protection Agency in *Characterization of Municipal Solid Waste in the United States, 1992 Update,* prepared by Franklin Associates, Ltd. This category includes all paper-based packaging materials, including corrugated containers.

For names of laws or ordinances, INFORM has used translations by Germany's Federal Environment Ministry, when available.

THE
REUNITED
GERMANY

DENMARK

SCHLESWIG-
HOLSTEIN

HAMBURG

MECKLENBURG-
WESTERN POMERANIA

NETHERLANDS

BREMEN

LOWER SAXONY

POLAND

BERLIN

Hanover

BRANDENBURG

NORTH RHINE-
WESTFALIA

Dortmund

Düsseldorf
Wuppertal

Kassel

SAXONY-
ANHALT

Leipzig

SAXONY

Dresden

Cologne

Bonn

BELGIUM

HESSE

THURINGIA

Wiesbaden
Frankfurt

LUXEM-
BOURG

RHINELAND-
PALATINATE

Mainz

THE CZECH REPUBLIC

SAARLAND

Heidelberg

FRANCE

Stuttgart

BAVARIA

BADEN-
WÜRTTEMBERG

Munich

AUSTRIA

SWITZERLAND

Note: Reunited Germany consists of 16 independent *Länder,* or states.
Three major cities, Berlin, Hamburg, and Bremen are also independent states.

Key: ━━━━━━ indicates the border between the former East and the
former West Germany, prior to reunification in 1990. The city of Berlin was divided between the two countries.

Chapter 1

Why Look at Germany?

The Federal Republic of Germany has initiated the world's most ambitious national solid waste policy. Aimed at promoting source reduction, reuse, and recycling, Germany's new legislation is having international repercussions. The Packaging Ordinance, passed in 1991, extends industry responsibility for its packages to the end of their life cycles, including the cost of recycling after consumers discard the packages. Germany is already circulating similar proposed legislation to extend industry responsibility for its products, specifically automobiles, electronic equipment, newspapers, and batteries. The idea of shifting responsibility for waste management from the public sector to private industry is sweeping Europe and is under consideration by some policymakers in the United States.

This report offers a detailed description of Germany's new approach — not to advocate adoption of the same policies here, but rather to increase our understanding of the German experience. This understanding can help us make informed judgments as to whether Germany's policies might help solve US problems and, if so, how they may be adapted to the specific needs of the United States.

What is Municipal Solid Waste?

The particular waste stream addressed in this report is municipal solid waste, commonly called garbage. In the United States, it consists of materials discarded by the residential, commercial, and institutional sectors, and includes paper, food, packaging, yard waste, clothing, and appliances. Commercial wastes such as corrugated boxes, wood pallets, lunchroom waste, and office paper waste are included in municipal solid waste, but industrial wastes, sludge, and ash are not. Thus, the term "packaging waste" does not include waste generated in the production of that packaging.

The definition of municipal solid waste is generally the same in Germany, but materials collected for recycling in Germany are not included in the waste stream data. Other discrepancies in definitions and methodologies of measuring waste preclude comparisons of waste generation between the two countries, as discussed in Chapter 2.

In this report, the term "waste" is used in its broadest sense: to describe materials discarded by their end users — households, businesses, and institutions. Packaging waste therefore includes all discarded packaging, including the portion that is ultimately recycled. This definition is used by the US Environmental Protection Agency and by the European Community, which divides waste into two categories: waste for recovery and waste for disposal. However, it differs from the German definition, which classifies discarded materials as either *Abfall* (waste) or *Wertstoffe* (valuable materials). The difficulty in using the German classifications in this report is that when used packaging is collected, it is often not known whether it will be recycled, burned, or landfilled. Many materials that are supposed to be recycled are dumped illegally. Therefore, for lack of better terminology at present, this report will refer to all discarded materials as waste and to recycling as one of the methods of handling this waste. Consistent terminology for materials discarded or recycled in the United States and internationally would be extremely useful for public and private sector analysts.

Municipal Solid Waste Problems in Germany and the United States

Germany is running out of disposal capacity for the waste it generates, and Germans are unwilling to site new incinerators and landfills. When the German Cabinet approved the Packaging Ordinance in November 1990, the Federal Environment Ministry (the Bundesministerium für Umwelt, Naturschutz und Reaktorsicherheit, or BMU) estimated that the former West Germany was disposing of about 32 million metric tons of municipal solid waste per year and that disposal capacity would run out in two to five years. "In order to head off a threatened waste disposal emergency as early as possible," the Ministry said, "it is necessary to take decisive waste avoidance measures."[1] (The name of this ministry includes "the environment, protection of nature and safety of nuclear reactors," but is referred to in this report simply as the Federal Environment Ministry.)

Many landfills in Germany are closing, either because they are filled or because they do not comply with strict new environmental regulations. The number of landfills in the former West Germany dropped from 4,000 in 1975 to 300 in 1991. In the former East Germany, there are 11,000 dump sites, but most of them are unregulated. About 24 percent of the waste that is disposed of in Germany is incinerated, and the remainder is landfilled. The former West Germany has 49 waste-to-energy (incineration) plants in operation, with 10 more planned or under construction, while the former East Germany has one.[2]

The crisis in Germany emanates primarily from a decline in disposal capacity, not from a surge in waste generation. Germany's population density makes it difficult to locate disposal facilities far from population centers. Opposition to the siting of new disposal facilities is so intense in Germany that election to local public office is virtually impossible for officials who support such facilities.[3] A proposal for one incinerator in Baden-Württemberg generated more than 100,000 complaints and lawsuits.[4] A new technical law mandates that valuable landfill space, in 10 years, be reserved for the residues from waste-to-energy plants, and will prohibit the direct landfilling of municipal solid waste.[5]

In the past, West Germany exported much of its waste to East Germany and other European countries. It shipped about 700,000 tons to France each year until August 1992, when France closed its borders to German garbage, leaving cities in southwest Germany — Heidelberg and Ulm, for example — searching for a place to dispose of their waste. Since the fall of Communism in Europe, Eastern Europe no longer provides cheap disposal options. The new European Community regulations on interstate shipment of waste, discussed in Chapter 12, aim at severely curtailing the export of waste for disposal and making countries self-sufficient in waste management. These measures will increase the pressure in Germany to solve its waste problem.

The United States also faces a solid waste problem. Parts of the United States are running out of places to dispose of garbage that are environmentally and politically acceptable. New York and New Jersey export waste across the country, while states such as Indiana, Michigan, Pennsylvania, and Kentucky that receive this waste are seeking to restrict these shipments. Legislation in California subjects localities to large fines if they do not reduce the amount of waste they send to disposal.

The US municipal solid waste stream has more than doubled since 1960, partly owing to increased population and partly because the average US resident produces 1.6 more pounds of garbage per day than 30 years ago, for a total of 4.3 pounds per day in 1990.[6]

As in Germany, landfills are closing in the United States, and the public has expressed intense opposition to the siting of new landfills and incinerators. Only 6,600 landfills were in operation in 1989, down from 20,000 a decade earlier. Between 1987 and 1991, plans for 121 proposed waste-to-energy plants were canceled, mainly as a result of public opposition to the siting of the facilities.[7]

Environmental concerns are feeding the popular antipathy to disposal facilities known as the NIMBY (not in my backyard) syndrome. Society has come to realize that the term "throwaway" is misleading: in practice there is no "away." Refuse can no longer be burned and dumped without intense scrutiny of the resulting environmental effects.

Solid Waste Policy Options

To address the solid waste problem, the US Environmental Protection Agency's hierarchy of solid waste policy options designates reduction of waste at source as the number one strategy, followed by recycling, with treatment and disposal last. Reducing the amount and/or toxicity of waste generated is called source reduction. Although source reduction has become a widely acclaimed strategy, it has been limited in practice.

In recent years, some municipalities have focused predominantly on recycling as the solution to their garbage problems. However, expanding recycling has not been simple because it requires additional collection, sorting, and processing systems. Moreover, the amount of materials collected has greatly outstripped the demand for these materials. Although it is desirable to recycle waste that has already been generated, there is no reason to devote scarce resources to recycling waste that need not have been generated in the first place.

Waste management professionals tend to focus on the environmental effects of disposal, but far greater environmental damage may result from the excessive and inefficient use of raw materials in the extraction and production processes. Thus the question of how to manage municipal solid waste may be seen as part of a broader issue: resource management. Resource management requires policies that encourage reduction, reuse, and recycling not only to curb the growing waste stream but also to conserve for future generations our natural resources: air, water, land, energy, and raw materials.

Learning from the German Approach

Germany's waste policy incorporates a new approach that, by shifting responsibility and incentives, aims to promote improved resource management through both source reduction and recycling. Understanding the German system in some detail is necessary if US policymakers are to learn from Germany's recent initiatives, particularly with respect to the top waste policy option in the United States — source reduction. What is Germany trying to accomplish? What strategies are being used? How much do the systems cost? What problems and successes can be documented? By pro-

---

Figure 1-1: The German Packaging Ordinance at a Glance

Underlying Principles

Goals: 1. Reduce packaging waste requiring disposal.
2. Develop a sound materials policy.

Concepts: Industry should pay for managing the waste generated by packages.
Strategy: Make industry take back, reuse, and/or recycle
packaging materials independent of the public waste
management system.

Implementation
- Government-mandated recycling rates
- Government-mandated refilling rates for beverages
- Materials industries' responsibility for recycling
- Industry-imposed packaging fees
- Convenient collection from consumers
- Installation of bins so customers can leave outer packaging
in stores
- Preservation of existing waste management system

---

viding such information, this report aims to contribute to the discussion of the
viability of the German approach as a model for policy in the United States.

Figure 1-1 provides a snapshot view of the "Ordinance on the Avoidance of Packaging Waste," *Verpackungsverordnung,* passed in 1991. In considering whether a similar law could be adapted to US needs, one should
view the ordinance's elements both collectively and separately, because
they are not always mutually dependent. Some of the policies and strategies might be applicable here, others less so. We might choose to shift
responsibility for waste management to industry but select a different way
of doing this, such as by imposing advanced disposal fees (charging producers for the cost of recycling and disposal), rather than making industry
take back what it produces.

Goals and Philosophy

The United States shares Germany's goals of reducing the amount of waste
sent to disposal and developing a sound materials policy. The German philosophy, however, raises a basic question for policymakers: who should be
responsible for waste?

The philosophy behind the Packaging Ordinance is based on what is known in Germany, and in the field of resource economics, as the "polluter pays" principle: those who produce waste are responsible for recycling and disposing of it. In the United States today, waste management is a public responsibility, like education and fire protection, funded by taxpayers. Some critics contend that funding waste management with public money subsidizes wastefulness.[8] By shifting responsibility for waste to private industry, Germany aims to influence industry as early as the design stage to make less wasteful packages and products. Shifting the responsibility, in effect, "internalizes" waste management costs — building them into package and product prices. Key policymakers in the United States, including Senator Max Baucus, chairman of the Senate Environment and Public Works Committee, are raising the crucial issue of shifting responsibility: Should it be done here? If so, how?[9]

Strategy

Germany's basic strategy is to make industry take back what it produces. Its approach permits industry to decide on the specific implementation mechanisms, rather than having the government micro-manage the system. The German government has imposed no taxes or fees and is not involved in creating markets for recyclable materials. In fact, industry has been allowed to develop and operate its own system for taking back and recycling packaging waste, provided it meets the government quotas for recycling and refilling. This strategy relies on two basic assumptions: 1.) Industry is key to waste and materials policy because it determines what packages and products are produced; and 2.) Incentives are a more effective public policy tool for modifying industry practices than extensive government regulations. Some of Germany's strategies may not be applicable to the larger, more populous United States, with its different political and legal constraints, and some may even prove unsuccessful in Germany.

Implementation Methods

The implementation methods outlined in Figure 1-1 could be used collectively or as stand-alone measures. For example, requiring retailers to provide bins so consumers can leave outer packaging in the stores could be one part of a comprehensive packaging law in the United States, as it is in

Germany. Or it could be a singular measure taken at the federal, state, or local level to give retailers an incentive to encourage their suppliers to reduce packaging. The methods need not be implemented in the United States as they are in Germany. For example, mandated recycling or refill rates could be set at different levels from Germany's, or the fees that have been set for German packaging could be a used as a model for advanced disposal fees in the United States.

Impact of the Packaging Ordinance

Although the Packaging Ordinance was not fully implemented until January 1993, some early indications of its impact were evident when this report was prepared for publication. Some companies have changed their packages in direct response to the ordinance, or in anticipation of its implementation.

From 1991 to 1992 in Germany — a period in which the economy was growing — packaging was reduced by more than 600,000 metric tons, or about 4 percent. This reduction indicates a reversal in the trend of annual increases and represents packaging that was eliminated, reused, or made of lighter materials. But changes in packaging are not limited to reductions in weight: some companies have switched to materials that are more easily and cheaply recycled, e.g., substituting paper for plastic.

Changes made by companies in Germany include:
- Eliminating outer boxes, blister packs, and wrappings
- Reducing the size of boxes or amount of outer wrappings
- Developing reusable shipping container systems
- Selling liquid and powdered products in concentrated form
- Using refill bags or bottles for cleaning products
- Replacing packaging made of mixed materials with a single material that is easier to recycle

Moreover, the new packaging fees based on material and weight (introduced in October 1993) are expected to accelerate packaging changes by providing stronger financial incentives for companies to reduce the weight of materials and switch to materials that are easier to recycle. Recycling of packaging materials has increased in Germany, and with it have come new technologies — particularly for recycling beverage cartons and plastics.

At the same time, refill rates for beverages have increased, exceeding the requirement that the volume of beverages sold in refillable containers not fall below the level when the Packaging Ordinance went into effect.

Besides packaging, some manufacturers have also changed their products in anticipation of legislation that would apply the "polluter pays" principle to products such as automobiles and electronic equipment. Companies in these industries are volunteering to take back some of their products and have extended their concern about their products to the end of the life cycle. Thus auto and electronics manufacturers are incorporating reuse and recycling considerations into their materials selection and design processes.

In sum, application of the "polluter pays" principle in Germany is linked to a change in the way manufacturers think. Many companies are thinking about the environment when designing packages and products, as demonstrated by the innovations on the market.

An International Laboratory

As might be expected with such a bold new approach, the German system has experienced substantial difficulties. Still, it contains elements that merit serious consideration in the United States. The system's problems may be due in part to the high level of the mandated recycling rates and the speed at which they must be achieved, not to the basic concepts underlying the system. For the United States, Germany serves as a laboratory for innovative municipal solid waste policies and will provide much useful data on their impact — even given the two nations' social, political, and cultural differences, described briefly in the next chapter.

The German legislation is relevant to the United States beyond the potential for applying similar steps to alleviate US municipal solid waste problems. Many US companies sell products on the German market and must comply with German laws. US companies also compete with German companies in the global marketplace and need to understand the new rules under which German industry is operating. Moreover, the German policies have already extended well beyond Germany. The "polluter pays" principle is sweeping Europe: legislation has already been enacted in France, Austria, and Belgium, and is under consideration in many other European countries; and the European Community is adopting a modified version of the German approach in its own Packaging Directive. The Canadian government is also using Germany as a model for its new system of shared responsibility for packaging waste.

Notes

1. Federal Environment Ministry (BMU), "Packaging Ordinance Approved: Abandoning the Throwaway Society," press release, Bonn, November 14, 1990.

2. Bureau of National Affairs, "New Directive Sets Parameters for Incineration, Landfill Disposal," *International Environment Daily,* Washington, DC, September 22, 1992.

3. Hubert Gehring (BMU), "The German Packaging Ordinance," Institute of Packaging Professionals Conference: Environmental Packaging Legislation, Baltimore, MD, July 16, 1993.

4. Hubert Gehring (BMU), telephone interview, April 22, 1993.

5. Hubert Gehring (BMU), interview, Baltimore, MD, July 15, 1993.

6. Franklin Associates, Ltd., for the US Environmental Protection Agency, *Characterization of Municipal Solid Waste in the United States: 1992 Update,* Prairie Village, KS, p. ES-6 and 5-2.

7. INFORM (Bette K. Fishbein and Caroline Gelb), *Making Less Garbage: A Planning Guide for Communities,* New York, 1992, p. 14.

8. Senator Max Baucus, keynote address, US Conference of Mayors: Reality-Based Recycling II Conference, Washington, DC, April 1, 1993.

9. *Ibid.*

Chapter 2
Putting Germany in Perspective

Noting the context in which the German policy was developed, and some key similarities and differences between the two countries that affect waste policy, will help US policymakers discern the relevance of Germany's legislation for the United States.

Higher Population Density

Germany is far more crowded than the United States. Its population density is more than eight times greater, as indicated in Table 2-1. This is comparable to one-third of the US population's living in an area the size of Montana. The United States has roughly three times as many people as Germany in an area 26 times larger. Consequently, Germany has less land available for disposing of its waste, and its solid waste crisis is far more acute. Germany's greater population density has also affected the level of environmental concern in that country.

Proximity to Other Nations

Germany's proximity to other countries and its suffering from their environmental problems have increased its residents' sensitivity to environmental issues. Unlike the United States, Germany is not geographically

**Table 2-1: A Comparison of the United States and Germany –
Selected Data (1991)**

	United States	Germany
Population (millions)	252	80
Land area (000s square miles)	3,539	135
People per square mile	71	588
Number of states	50	16
GDP ($ trillions)*	5.61	1.25
GDP per capita ($)	22,204	19,500

* *Based on new measures developed by the International Monetary Fund to compare Gross Domestic Product based on purchasing power parity rather than exchange rates.*

Sources: 1.) United States Census Bureau, *Statistical Abstract of the United States, 1992;*
and 2.) Organization for Economic Cooperation and Development, *National Accounts Main
Aggregates Volume 1 (1960-1991)*, 1993.

isolated by oceans; rather, it borders nations that generate pollution, including airborne and water-borne toxics, without regard to national boundaries.

The 1986 Chernobyl nuclear accident in the former Soviet Union produced serious consequences in Germany — particularly in Bavaria, which
suffered extensive radioactive contamination. Cesium 137 activity, which
may induce genetic mutations, increased by a factor of four to six throughout Germany but by a factor of 15 in Bavaria.[1] Milk and milk products
were contaminated, as was the water in the Baltic Sea. Such events have
contributed to a greater awareness among Germans of the fragility of the
earth's environment, together with a sense of urgency to solve environmental problems. The Chernobyl accident led Germany to establish a Federal Environment Ministry.

Concern Over Damaged Forests

The Germans' love of their forests runs deep and has a long historical tradition. According to a study of green consumerism, "the upsurge in concern about the environment (in Germany) really began…when it became

clear that acid rain was destroying the much loved forests."[2] German forests are not abundant: forest area per capita there is 1.3 square kilometers as compared to 11.8 in the United States.[3] The visual impact of dying forests has played a major role in developing a consensus on the need for environmental protection policies. The problem is particularly serious at higher altitudes, where large expanses of forest on mountain summits and crests are disappearing, presenting highly visible evidence of environmental damage.[4] In the former East Germany, one-third of the forests are damaged; in the former West Germany, 16 percent.[5]

Comparable Economic Strength

A country's per capita gross domestic product (GDP) — its output of goods and services — is an indicator of its economic well-being and capacity to fund waste management. In this respect, the United States and Germany are similar. GDP in the United States in 1991 was $5.61 trillion — about four times Germany's GDP of $1.25 trillion — but per capita GDP in the two countries was $22,204 in the United States and $19,500 in Germany, as shown in Table 2-1.

The financial commitment to environmental protection was similar in the former West Germany and the United States. West Germany spent about 1.6 percent of GDP on environmental protection in 1990, compared with about 1.4 percent in the United States. In both countries, industry contributed 59 percent of this expenditure.[6] Data for the former East Germany are not available.

Strong Environmental Commitment

Germany's raw material and energy resources are more limited than those of the United States; consequently, it has a tradition of conservation. Through a month-long series of personal interviews with German industry, business, government, consumer, and environmental representatives, INFORM found a general commitment to protecting the environment and working collectively and individually to that end.

INFORM's impressions are consistent with survey findings in Europe that "for German consumers environmental awareness is the norm not the exception" and that "German consumers are much 'greener' than the Dutch or the British."[7] A world environmental survey found that Germany was not quite in the same league as Sweden, which the survey rated the "greenest" nation worldwide, but that Germany has been "recognized as a green opinion leader for many years" and that "West German regulations have been among the toughest in the world."[8]

Consumer participation in environmentally favorable practices is widespread in Germany. As discussed in Chapter 7, Germans bring back most of their beverage bottles for refilling. They are accustomed to depositing recyclable materials such as glass and paper at the drop-off containers conveniently placed throughout cities and towns. Even in cities, Germans use bicycles as a mode of transportation more than US residents do.

In German hotels, signs in the bathrooms note that, to help the environment, fresh towels are provided only on request. Plastic bags are not generally provided in hotel rooms, nor are the free bath and beauty products commonly provided in the United States. Furthermore, Germany's industrial output per unit of energy is higher than that of the United States, partly owing to policies that favor efficiency.[9] Gasoline, for example, is taxed much more heavily in Germany and in all of Europe than in the United States, resulting in higher prices and thus incentives to make or buy more fuel-efficient cars.[10]

While not comprehensive, these examples indicate the context in which the Packaging Ordinance was passed: in a country marked by pervasive concern for conserving materials and energy at the individual, institutional, and national levels and driven by a high level of general environmental concern.

Waste Generation: Difficult to Make International Comparisons

According to data published by the Organization for Economic Cooperation and Development (OECD), waste generation in Germany is 318 kilograms per person per year as compared to 864 kilograms per person per year in the Unites States.[11] This might suggest that the average person in the United States generates two to three times as much garbage as the average person in Germany. However, data for the two countries are not comparable: the German data do not include materials collected for recycling, nor do they include some commercial waste, both of which are included in the US data. International comparisons of waste generation are usually unreliable because countries use different data collection methodologies and different definitions of waste.

An estimate of per capita generation in Germany that is somewhat more comparable to that in the United States can be made by adding recycling quantities to the German data. Germany disposes of about 40 million metric tons of municipal solid waste each year and recycles an estimated 10 million metric tons, meaning generation is about 50 million metric tons, for an estimated 625 kilograms per person per year (compared with 864 in the United States).[12] Nonetheless, other discrepancies remain, and reconciling waste generation data for the two countries is beyond the scope of this report. INFORM's observations in Germany support the hypothesis that, on average, less waste is generated per person in Germany than in the United States, but accurate data to confirm this are lacking.

Germany's attempts to compile waste statistics were complicated by the unification of the country in 1990. Until then, West Germany collected data, but East Germany collected very little. German reports indicate that the average household waste per person per year, prior to unification, was twice as high in West Germany as in East Germany, but generation in the former East Germany has increased rapidly, reducing the disparity.[13] A reminder: throughout this report, data for Germany refer to the unified country unless otherwise specified.

Similar Solid Waste Management Structures

Both the United States and Germany are federal democracies. Germany is a federation of 16 *Länder* that have a role roughly comparable to the 50 US states. The allocation of responsibility for solid waste management across the levels of government is similar in the two countries. Solid waste management is primarily the responsibility of local and regional governments (cities and counties), although the federal government has played a much larger role in waste policy in Germany.

Green Party Promotes Environmental Agenda

In the 1980s, Germany was home to the world's largest, most dynamic, and most successful Green Party (Die Grünen).[14] Founded in the late 1970s as a protest group opposed primarily to nuclear power, the Greens broadened their environmental agenda and increased their vote from 5.6 percent in 1983 to 8.3 percent in 1987 — giving them 42 seats in the Bundestag (Parliament) in 1987.[15] The Greens greatly increased Germans' awareness of environmental issues and promoted environmental legislation. However, they suffered from internal dissension which ultimately caused the Green Party's decline.

Nonetheless, much of the Green agenda has been adopted by the traditional parties. Indeed, Environment Minister Klaus Töpfer of the conservative Christian Democratic Union (CDU) is driving the innovative policies on municipal solid waste. The Greens still hold elective office at the state and local levels and remain powerful in some regions.

In May 1993, the Green Party of the former West Germany and the former East German party Alliance '90 merged. The new party is called Alliance '90/ Greens, but will use Greens as its abbreviated name. The merger's purpose was to enable the Greens to regain enough political strength in the 1994 elections to become the country's third largest political party after the Christian Democratic Union and the Social Democratic Party (SPD). The new party will be committed to "human rights, ecology, democracy, social justice and the equality of men and women," and will try to reconcile the agenda of the ecology-minded western Greens with that of the former East German group, which was founded to support human rights and oppose the former Communist regime.[16]

Notes

1. Federal Environmental Agency (UBA), *Facts and Figures on the Environment of Germany: 1988/89,* Berlin, p. 218.

2. Michael Peters Brand Development Division and Diagnostics Market Research Ltd., *Green, Greener, Greenest: The Green Consumer in the UK, Netherlands and Germany,* London, September 1989, p. 19.

3. Organization for Economic Cooperation and Development, *OECD Environmental Data 1991,* Paris, 1991, p. 87.

4. Federal Environmental Agency (UBA), *op. cit.,* p. 89-90.

5. "German Forests Continue to Die," *Europe Environment No. 398,* Europe Information Service, Brussels, November 17, 1992, p. 12; and Federation of German Industries (BDI), "International Environmental Policy — Perspectives 2000," Cologne, May 1992, p. 11.

6. INFORM estimates based on GNP data in BDI, "International Environmental Policy," *op. cit.,* p. 8.

7. Michael Peters Brand Development Division, *op. cit.,* p. 127 and 146.

8. John Elkington, *The Green Wave: A Report on the 1990 Greenworld Survey,* compiled by Sustainability, London, 1990, p. 51-52.

9. Organization for Economic Cooperation and Development, *op. cit.,* p. 193.

10. US Energy Information Administration, *International Energy Annual,* Washington, DC, 1992; and International Energy Agency, *Energy Prices and Taxes 1992,* Paris, 1993.

11. Organization for Economic Cooperation and Development, *op. cit.,* p. 133.

12. Hans-Jurgen Oels (Federal Environmental Agency [UBA]), telephone interview, April 27, 1993.

13. Thomas Rummler and Wolfgang Schutt, *The German Packaging Ordinance: A Practical Guide with Commentary,* Hamburg: B. Behr's Verlag GmbH & Co., 1990, p. 3.

14. Jonathan Porritt and David Winner, *The Coming of the Greens,* London: Fontana Collins, 1988, p. 212.

15. *Ibid.,* p. 214.

16. Stephen Kinzer, "Green Party Merges with an East German Group," *The New York Times,* January 20, 1993, p. A7.

Chapter 3

German Ordinance on the Avoidance of Packaging Waste

On June 12, 1991, the German Packaging Ordinance requiring industry to take back, reuse, and/or recycle packaging materials went into effect. Klaus Töpfer, head of the Federal Environment Ministry (Bundesministerium für Umwelt, Naturschutz und Reaktorsicherheit, or BMU), had earlier claimed that "this ordinance, unlike any other regulation taken up to now, marks the final abandonment of the throwaway society."[1] By making industry take back its packaging, the ordinance shifts the burden of managing packaging waste from municipal authorities to manufacturers, distributors, and retailers. The goal is to give private industry the incentive to consider the solid waste consequences when it designs packages — to envision how the package will be reused or recycled, and what that will cost. Clearly, the company can benefit financially if the package is eliminated or reduced.

Making the "Polluter Pay"

For the first time anywhere, the ordinance applied the "polluter pays" principle to municipal solid waste. According to the Federal Environment Ministry, "Public financing of all environmental protection measures from taxpayers' money is not the way to go. The German key concept, rather, is the polluter-pays principle. The costs of preventing and reducing damage to the environment must be born by those who make use of it."[2] Public funds will no longer be used to manage packaging waste.

Under this pioneering legislation, industry retains responsibility for its packages after they have been discarded by consumers. Consumers, however, share the cost. Industry is expected to incorporate the collection, sorting, recycling, and disposal costs into the price of packages and products. The legislation contains no specific mandates for consumers.

The mandate for industry to "take back" packaging is not meant literally; very few companies will physically take back their own packages under the Packaging Ordinance. To this extent, take-back is more of a theoretical concept than a practical strategy. Government, business, and environmentalist leaders agree it is impractical to require the extra shipping that would be entailed in making producers literally take back billions of packages each year. The strategy entails a shift in financial responsibility to industry, but companies may arrange for third parties to actually manage the waste. Thus waste continues to be collected by a combination of municipal workers and private carters.

Background on the Passage of the Ordinance

The authority for the Packaging Ordinance is Germany's "Waste Avoidance and Waste Management Act," *Abfallgesetz*, of August 1986, which empowered the federal government to regulate the flow of packages and products so they can be returned for "environmentally friendly" reprocessing. At first, Germany tried a voluntary approach, asking industry to reduce packaging and increase recycling. When this tactic failed, the government introduced the legislation that became law on June 12, 1991.[3]

When the Bundesrat, the upper house of Parliament, was considering the proposed new law, the *Länder*, or states, demanded stricter measures, including regulation of excessive and environmentally damaging packaging, labeling of plastics, and higher mandated rates for refilling beverage containers. The federal government argued that such regulations required notification to the European Community and would cause lengthy delays in passing the ordinance. The states' representatives in the Bundesrat agreed to drop their proposed amendments but adopted a resolution calling for supplementary measures to strengthen the ordinance. One such proposal, on refillable beverage containers, was being circulated in mid-1993, as discussed in Chapter 7.

The driving force behind the Packaging Ordinance was Dr. Klaus Töpfer, who has been Germany's Environment Minister since May 7, 1987, longer than any other environment minister in the European Community. Töpfer, a former professor of economics and regional planning, has also held high-level leadership positions in the Christian Democratic Union (CDU) — the party of Chancellor Helmut Kohl.

The Packaging Ordinance is but the first in a series of German ordinances based on the "polluter pays" principle. It is the prototype for proposed ordinances that would require industry to take back automobiles, electronic equipment, newspapers, and batteries — to "internalize" the costs of waste management, an approach long advocated by economists but never before implemented for municipal solid waste on such a broad scale.

Internalization of costs is an economics term used, in this case, to mean that producers of packages and products are made to pay the costs of collecting, sorting, recycling, and disposing of their materials. They are prohibited from placing the financial burden on the public waste management system. However, these internalized costs are expected to show up in increased prices of those packages and products.

Why Target Packaging?

Packaging was targeted in Germany because it accounts for about 50 percent of the volume and 30 percent of the weight of municipal solid waste, making it one of the largest sources of municipal solid waste in Germany. Of the packaging sent to disposal, about 70 percent is landfilled and 30 percent incinerated. The capacity of these disposal facilities is fast running out.[4]

Another reason for targeting packaging was the long dispute with the European Commission — the European Community's executive body — over Germany's ordinance requiring the return of and mandatory deposits on one-way plastic beverage containers. The EC Commission argued that legislation singling out one type of packaging was discriminatory. To avoid such charges, the Packaging Ordinance extends the return and deposit mandates to all packaging.[5]

Provisions of the Ordinance

The Packaging Ordinance, which is reprinted in full in Appendix A, requires that industry, not the public waste management system, take back, reuse, and/or recycle all one-way packaging, including packaging on imported products. It applies to all one-way packaging on the German market except materials with hazardous residues, subject to other regulations. Hazardous residues include waste contaminated by pesticides, disinfectants, solvents, acids, and mineral oils.

The ordinance sets out four major objectives:[6]

1. Packaging should be made from "environmentally responsible" materials compatible with recycling.
2. Weight and volume should be minimized.
3. Packaging should be refillable, if feasible.
4. Packaging should be recycled if it cannot be refilled.

While these are objectives rather than legal obligations, they do indicate the high priority the government gives to waste avoidance and refilling.

The ordinance divides packaging into three categories:

1. **Transport** — packaging used to ship goods to retailers (e.g., crates, pallets, corrugated containers).
2. **Secondary** — additional packaging designed to facilitate self-service sales, to prevent theft, or to advertise and market the product (e.g., outer boxes, foils, blister packs).
3. **Primary** — the basic package that contains the product (e.g., soup can, jam jar, soap powder box).

The Federal Environment Ministry distinguishes among these categories based on when the package "loses its function." Transport packaging loses its function at the store when goods are stacked on the shelves. Secondary packaging, always a second or third layer around a primary package, loses its function at the retail cash register. Primary packaging, typically used until the product is consumed, loses its function with the consumer.

The ordinance sets deadlines for industry to begin taking back, reusing, or recycling each of the three packaging categories:

- **December 1991.** Manufacturers and distributors had to take back transport packaging.
- **April 1992.** Retailers had to install marked bins so customers could leave secondary packaging in the stores.
- **January 1993.** Customers could return primary packaging to retailers. A minimum mandatory deposit is imposed on nonrefillable beverage containers, washing and cleansing agent containers, and emulsion (water-based) paint containers. The deposit on beverage and cleansing agent containers of 0.2 liter and over = DM0.50 ($0.30), 1.5 liter and over = DM1.00 ($0.60); the deposit on paint containers of 2 kg and over = DM2.00 ($1.20).

The regulation of transport and secondary packaging went into effect as scheduled. However, the ordinance provided an exemption to the primary packaging regulations if industry proposed an alternative, privately financed plan that could meet the specified goals for collecting and sorting packaging materials and for refilling beverage containers.

That exemption was granted for such an alternative industry plan. Known as the "Dual System," it is run by the private company Duales System Deutschland GmbH (DSD), which is described in Chapter 6. The exemption means stores need not take back primary packaging and collect the mandatory deposits described above, provided that the collection, sorting, and refill quotas specified in the ordinance are met. If DSD fails, retailers will have to accept primary packages returned to the store.

The ordinance specifies two sets of goals related to one-way primary packaging in Germany: the quotas for collecting packaging waste and the quotas for sorting the collected materials. Assuming all sorted materials are delivered to recyclers, the recycling quota is the product of the collection and sorting quotas set out in the ordinance. These goals are illustrated in Tables 3-1 through 3-3.

Table 3-1: The Ordinance's Collection Quotas for One-Way Packaging

Material	January 1993 (% by weight)	July 1995 (% by weight)
Glass	60	80
Tinplate	40	80
Aluminum	30	80
Paper/Paperboard	30	80
Plastic	30	80
Composite*	20	80

Mixed materials as described on page 30.

Source: Federal Environment Ministry (BMU), *Ordinance on the Avoidance of Packaging Waste,* June 12, 1991.

Table 3-2: The Ordinance's Sorting Quotas for Collected One-Way Packaging

Material	January 1993 (% by weight)	July 1995 (% by weight)
Glass	70	90
Tinplate	65	90
Aluminum	60	90
Paper/Paperboard	60	80
Plastic	30	80
Composite	30	80

Source: same as Table 3-1.

Table 3-3: Implied Recycling Quotas Calculated from the Ordinance's Collection and Sorting Quotas for One-Way Packaging

	January 1993 (% by weight)	July 1995 (% by weight)
Glass	42	72
Tinplate	26	72
Aluminum	18	72
Paper/Paperboard	18	64
Plastic	9	64
Composite	6	64

Source: INFORM. The recycling quota is the product of the collection and sorting quotas shown in Tables 3-1 and 3-2.

Collection Quotas

The collection quotas stipulate, for example, that by January 1993, 60 percent of glass containers and 30 percent of paper (by weight) had to be collected. These lower initial rates represented the transitional phase for operating the Dual System, allowing time for establishment of an expanded recycling system. From January 1993 through June 1995, the individual quotas are to be waived if 50 percent (by weight) of the collective sum of these packaging materials are collected. By July 1995, 80 percent by weight of each of the materials must be collected. This ambitious figure assumes that, if waste is collected from every household, German consumers will have placed 80 percent of these recyclable packaging materials into the proper bins for collection.

Sorting Quotas

After collection, packaging materials must be sorted (separated) and sent to recyclers at the rates specified in Table 3-2. For example, by January 1993, 60 percent of the collected paper had to be sorted for recycling; by July 1995, 80 percent must be sorted. As in the case of collection quotas, lower initial rates, particularly for plastics and composites, allowed time to set up new sorting and recycling facilities and took into account the contamination of some of the materials collected. Given the July 1995 sorting quotas of 80 to 90 percent, the ordinance allows a 10 to 20 percent margin for nonrecyclable, or contaminated, materials.

A major dispute erupted in June 1993 over whether the sorting quota for plastics applied to the amount of material required to be collected or the amount actually collected; i.e., how should the system handle the plastics collected in excess of the collection quota? The dispute and its resolution are discussed in Chapters 6 and 8.

Implied Recycling Quotas

Although the legislation does not include explicit recycling quotas, the effective recycling quota (as shown in Table 3-3) can be calculated because the ordinance calls for all sorted material to be delivered to recyclers. Thus, the recycling quota is the product of the collection and sorting quotas. By July 1995, for example, 80 percent of glass containers must be collected and 90 percent of that amount must be sorted, for an effective recycling rate of 72 percent. The recycling rate in this context is the percentage of primary packaging delivered to recyclers and does not take into account processing losses in recycling facilities.

Incineration, called "thermal recycling" by some industry advocates when it is used to recover energy from burning waste, is not permitted as a method to meet the quotas. However, "chemical recycling" of plastics, a set of processes that break down plastics into their basic components, such as liquid petrolem (as described in Chapter 8), will be permitted. No quotas were set for materials whose contribution to packaging waste is small, such as wood, ceramic stoneware, and fabrics.

To qualify for the exemption from the primary packaging take-back and deposit mandates in the ordinance, Duales System Deutschland (DSD) must ensure that the refill rates for beverages do not decline below the average refill rates in West Germany in 1990. The refill rate for milk must not fall below 17 percent, and the refill rate for all other beverages (beer, bottled water, soft drinks, juices, wine) must not fall below 72 percent nationwide. Moreover, the refill rates in each state must not fall below the average rate in that state in 1991, when the ordinance took effect.

Packaging Statistics

The ordinance requires the federal government to publish packaging statistics in the *Bundesanzeiger (Federal Bulletin)* every three years. These must include the average amount of packaging consumed per person in each state, classified by type of packaging material. The statistics will form the baseline data against which the amounts collected will be compared; the data may be used to calculate changes in the amount of packaging used. The official 1991 data were published, several months behind schedule, in January 1993. Tables 3-4 and 3-5 summarize those data, which were prepared by the Group for Packaging Market Reserach (Gesellschaft für Verpackungsmarktforschung, or GVM), a private firm under contract with the government. The German government is also required to publish annual data on the percentage of beverages sold in refillable containers. These data, also prepared by GVM, are presented in Chapter 7.

Table 3-4: Packaging Consumption* in Germany 1991

(thousands of metric tons)

[Total packaging, less toxics, less refillables = packaging covered by the ordinance]

Material		Total Packaging		Toxics
Glass		4636.8		4.7
Tinplate**		793.1		77.1
Aluminum		124.0		1.3
Plastic		1606.5		60.1
Paper/Paperboard		5206.6		18.7
Composite				
a. Beverage cartons	198.2		–	
b. Paper-based	177.9		2.8	
c. Plastic-based	28.0		–	
d. Aluminum-based	6.8		0.1	
Composite total		410.9		2.9
Subtotal (quota materials)		*12,777.9*		*164.8*
Steel***		305.8		99.7
Wood, cork		2249.9		–
Other		13.5		–
Subtotal (non-quota materials)		*2569.1*		*99.7*
TOTAL		15,347.1		264.5

*   *As discussed in Chapter 1, Germany classifies discarded materials as waste (Abfall) or valuable materials (Wertstoffe). The total amount of packaging consumption includes both Abfall and Wertstoffe, and corresponds to the US term "packaging waste."*

**   *Coated steel cans for consumer goods, mostly food and beverages.*

***   *Steel barrels, drums, transport containers, pallets, and straps.*

Source: Federal Environment Ministry (BMU), prepared by Gesellschaft für Verpackungs-marktforschung (GVM), *Bundesanzeiger*, January 16, 1993.

Refillables	Packaging Covered by Ordinance
819.3	3812.8
–	716.0
–	122.7
172.4	1374.0
19.6	5178.3

Refillables	Packaging Covered by Ordinance
198.2	–
175.1	–
28.0	–
6.7	–

Refillables	Packaging Covered by Ordinance
–	408.0
_1001.3_	_11,611.8_
187.3	18.8
1188.2	1061.7
–	13.5
_1375.5_	_1094.0_
2376.8	12,705.8

Table 3-5: Packaging Consumption* Covered by the Ordinance 1991

(thousands of metric tons)

[Secondary + transport + primary packaging = packaging covered by the ordinance]

Material	Secondary	Transport
Glass	–	–
Tinplate**	–	1.8
Aluminum	–	–
Plastic	9.5	314.4
Paper/paperboard	46.5	2867.3
Composite		
a. Beverage cartons	–	–
b. Paper-based	–	0.3
c. Plastic-based	–	0.2
d. Aluminum-based	–	–
Composite total	–	0.5
Subtotal (quota materials)	*56.0*	*3184.0*
Steel***	–	9.7
Wood, cork	0.7	1030.5
Other	–	–
Subtotal (non-quota materials)	*0.7*	*1040.2*
TOTAL	56.7	4224.2

*   *As discussed in Chapter 1, Germany classifies discarded materials as waste (Abfall) or valuable materials (Wertstoffe). The total amount of packaging consumption includes both Abfall and Wertstoffe, and corresponds to the US term "packaging waste."*

†   *Primary packages for goods shipped to large companies.*

**   *Coated steel cans for consumer goods, mostly food and beverages.*

*** *Steel barrels, drums, transport containers, pallets, and straps.*

Source: Federal Environment Ministry (BMU), prepared by Gesellschaft für Verpackungsmarkt-forschung (GVM), *Bundesanzeiger,* January 16, 1993.

	Primary	Industrial Primary[†]	Packaging Covered by Ordinance
	3812.8	–	3812.8
	703.4	10.8	716.0
	122.7	–	122.7
	927.6	122.5	1374.0
	1553.5	711.0	5178.3
198.2		–	198.2
174.7		0.1	175.1
27.7		0.1	28.0
6.7		–	6.7
	407.3	0.2	408.0
	_7527.3_	_844.5_	_11,611.8_
	1.7	7.4	18.8
	28.7	3.8	1061.7
	6.1	7.4	13.5
	_36.5_	_18.6_	_1094.0_
	7561.8	863.1	12,705.8

As shown in Table 3-4, the take-back requirement of the ordinance covers approximately 12.7 million metric tons of packaging, of a total 15.3 million metric tons consumed. The difference is accounted for by packaging that has been contaminated by toxics and refillable packaging not subject to the take-back provisions.

Table 3-5 shows the breakdown of packaging covered in the ordinance by package category and material type. About one-third of this total is transport packaging, and about two-thirds is primary packaging. Secondary packaging represents less than 0.5 percent of the total. The materials aggregated in the subtotal for non-quota materials will be collected by DSD but are not subject to specific collection and sorting quotas.

Throughout this report, "composite" describes packaging made of mixed materials — called *Verbunde* in German. Packaging falls into this category when the consumer cannot separate the constituent materials: for example, the layers of plastic and metal bonded together in an aseptic milk or juice carton. (Aseptic processing entails ultra-high heating of a product and immediate cooling. The sterilized product is packaged in a sterilized multilayer container, which can preserve its contents for months without refrigeration.) Mixed-material packaging that can be separated — for example, foil and paper wrappers around a chocolate bar — are not composite packaging. Composite packaging has been differentiated into four groups (shown in Table 3-5).

Role of Consumers

As noted earlier, the Packaging Ordinance imposes no direct obligations on consumers. The ordinance's success, however, depends on their cooperation in putting used packaging in the proper bins and returning refillable containers. Some local laws prohibit placing recyclable materials into regular garbage bins, but there is no such federal law.

The Ordinance and the
European Community (EC)

The German government took great care to ensure that the Packaging Ordinance did not conflict with EC law; the ordinance contains no technical provisions that would require formal notification of the European Community, as this would have delayed implementation. An unofficial guide to the ordinance, *The German Packaging Ordinance — A Practical Guide with Commentary,* states: "The ordinance does no more than impose behavioural obligations on manufacturers and distributors and does not additionally establish restrictions on packaging. For this reason there are no rules relating to mandatory identification of packaging, nor to the composition of packaging. If it is decided in the future that regulations need to go further, as requested by the Bundesrat on 19 April 1991, the need for such regulations to be notified in accordance with [an EC directive]... should be taken into account."[7] The relationship of the Packaging Ordinance to the European Community is discussed more fully in Chapter 12.

The guide from which this quotation was taken was written by Dr. Thomas Rummler, who is responsible for administering the Packaging Ordinance within the Federal Environment Ministry, and Wolfgang Schutt, an industry consultant, who played a major role in developing the Dual System. Published in English and German, the guide explains in detail the ordinance's provisions and provides commentary on why certain provisions were included. Environment Minister Klaus Töpfer, in his introduction to the guide, wrote: "I am convinced that the book looks set to become a standard reference work for the practical implementation of the Packaging Ordinance." Although the guide was published privately and is not an official government document, it offers the best material available on the ordinance and the thinking behind it. It is a principal source in this report.

Notes

1. Federal Environment Ministry (BMU), "Packaging Ordinance Approved: Abandoning the Throwaway Society," press release, Bonn, November 14, 1990.

2. Federal Environment Ministry (BMU), "Germany – The Federal Environment Ministry," Bonn, August 1992 edition, p. 7.

3. Hubert Gehring (BMU), "The German Packaging Ordinance," Institute of Packaging Professionals Conference: Environmental Packaging Legislation, Baltimore, MD, July 16, 1993.

4. Federal Environment Ministry (BMU), "Packaging Ordinance Approved," *op. cit;* and Thomas Rummler and Wolfgang Schutt, *The German Packaging Ordinance: A Practical Guide with Commentary,* Hamburg: B. Behr's Verlag GmbH & Co., 1990, p. 4.

5. Rummler and Schutt, *ibid.,* p. 12.

6. Federal Environment Ministry (BMU), "Ordinance on the Avoidance of Packaging Waste" *(Verpackungsverordnung)* of June 12, 1991.

7. Rummler and Schutt, *op. cit.,* p. 33.

Chapter 4

Transport Packaging

The first part of the German Packaging Ordinance, the rules for transport packaging, took effect in December 1991. Transport packaging accounts for about one-third of packaging waste covered by the ordinance. It is defined as "drums, containers, crates, sacks, pallets, cardboard boxes, foamed packaging materials, shrink wrapping and similar coverings which are component parts of transport packaging and which serve to protect the goods from damage during transport from the manufacturer to the distributor or are used for reasons of transport safety."[1]

The ordinance requires manufacturers and distributors to "take back" transport packaging and reuse or recycle it independent of the public waste management system. However, the requirement to "take back" is not meant literally, as unnecessary shipping of waste is undesirable for economic and environmental reasons. It makes little sense for a supermarket to return shipping containers to a consumer product company, which would then have to send them to a recycler. Instead, the law allows manufacturers and distributors either to arrange for third parties to pick up used packaging or to pay the retailers to arrange for recycling.

Before the ordinance was passed, retailers had to pay to recycle or dispose of transport packaging. Under the new legislation, transport packaging must be reused or recycled, rather than burned or landfilled, and the manufacturing sector — which controls packaging decisions — is financially responsible for these steps. Although the take-back provision is intended to make manufacturers and distributors financially responsible for the reuse or recycling of the packaging, the law does not specify how payments are to be allocated; industry is free to decide how to fulfill its obligation. Companies need not take back the specific packages they shipped; rather, "the take-back obligation is limited to packages of the quantity, type, form and size" that they shipped.[2] The Federal Environment Ministry (Bundesministerium für Umwelt, Naturschutz und Reaktorsicherheit, or BMU) recommends that manufacturers obtain a certificate of recycling or reuse from third parties to prove that they have complied with the law.[3]

The manufacturers and distributors responsible for transport packaging have proposed the establishment of a company, the Group for Take-Back and Recycling of Transport Packaging (Gesellschaft zur Rücknahme und Verwertung von Transportverpackungen, or RVT), to manage the recycling of transport packaging waste nationwide. Modeled after Duales System Deutschland (DSD), RVT would collect fees from manufacturers and distributors for this service. The possibility of having DSD manage the transport waste was discussed, but the Federal Cartel Office (Bundeskartellamt) ruled this out.

Manufacturers and distributors, in general, have chosen to compensate retailers for managing the waste. Fee schedules are generally based on the materials and quantities involved. For example, Procter & Gamble GmbH, the German subsidiary of the large US-based consumer product company, pays retailers approximately DM785 ($471) per metric ton to arrange for plastics recycling and approximately DM250 ($150) per metric ton for corrugated recycling.[4] Some smaller producers have arranged to compensate the retailers about 0.1 – 0.3 percent of the value of the goods shipped.

Transport insurers have reevaluated their insurance rates out of concern for an increase in damages that might result from over-reduction of packaging.[5] However, the ordinance has spurred innovation that could reduce product damage in transport: the design of new reusable shipping container systems that are sturdier than the one-way containers they replace. According to information sheets published by the Federal Environment Ministry, "the most sensible ecological and economic solution may be multi-use [i.e., reusable] packaging."[6]

No data are available on changes in transport packaging waste resulting from the Packaging Ordinance. However, many new reusable packaging systems have been developed in response to the ordinance. Different systems have been developed for particular products such as fish, fruits and vegetables, medicine, bicycles, and furniture, as well as a system for the general line of consumer products sold in supermarkets. Two of these systems are described in the following case studies.

Case Studies: Reusable Transport Containers

Multi-use Returnable Transport Packaging System (MTS)

MTS is an example of a reusable transport packaging system, developed in response to the Packaging Ordinance by Schoeller International at the suggestion of Tengelmann. Schoeller and Tengelmann are privately held companies with international operations. Schoeller, which manufactures plastic packaging, developed the ubiquitous plastic crate for refillable bottles that it manufactures and distributes throughout the world for beverage companies, including Coca-Cola and PepsiCo. Tengelmann, described more fully in Chapter 6, owns large supermarket chains in Germany, the United States, Canada, the Netherlands, and Austria.

The MTS system, shown on the following pages, consists of modular plastic containers designed to maximize use of the standardized European shipping pallets. The crates and the straps that bind them are made of a single plastic resin, polypropylene, to facilitate recycling. The containers consist of trays on top and bottom with side frames that enable users to stack them to different heights; their five basic sizes can be built up to five different heights. The pieces disassemble and collapse to facilitate storage, and the trays may be used for displaying products on retail shelves.

A promotional videotape for MTS claims that its primary purpose is its "immense ecological advantage" over single-use containers, because the system fulfills the three "Rs" — reduce, reuse, and recycle. Use of MTS as a display tool at retail stores is being promoted as a major improvement over existing shipping containers. The system also eliminates the need for cutting corrugated cartons with a knife, a significant cause of personal injury and product

The system components:
1. Tray for bottom and lid
2. Frame for side walls

Closed container:
2 trays, 2 frames

Open container:
1 tray, 1 frame

Source: Tengelmann and Schoeller International, Munich. (Patent pending.)

Open and closed frame

Closed container:
2 trays, 1 frame

Self-supporting
packaging with
2 trays

damage in supermarkets.[7]

According to Schoeller, the MTS crates are expected to last 10 years and complete six to eight cycles a year, for a total of 60-80 cycles. The material can then be recycled four or five times into new MTS containers. Schoeller estimates that widespread use of MTS could help reduce transport packaging waste by 1 million metric tons per year.[8] Primary packaging may also be reduced, because the sturdy MTS crates will permit use of less primary packaging without causing product damage.

Schoeller has patented the crates, which are to be leased by the piece for each cycle and are not for sale to manufacturers. The containers will be serviced by MTS Ökologistik GmbH & Co. KG, a company comprised of partners in industry and trade, including major chain stores such as Tengelmann, Metro, and Rewe. The service company plans to buy the MTS containers from Schoeller and its licensees, deliver them to manufacturers, and retrieve the empty containers from the store after a single use. The MTS containers would then be transported to depots all over Europe, where they would be sorted, washed, and stored for the next delivery.

Schoeller estimated that rental costs of the MTS containers would be lower than current purchase costs for single-use corrugated, as shown in Table 4-1. For the sizes shown, the purchase price of cardboard ranges from DM0.51- 0.85 ($0.31- 0.51). This price includes the cost of disposing of the cartons, which ranges from DM0.02- 0.05. ($0.01- 0.03). The rental fee per trip of the MTS containers is lower, ranging from DM0.36- 0.80 ($0.22- 0.48). This fee includes all servicing plus amortization and administrative costs. The deposits on the MTS containers are about six times the rental fee; however, these deposits are generally accounting transactions, with no money changing hands unless MTS containers are lost or stolen. Given that stores must pay to recycle or dispose of one-way containers, and waste management costs are rapidly rising, Schoeller claims its system will be cheaper, stating that the "growing disposal expenses of one-way packages result in a growing cost advantage of MTS."[9]

Pilot tests have been conducted with such major companies as Hertie, Karstadt, Rewe, Woolworth, Colgate Palmolive, Henkel, Kraft, Lever, and Procter & Gamble. More than 70,000 trays and frames have been tested for products ranging from food to office supplies. Life-cycle analysis has been

Table 4-1: Comparative Prices for One-Way Corrugated Containers vs. Multi-use Returnable Transport Packaging System (MTS) Containers

Selected Container Sizes	Corrugated (including disposal costs)*		MTS Rental Fee		MTS Deposit	
(millimeters)	DM	($)	DM	($)	DM	($)
300 x 200 x 150	0.51	(0.31)	0.36	(0.22)	2.10	(1.26)
300 x 200 x 225	0.58	(0.35)	0.45	(0.27)	2.80	(1.68)
400 x 300 x 150	0.77	(0.46)	0.65	(0.39)	4.20	(2.52)
400 x 300 x 225	0.85	(0.51)	0.80	(0.48)	5.40	(3.24)

*Disposal costs included range from DM0.02 to 0.05.

Source: INFORM, based on estimates by Schoeller International, June 1993.

conducted by the Fraunhofer Institute for Food Technology and Packaging in Munich (Fraunhofer Institut für Lebensmitteltechnologie und Verpackung), an independent institute specializing in food technology and packaging. The institute, which studied raw materials use, air pollution, water consumption, water pollution, and waste, found MTS harms the environment less than cardboard cartons in all of these areas. INFORM has not assessed the assumptions on which the life-cycle analysis was based.

Schoeller expected MTS containers to be on the market in early 1994, and predicted they would become a standard shipping container throughout Europe, similar to the standardized European shipping pallets.[10] Schoeller is in contact with leading chain store groups, some of which have already tested MTS in Scandinavia, Belgium, the Netherlands, Luxembourg, Switzerland, and the United Kingdom.[11]

Procter & Gamble GmbH (P&G), a major consumer goods manufacturer, points out that it would have to invest in new filling equipment and redesign consumer packages to fit the new containers. Although MTS conforms to the outside measurements of the standardized European shipping pallets, the walls of the MTS containers are thicker than those of corrugated, reducing the inside container measurements and requiring a change in the dimensions of the packages shipped. P&G believes a reusable container system like MTS may be viable if it is economical and internationally usable, and if it becomes standard throughout Europe. According to P&G, MTS has not yet met these conditions.[12]

Schoeller says it will take 10 to 15 years for MTS to gain its expected market share of 50 percent for "suitable products." (MTS will not be used to ship fish or produce.) Schoeller "assumes that, owing to the growing demand for standardized packaging dimensions and to the continuing brand innovations, most producers will redesign the consumer packages of their products anyway in the next years. These consumer packages can then be changed according to the inside dimensions of MTS without additional cost. The same applies to filling equipment and other machinery."[13]

International Fruit Container (IFCO)

Schoeller has also developed an International Fruit Container (IFCO) — a reusable, collapsible food container for fruits and vegetables that is also made of polypropylene. Like MTS, this shipping system was developed in direct response to the Packaging Ordinance. Schoeller expected that the IFCO crates, which entered the market in 1992, would have a delivery capacity of 20 million per month by the end of 1993.[14] The rented IFCO containers come in eight sizes and will have their own service company — IFCO-International Fruit Container Organization GmbH.

Fruit and vegetable suppliers' complaints about IFCO may portend difficulties for other reusable container systems. When a major German supermarket chain, Metro International, sent letters to its fruit and vegetable suppliers saying it would "whenever possible buy only goods delivered in IFCO crates," the suppliers directed a deluge of protests to the European Community. Metro, in response, gave assurances that the system would not be "compulsory" or "exclusive."[15] Standardization is required for the economic viability of reusable systems: the challenge lies in reconciling standardization with antitrust and free trade concerns.

Besides working with Schoeller to develop MTS, Tengelmann has published a packaging guide for the producers from which it purchases goods. With respect to transport packaging, it advises producers to use standardized, reusable shipping containers and to minimize packaging. It also suggests that, if one-way packaging is used, it be made of recyclable materials and be labeled to identify the materials used.[16]

Notes

1. Federal Environment Ministry (BMU), "Ordinance on the Avoidance of Packaging Waste" (*Verpackungsverordnung*) of 12 June 1991, p. 4.

2. Thomas Rummler and Wolfgang Schutt, *The German Packaging Ordinance: A Practical Guide with Commentary,* Hamburg: B. Behr's Verlag GmbH & Co., 1990. p. 79.

3. Federal Environment Ministry (BMU), "Key Point: On the Spot Recycling and Reuse of Transport Packaging," Bonn, p. 2.

4. Klaus Draeger (Procter & Gamble GmbH, Germany), telephone interview, April 19, 1993.

5. Michael Scriba, "Pack Leaders," *Environment Risk,* May 1992.

6. Federal Environment Ministry (BMU), "Key Point," *op. cit.,* p. 2.

7. Schoeller International (Munich), "Multi-use Returnable Transport Packaging System (MTS)" video.

8. *Ibid.*

9. Tengelmann and Schoeller International (Munich), "MTS Returnable Transport Packaging System," p. 10.

10. Sibille Kohler (Schoeller International, Munich), written communication, June 16, 1993.

11. Kohler, *ibid.*

12. Klaus Draeger (Procter & Gamble GmbH, Germany), telephone interview, April 15, 1993.

13. Kohler, *op. cit.*

14. International Fruit Container Organization (Düsseldorf), "A System of the Food Trade."

15. "Germany's Fruit and Vegetable Suppliers in Plastic Crate Scare," *European Environment,* No. 411, Europe Information Service, Brussels, June 8, 1993, p. IV-8.

16. Unternehmensgruppe Tengelmann, "ÖKO-Logistische Verpackungsanforderungen" ("Environmental Packaging Requirements 1990"), p. 8.

Chapter 5
Secondary Packaging

The German Packaging Ordinance's rules for secondary packaging took effect in April 1992. Secondary packaging consists of materials, beyond those needed to contain and safeguard a product, that are designed to advertise, facilitate self-service, or prevent theft. It is distinct from second layers of packaging that are necessary to protect goods, or that insure durability or sterility — these are classified as primary packaging. Secondary packaging includes outer boxes, blister packs, or wrappings around the primary package, e.g., a box for a bottle of whiskey. (Blister packs are made of rigid plastic that is heat-sealed to paperboard, as shown in the first photograph on page 44.)The 56,000-plus metric tons of secondary packaging waste in Germany in 1992 accounted for less than one half of one percent of all the packaging waste covered by the ordinance.

The ordinance requires that retailers either remove the secondary packaging or provide marked bins near the point of sale so that customers may leave secondary packaging in the store. Like transport packaging, retailers must reuse or recycle secondary packaging independent of the public waste management system. For health and safety reasons, pharmacies are exempt from this provision.

The provisions for secondary packaging are aimed at waste avoidance in the belief that much secondary packaging is unnecessary. The guide to the ordinance says, "Decisions about dimensions of packaging should not be based primarily on marketing criteria. Packaging should not be used if it is there purely for marketing reasons."[1]

Secondary Packaging is Reduced

Making retailers responsible for secondary packaging waste gives them an incentive to pressure suppliers to reduce or eliminate these materials — and retailers have done just that. Duales System Deutschland (DSD) claims that secondary packaging has been reduced by 80 percent.[2] The Munich Department of Sanitation estimates reductions in secondary packaging of about 40 percent.[3] Environment Minister Klaus Töpfer claimed in January 1993 that secondary packaging had "largely disappeared."[4]

DSD has published before-and-after photographs of secondary packaging reductions. Some of these photos appear on the next page.

Although official statistics are not yet available, it is evident that secondary packaging is being reduced as a result of retailer pressure on manufacturers. Food industry retailers are powerful in Germany because they are highly concentrated: seven or eight leading companies control about 75 percent of the market. Tengelmann, one of the major food retailers, claims it has been urging suppliers to reduce packaging for years but that manufacturers have been more responsive since the ordinance was passed. Tengelmann says it cannot refuse to carry products with secondary packaging that has not been reduced, as this would prevent it from getting the amount of merchandise it needs, but it continues to pressure its suppliers and has published brochures advising them how to reduce their packaging.[5] Large department store chains such as Hertie and Karstadt have announced their intention to eliminate all secondary packaging from their stores.

Toothpaste has become a symbol of the reduction in secondary packaging. Shortly after the ordinance was passed, Colgate began marketing toothpaste in its tube only, without the box. Other companies have followed suit, and industry observers expect most toothpaste will soon be sold without the box in Germany.[6] The tubes are displayed on the shelf in

Celaflor GmbH plant food: eliminated blister pack.

Croldino Schneider hand creme: eliminated box.

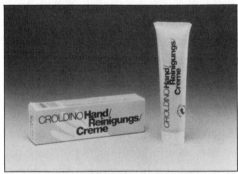

Canon GmbH "Prima" camera: reduced size of box and substituted used paper for polystyrene casing.

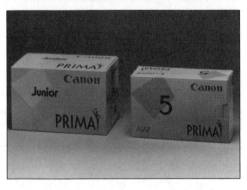

Sources: Duales System Deutschland, "Daten und Fakten zum Grünen Punkt: Der Ökologische Wandel bei Verpackungen" ("Data and Facts about the Green Dot: The Ecological Change in Packaging"). November 1992. Denta-Clin toothpaste photographed by B. Fishbein.

Asbach & Co. brandy: eliminated plastic wrap.

Brilliant AG hair dryer: substituted paperboard for blister pack.

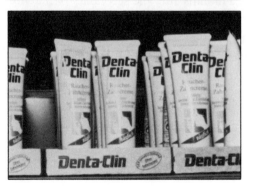

Denta-Clin toothpaste: eliminated box; developed display tray.

different ways: some stand on their caps and are inserted into holes in display trays; others lie in open cartons like candy bars.

Just a Few Problems

According to Tengelmann and the Bavarian Retailers Association (Landesverband des Bayerischen Eizelhandels e.V.), problems due to reductions in secondary packaging have been few and manageable. The Bavarian Retailers Association at first expressed concern about product damage resulting from packaging reductions.[7] Tengelmann reported that when the wooden box was eliminated from Camembert cheese, and it was sold in a film wrap only, sales dropped 30 percent. They have since recovered by about 20 percent, leaving a net reduction of 10 percent. It may be that consumers are more sensitive to changes in packaging for food than for non-food items: consumer reaction to other packaging reductions has been slight. Tengelmann's discount stores reported some increase in theft, but the retailer countered by placing products in different locations.[8]

Supermarkets and department stores seem to have their bins in place, but many smaller retailers were not immediately complying. A July 1992 survey by the National Retailers Association (Hauptverband des Deutschen Einzelhandels or HDE), showed that, of 1,480 stores surveyed, only 51 percent had the required bins, three months after the secondary packaging requirements went into effect. A survey in Munich indicated that 66 percent of retailers had bins, but some were not placed correctly. Munich imposes fines up to a maximum of DM100,000 ($60,000) on retailers who refuse to set up bins or fail to inform customers about leaving packaging in the store.[9]

Notes

1. Thomas Rummler and Wolfgang Schutt, *The German Packaging Ordinance: A Practical Guide with Commentary,* Hamburg: B. Behr's Verlag GmbH & Co., Germany, 1990, p. 57.

2. Michael Scriba, "Pack Leaders," *Environment Risk,* May 1992.

3. Helmut Paschlau (Landeshauptstadt München, Amt für Abfallwirtschaft [City of Munich, Department of Sanitation]), interview, October 9, 1992.

4. *Reuter European Community Report,* "German Anti-Rubbish Law Cuts Down on Excess Packaging," January 4, 1993.

5. Anja Raffalsky (Tengelmann, Mülheim) interview, October 27, 1992.

6. Rafaella Schuster (Landesverband des Bayerischen Eizelhandels e.V. [Association of Bavarian Retailers] Munich), interview, October 9, 1992.

7. Schuster, interview, *ibid.*

8. Raffalsky, interview, *op. cit.*

9. Schuster, interview, *op. cit.*

Chapter 6

Primary Packaging and the Dual System

Primary packaging is by far the largest component of packaging waste in Germany, accounting by weight in 1991 for about two-thirds of the total covered in the ordinance, or 8.4 million metric tons. Primary packaging includes closed or open receptacles and coverings used to contain goods until they are consumed (e.g., the can for soup, jar for jam, box for soap powder). Disposable dishes and cutlery are also considered primary packaging. In short, primary packaging is basically the packaging that consumers actually take home.

The Packaging Ordinance states that retailers had to "take back" primary packaging as of January 1, 1993, and reuse and recycle it independent of the public waste management system. The ordinance also mandates deposits on nonrefillable containers for beverages, detergents, and paints as described in Chapter 3.[1]

However, the ordinance allows an exemption from the mandatory deposits and from the requirement to take back primary packages if industry devises an alternative system that will meet the specified collecting, sorting, and refilling quotas. With the exemption, the German government gave industry the option to design and operate its own system. Called the "Dual System," the alternative is run by an industry-operated company, Duales System Deutschland (DSD). (The provisions for the exemption are described in Article 6(3) of the Packaging Ordinance, reprinted in Appendix A.)

Table 6-1: Share of Primary Packages by Material

Material	Number of Packages (percent)	Weight of Packages (percent)
Glass	8.87	45.6
Tinplate	5.94	8.5
Aluminum	1.83	1.5
Plastic	28.69	12.5
Paper/paperboard	34.49	26.9
Composite	20.12	4.8
Other	0.06	0.6
Total	100.00	100.0

Source: INFORM, based on Gesellschaft für Verpackungsmarktforschung (GVM) data.

The Primary Packaging Waste Stream

In 1991 there were an estimated 183 billion primary packages in Germany's waste stream — 160 billion discarded by households and 23 billion by industry. Table 6-1 shows the share of packaging for each material by number of packages and weight.

At 46 percent of packaging, by weight, glass accounts for the most tonnage of the materials to be collected, although it comprises less than 9 percent of the number of packages. Paper is the next largest contributor of tonnage; it represents 27 percent, by weight, and more than one-third of the number of packages. Packaging materials other than glass and paper are often referred to in Germany as the "light fraction." These include plastics, metals, and composites and account for 27 percent, by weight, and 57 percent of the number of packages. Plastics alone account for 29 percent of the packages, although they contribute only 12.5 percent of total packaging weight.

Establishing the Dual System

Getting the Exemption

Implementation of Duales System Deutschland's proposed alternative plan for taking back primary packaging was dependent on approval from

Germany's 16 *Länder*, or states. The states have the authority to grant or deny the exemption for an industry-run system and may revoke approvals if they determine that the quotas are not being met.

With support widespread in Germany for the underlying principle of the Packaging Ordinance — making the "polluter pay" — some critics argue that the ordinance is not strong enough; they are particularly critical of the industry-run Dual System. Several states, notably Bavaria, had threatened to deny the exemption for reasons discussed in Chapter 9, such as its lack of sufficient attention to waste prevention. Despite the criticisms, all states granted the exemption by January 1, 1993, and the Dual System went into effect as scheduled.

Implementation of the Dual System relieved retailers of the task of taking back more than 100 billion packages each year, averted the high deposits on one-way packages mandated by the ordinance, and provided consumers with curbside collection of a portion of primary packaging. Under the ordinance, the minimum deposit for a soda can would have been DM0.50 ($0.30) — two-thirds the price of the soda itself, and more than three times current deposits on a refillable bottle.

Still, the political battles are by no means over. The states of Bavaria, Lower Saxony, and Baden-Württemberg gave the exemption with limitations that will be very difficult for DSD to meet. In June 1993, DSD faced a crisis with many of the states, led by Rhineland Palatinate and Lower Saxony, threatening to withdraw the exemption. Intense negotiations between DSD and the states appeared likely to continue.

Membership in DSD

In September 1990, 95 companies, including retailers, consumer product manufacturers, and packaging manufacturers, founded DSD to operate the Dual System for reducing and recovering primary packaging waste. As of April 1993, nearly 600 companies had joined.[2] Members contribute working capital to DSD, each paying a onetime fee of DM5,000 ($3,000), but they reap no direct profits, as DSD is a not-for-profit company. Members do, however, receive valuable information and participate in decisions important to their industries. DSD notes that it "enjoys the support of" the Federation of German Industries (Bundesverband der Deutschen Industrie, or BDI) and the Association of German Chambers of Industry and Commerce (Deutscher Industrie- und Handelstag, or DIHT) — the major industry organizations in Germany.[3]

Drop-off and Curbside Collection

To meet the ordinance's ambitious goals for recycling, collection must be convenient for consumers. The DSD system includes a combination of drop-off and curbside collection. Figure 6-1 illustrates the flow of materials through the Dual System for different types of packaging.

Many of the igloos and containers for collecting glass and paper shown under the "Drop- off" section of the figure were in place long before DSD was created, as municipal governments had previously collected glass and paper for recycling. DSD has required expansion of the extensive existing system for glass to a ratio of one group of drop-off bins for every 500 people. There are separate bins for clear, green, and brown glass. DSD also required expansion of the number of the existing drop-off bins for paper to one for every 500 people. Other existing paper collection systems, which differ by locality, will be maintained. Materials other than paper and glass, including plastics, aluminum, tinplate, and composites, are collected curbside — like regular household garbage. DSD provides yellow bins and bags for this waste and picks it up free of charge to the households, as the funding is provided by the green dot fees, discussed later in this chapter.

DSD's plan to pick up primary packaging from businesses was challenged by the German Cartel Office (Bundeskartellamt), as described in Chapter 9.

Recycling and the Dual System

Guaranteeing Recycling

Duales System Deutschland is licensing its trademark green dot *(der Grüne Punkt)* — shown on the cover of this report — as a symbol to be placed on primary packages, signifying that they will be recycled. Most retailers in Germany will not carry packages without the green dot. A company must meet two prerequisites to qualify for a green dot on its packages: a guarantee from a designated recycling company that the specific type of packag-

Figure 6-1: The Dual System

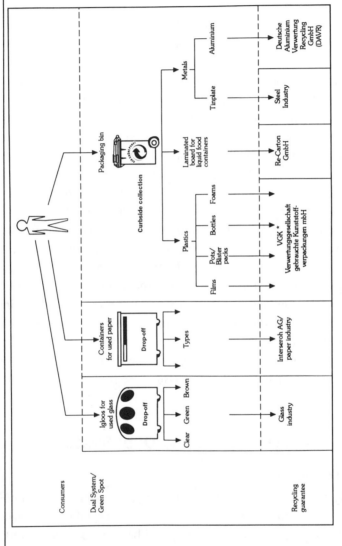

* In June 1993, DSD established a new company, called DEKUR-Kunststoff Recycling GmbH, to assume the tasks of plastic recycling formerly performed by VGK.

Source: Thomas Rummler and Wolfgang Schutt, *The German Packaging Ordinance: A Practical Guide with Commentary*, Hamburg: B. Behr's Verlag GmbH & Co., 1990.

A Munich resident uses the typical recycling "igloos" for glass and paper.

ing material will be recycled, and a contract with DSD indicating that the license fee has been paid. DSD says its members receive no preference in the awarding of the green dot.

DSD has designated recyclers for six different materials: glass, tinplate, aluminum, plastics, paper, and composites. When these recyclers make general guarantees that packages made of certain materials will be recycled, individual agreements for these materials are not necessary. For materials without general guarantees, the manufacturer must provide detailed information on the materials in the package; the recycler then determines whether to guarantee that the material will be accepted for recycling. If the guarantee is not given, the manufacturer — to keep its retailers — will most likely have to change the package. From the outset, general guarantees have been given for glass, tinplate, aluminum, some composite beverage containers, and most paper packaging. Guarantees for plastics have changed over time. As of April 1993, 60-70 percent of the packages on the German market already carried green dots.[4] About 12,000 companies had already signed contracts for the green dot, among them 1,900 companies based outside of Germany.[5]

Fees for Plastics

Companies have not always been given their recycling guarantees free of charge. While the general guarantees have all been free, the recycler originally designated for plastics, the Recycling Group for Used Plastic Packaging (Verwertungsgesellschaft Gebrauchte Kunststoff Verpackungen mbH, or VGK), charged 25 percent of the green dot fee for the guarantee, owing to the high cost of recycling plastics. Thus consumer product companies incurred additional costs by using plastic packaging. Because the plastics industry was not making sufficient progress in creating additional recycling capacity, a new company, DEKUR-Kunststoff Recycling GmbH (DKR), was formed in June 1993 to assume the tasks previously performed by VGK, as discussed in Chapter 8.

Recycling Incentives

The German legislation mandates recycling even if it is not economical. The theory is that if industry must pay for recycling, it will have an incentive to build up markets for recycled materials by increasing use of recycled content and by using materials that are more economical to recycle. The ordinance relies on incentives to industry for the creation of markets for secondary materials; the government is not involved in creating these markets. According to a DSD brochure, "Recycling costs are charged to packaging manufacturers, included in their cost calculations and passed on to the consumer goods manufacturer."[6]

Theoretically, the cost of recycling is incorporated in the price of packaging. As consumer product companies start paying less for packaging materials that are easily and economically recycled, and more for materials that are difficult and expensive to recycle, the Dual System, by internalizing the costs of recycling, should alter the relative competitive advantages of the different packaging materials.

Monitoring Recycling

A group of private companies, called Technische Überwachungsvereine, or TÜVs, that perform technical inspections and certify products that must meet government specifications, will monitor DSD's recycling activities to assure that materials collected are actually recycled. DSD established a working group of TÜVs "to inspect the sorting and recycling plants and to submit regular reports on incoming and outgoing materials."[7]

By March 1993, the TÜV in Cologne had investigated 120 plastics recycling facilities, 85 in Germany and 35 around the world. The TÜV in Essen was inspecting paper-recycling facilities, and the TÜV in Munich was inspecting glass facilities.[8]

Recycling Capacity

Estimates of capacity compared with quotas

Consumer and environmental groups have criticized DSD for licensing its green dots before sufficient recycling capacity was in place. DSD claimed that recycling capacity in 1993 would exceed the amount of materials required to be recycled under the quotas set by the ordinance. Figure 6-2 shows estimates of the amount of each material required to be recycled in 1993 and 1995 and DSD's estimate of the recycling capacity for that material in 1993.

DSD has not indicated how much of this capacity is outside of Germany. As discussed in Chapter 9, green dot packaging materials are flooding the world markets and lowering prices for secondary materials. Countries that are receiving these materials, particularly those that are members of the European Community (EC), have protested the shipments and may curtail them in the future, thereby reducing DSD's recyling capacity.

The 1993 recycling quotas (shown in Table 3-3) ranged from a low of 6 percent for composites to a high of 42 percent for glass. For 1995, the mandated rates range from 64 percent to 72 percent. Thus, even if the recycling capacity exceeds what is needed to meet the 1993 quotas, it is far short of what will be needed for some materials in 1995. For example, about 600,000 metric tons of plastic will have to be recycled in 1995, far exceeding the 1993 recycling capacity DSD estimated at about 200,000 metric tons. Paper and tinplate are the only materials for which DSD's estimated 1993 recycling capacity exceeds the 1995 recycling quotas. Plastics are the only materials for which DSD has acknowledged difficulties in reaching the recycling quotas.

Figure 6-2: Comparison of Recycling Quotas with Recycling Capacity

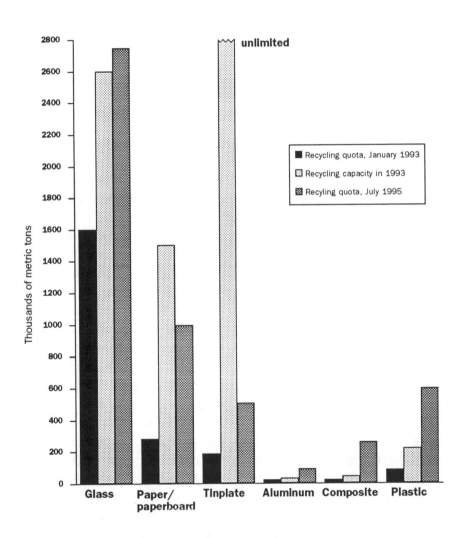

Sources: Estimates of 1993 recycling capacity from Duales System Deutschland GmbH, September 1993. Estimates of 1993 and 1995 recycling quotas by INFORM based on 1991 packaging consumption.

Recycling of Specific Materials

Beverage Cartons
DSD appears to have had considerable success in beverage carton recycling, which is guaranteed by Re-Carton GmbH. Two companies are recycling beverage cartons: Strepp, with a capacity of 20,000 metric tons per year in 1993 and 35,000 in 1995, and PWA Industriepapier GmbH, with a capacity of 25,000 metric tons per year in 1993 and 58,000 in 1995.[9] The typical composition of these cartons is: 70 percent paper; 22 percent polyethylene; 5 percent aluminum; and 3 percent binding agents. The recycling companies employ two recycling methods. One method separates the materials before recycling. DSD expected that technology would be operative by 1994 to recycle not only the paper components, but the plastic and aluminum as well.[10] The second method shreds the mixed-material cartons and presses them into plates similar to chipboard. The plastic melts in this process and acts as a bonding agent. The end product can be used in furniture and construction.[11] Despite the progress made in recycling beverage cartons, the estimated recycling capacity falls far short of the 1995 quota.

Glass
In 1992, 2.31 million metric tons of glass packaging was recycled in Germany and 170,000 tons was exported for recycling. This amounted to a total glass packaging recycling rate of 62 percent and a domestic recycling rate of 61 percent. The Packaging Ordinance requires that 42 percent of glass packaging be recycled in 1993 and 72 percent in 1995. The production of one-way glass packaging is decreasing in Germany owing to increased use of refillable bottles and substitution of other packaging materials for glass. DSD says temporary reprocessing problems could be solved by better color separation and increased reprocessing of used glass abroad.[12] Given the decline in the use of glass packaging, the 1993 recycling capacity may be adequate to meet the 1995 quota.

Paper/Paperboard
The three DSD-authorized guarantors for paper recycling in Germany are recycling paper within the country and exporting used paper packaging to

TÜV-certified recycling facilities in Hungary, Poland, Austria, Italy, Taiwan, Thailand, and Indonesia. Evidently, Germany is also shipping to other countries, as France and the United Kingdom have complained about German paper being dumped on their markets, as described in Chapter 9. DSD claimed to have the capacity to recycle 1.5 million metric tons of paper in 1993 — more than the ordinance requires by 1995.[13]

Metals (Aluminum and Tinplate)

DSD estimated that 25,000 metric tons of aluminum would be collected in 1993, and that a recycling capacity of 30,000 tons would be available. DSD asserts that "this capacity can be increased rapidly."[14] Tinplate containers do not appear to pose a recycling problem. According to DSD, capacity for recycling tinplate, which has traditionally been recycled by the steel industry, is unlimited in the long run because it is a small percentage of the scrap steel recycled in Germany.[15]

Plastics

DSD faced a crisis in June 1993 because it was collecting far more plastics than anticipated and lacked the capacity to recycle it, and because 20 percent of plastic material collected did not have the green dot.[16] DSD claimed it was being overwhelmed by its success and that it collected four times as much plastic packaging (400,000 metric tons) as it was required to recycle in 1993. A major political debate erupted over what to do with the additional plastics. The state of Rhineland-Palatinate threatened to withdraw the exemption for plastics, but DSD claimed it would be unfair to punish the system for collecting more plastic packaging than the ordinance required.[17] A detailed discussion of the plastics crisis is presented in Chapter 8.

Financing the Dual System

DSD Revenues and Costs

DSD originally estimated the costs of collecting and sorting primary packaging at DM2 billion per year ($1.2 billion) and calibrated the 1992 fee schedule to generate this level of revenue. In April 1993, DSD raised its cost estimate to DM4.2 billion ($2.5 billion) for 1994.[18] Much of this in-crease was due to DSD's decision to assume some of the cost of recycling plastics, which was not included in the prior estimate. Estimates of what the Dual System would actually cost have been uncertain. A study con-ducted at the Berlin Technical College (Technische Fachhochschule in Berlin, or TFB) concluded that DSD's 1992 green dot fees were not suffi-cient to cover its collecting and sorting costs, which TFB estimated could reach DM6-9 billion ($3.6-5.4 billion) annually by 1995.[19] In July 1993, the Federal Environment Ministry (Bundesministerium für Umwelt, Naturschutz und Reaktorsicherheit, or BMU) estimated DSD costs at DM5-6 billion ($3-3.6 billion) per year.[20]

Revenues from the green dot license fees cover DSD's administrative costs, as well as operating costs for collecting and sorting packaging waste. DSD employs about 200 people in an administrative system costing more than DM2 million ($1.2 million) per year.[21] The fees also cover expenses for public education and advertising. As discussed in Chapter 8, DSD pays part of the cost of recycling plastics. All other recycling costs are the re-sponsibility of the materials industries. To the extent that recycling gener-ates profits or incurs costs for manufacturers, these will be reflected in lower or higher materials prices. The sorted packaging materials, including valuable materials such as glass and aluminum, are given to manufacturers free.

Aside from DSD's operating costs, the organization estimates that the waste management industry will incur DM7 billion ($4.2 billion) in invest-ment costs in infrastructure, including sorting facilities. It had already in-vested DM5 billion ($3 billion) in the 18 months prior to May 1993.[22] More-over, the materials industries have to expand the infrastructure for recycling glass, metal, and paper, and develop a system for plastics and composites almost from scratch.

DSD's Financial Crisis

DSD faced a financial crisis in May 1993. Announcing a shortfall of DM500 million ($300 million) for the remainder of 1993, DSD began to negotiate a solution. As industry operates the Dual System and did not want it to fail, it agreed to make up the shortfall. First the retailers, who feared they would have to take back packaging if the system failed, agreed to contribute DM200 million ($120 million).[23] Private agreements determined how much each company would pay. The waste management and utilities industries that manage the waste under DSD contracts agreed to contribute DM180 million ($108 million).[24] The Federation of German Industries (BDI) and DSD decided that users of the green dot (primarily consumer product manufacturers) would be asked to pay their dot fees two months in advance — thereby giving DSD an interest-free loan. As a result of the agreements, DSD announced in June that its finances were "assured."[25]

Industry's contributions, however, were conditioned on DSD's reducing its costs, and on June 25 DSD announced "a drastic, unparalleled cost cutting program" aimed at saving DM240 million ($144 million) in the remaining six months of 1993.[26] DSD began renegotiation of contracts with waste management firms and localities. In the latter case, DSD claimed that 40 percent of the materials placed in the DSD yellow bins were not packaging and that the localities would have to pay DSD to collect this portion.[27] The localities claimed that only 20 percent of the materials in the bins was not packaging, and both sides ultimately agreed that waste composition studies would be undertaken to resolve the dispute.

When DSD made its financial problems public, it claimed that it was a victim of its success in that it was collecting far more than the ordinance required. But there were other causes of the financial difficulties: operational costs were high, and many companies were delinquent in paying the green dot fees. While printing the green dot on their packages, some companies were paying their fees late and, in some cases, not at all. DSD claimed it was receiving fees for only 50 percent of the primary packages on the market, even though 90 percent of the packages carried the green dot symbol in August 1993.[28] To address this problem, DSD announced that it intended "to take action against 'joyriders' [sic] who use the green dot without paying for it by introducing a computer-aided controlling system and tightening up surveillance."[29]

In early September 1993, DSD was again teetering on the brink of insolvency. This crisis, and its resolution, is discussed in the Epilogue.

Setting the Green Dot Fees

DSD originally based the green dot fees on the filling volume of individual packages, but in March 1993 it announced a new schedule based on weight and package material. According to DSD, the new 1993 fees were designed to reflect the actual cost of handling the different materials. A comparison of the two fee schedules is of interest from a US policy perspective because they could be used as guides for packaging taxes or advanced disposal fees.

The new fee schedule differs from the old one in three key respects: 1.) the fee is different for each material; 2.) fees are based on the weight of the package, not the volume of the product; and 3.) the total projected revenues from the fees have doubled. DSD estimated that green dot fees would generate DM4.2 billion in 1994 ($2.5 billion) compared with about DM2 billion ($1.2 billion) previously.

The 1992 Green Dot Fees

In 1992, the DSD licensing fees per package ranged from DM0.01 to 0.20 ($0.006-0.12), based on the filling volume of each package as shown in Table 6-2. These green dot fees provided the revenues to fund the collection and sorting of packaging waste. Recycling costs were not included because they were to be born by the individual materials industries. Although the Dual System did not officially go into effect until January 1, 1993, green dots became prevalent in 1992 when companies began applying for the dots and DSD began collecting the fees it needed to begin operating the system.

About three-quarters of the packages on the German market fall into the 200-milliliter to three-liter category, meaning most packages had a green dot fee of DM0.02 ($0.012). For example, a 330-milliliter can of Coca-Cola that cost DM0.70 ($0.42) had a green dot fee of DM0.02 ($0.012), amounting to about 3 percent of the price, while a two-liter bottle of fabric softener that cost DM3 ($1.80) also had a green dot fee of 0.02 DM, in this case amounting to only 0.7 percent of the price. As the 1992 fee schedule was based on filling volume, all packages containing the same amount of product incurred the same fee, regardless of the material or weight of the

Table 6-2: 1992 Green Dot Fees

Packaging Volume	DM per package
<50 milliliters	.0
50 – 200 milliliters	.01
>200 milliliters – 3 liters	.02
>3 – 30 liters	.05
>30 liters	.20

Note: See Appendix B for table converted to ounces and dollars.

Source: Duales System Deutschland, "The Green Dot: Don't Let Packaging Go to Waste!"

Table 6-3: 1993 Green Dot Fees
(Effective October 1, 1993)

Material	DM per kilogram
Plastic	3.00
Composite	1.66
Aluminum	1.00
Tinplate	0.56
Paper/paperboard	0.33
Natural materials	0.20
Glass	0.16

Note: See Appendix B for table converted to dollars per pound.

Source: Duales System Deutschland.

package. The fees, therefore, did not affect manufacturers' choice of packaging materials.

The 1993 Green Dot Fees

A new fee schedule based on material and weight went into effect October 1, 1993. The fee for plastics was originally set at 2.61 DM per kilogram in March 1993, but was raised to 3.00 DM per kilogram in July 1993. Some of the supporting data in this section are based on the 2.61 DM-per-kilogram fee.

The 1993 fees, shown in Table 6-3, reflect DSD's actual costs for managing materials. For example, glass bears the lowest fee because it requires virtually no sorting, as consumers drop off different-colored glass in separate bins.

Because the new fees are based on package weight, they provide an incentive for source reduction — reducing package weight. DSD asserts that weight-based fees are fairer than those based on product volume, because, for a given material, lighter packages will have lower fees.[30]

Table 6-4 shows DSD estimates of the tonnage and costs for each material. These are the figures DSD used to calculate the green dot fees in March 1993. For example, DSD estimated the costs for paper at DM587

Table 6-4: Estimated DSD Costs and Green Dot Fees for 1994, by Material

Material	DSD Costs (in millions of DM)	Packages* with green dot (per 1000 metric tons)	Average Fee (DM per ton)	Fee (DM per kg**)
Plastic	2197	842	2,610	2.61***
Composite	523	314	1,660	1.66
Aluminum	99	100	1,000	1.00
Tinplate	335	594	563	0.56
Paper/ paperboard	587	1,753	334	0.33
Glass	458	2,870	160	0.16
Total	4,198	6,473		

* Based on DSD's estimate that 75 percent of packaging, by weight, would bear the green dot.
** 1 metric ton = 1000 kilograms.
*** Later estimates raised the fee to DM3.00.

Source: INFORM, based on "Informationen zur neuen Gebührenordnung" ("Information about the New Fee Schedule"), Duales System Deutschland, April 1993.

million ($352 million). Dividing by the tonnage of paper packaging bearing the green dot (about 1.7 million metric tons) yields a per-ton fee of DM334, or DM0.33 per kilogram — the amount of the green dot fee. The green dot fees differ from DSD's actual per-kilogram collecting and sorting costs because they are based on the number of packages bearing the green dot, which is greater than the actual number that DSD will collect. Moreover, the costs represented in the fees include not only waste management, but also general administrative, operating, and public education costs, allocated to each material. DSD has estimated the costs for collecting and sorting at DM198 ($119) per metric ton for glass, DM349 ($209) for paper, and DM1915 ($1149) for all other materials combined.[31]

Plastics account for more than half of the estimated DSD costs because they are expensive to collect and sort and include some recycling costs, whereas the cost of handling other materials includes collecting and sorting only.

Material and Weight vs. Filling Volume

Because the new fees are based on the weight of the package, not the filling volume of the product, it is difficult to compare the 1992 and 1993 fee schedules. For example, in 1992 the fee for a one-liter bottle of soda made of either glass or plastic was DM0.02 ($0.012). The 1993 schedule sets the fee for plastic 19 times higher than for glass: DM3.00 as compared to DM0.16. However, this comparison is misleading, because the fees are based on the weight of the package, and plastic is lighter than glass. A better perspective is that of a company deciding what packaging material to use to deliver a certain amount of product.

To illustrate this comparison, Table 6-5 shows examples of the 1993 green dot fees for different packaging materials containing one liter of beverage, based on the weight of the package. These package weights, from the Berlin Technical College (TFB) study of DSD costs, are not necessarily representative of all beverage containers.[32] Most of these materials are not sold in the one-liter size, but they have been standardized here for comparison. For example, the weight for aluminum is based on three 0.330-liter soda cans.

In the table, the glass bottle weighs more than 12 times as much as the plastic bottle — 0.360 kilograms compared with 0.029 kilograms. Under the 1993 fee schedule, the green dot fee for this one-liter glass beverage bottle will be DM0.058 and the fee for the one-liter plastic beverage bottle will be DM0.087. In this case, the fee for the plastic bottle is 50 percent higher than the fee for the glass one — a difference far lower than what the fee chart might indicate at first glance. The lowest fee corresponds to the lightest package — the composite (aseptic) beverage carton. Note that the highest green dot fee for delivering one liter of beverage is only two and a half times the lowest — a much narrower range than the per-kilogram fees for the various materials themselves, which vary by a factor of 19:1.

Note also that the relative weights of the different packaging materials may vary by type of package and product. For example, according to Coca-Cola Foods data on the different materials used to package orange juice, a glass bottle weighs about 10 times as much as a plastic bottle, whereas the TFB data in Table 6-5 puts glass at 12 times the weight of plastic.[33] Likewise, the ratio of the weight of a plastic jar to a glass jar could vary for

Table 6-5: 1993 Green Dot Fees for Packaging One Liter of Beverage

Material	Type of package	Package weight (kilogram per liter)	Fees per kilogram (DM)	Fees per liter (DM)
Plastic	bottle	0.029	3.00	0.087
Composite	box	0.021	1.66	0.035
Aluminum	can	0.048	1.00	0.048
Tinplate	can	0.106	0.56	0.059
Glass	bottle	0.360	0.16	0.058

Source: INFORM. Package weight in kilograms per liter from Technische Fachhochschule Berlin, (Dr. Dieter Berndt, et. al.), Abschätzung der gegenwärtigen und zukünftigen Kosten für das Sammeln und Sortieren von Verkaufsverpackungen im dualen System (Transparente Modellrechnung) (Estimate of Present and Future Costs for Collecting and Sorting of Sales Packaging in the Dual System), Berlin, August 1992. The last column is the product of the package weight and green dot fees.

different products, such as cleaning fluids and peanut butter.

Despite these variations in relative weights, the new fees are generally higher for plastics on a per-package basis and may cause shifts from plastics to other materials. Figure 6-3 compares new and old green dot fees for selected packages in Germany. These comparisons are based on the DM2.61-per-kilogram fee for plastics. In the case of a light plastic bag for potato chips, the increase from the 1992 fees to the 1993 fees is small: from DM0.0200 to DM0.0206. For a heavy plastic bottle of fabric softener, however, the fee increases from DM0.0200 to DM0.1623. This illustrates the disadvantage of heavy plastic packaging under the new fee schedule. Obviously, DSD's increase of the plastics fee to DM3.00 per kilogram will augment these differences.

According to the Rudolph Wild Company in Heidelberg, the Packaging Ordinance, and particularly the new fee schedule, has led to a stagnation in the market for one-way packages and a boom in refill pouches for a variety of products. Wild says the higher fees for heavy plastic detergent bottles may encourage the use of composite refill pouches.[34] When a question arose about how to assess the green dot fees for composite packages that are mostly plastic, DSD ruled that if plastic accounts for more than half of the package weight, it incurs the DM3.00 fee for plastics rather than the DM1.66 fee for composites.

Figure 6-3: Comparison of 1992 and 1993 Green Dot Fees for Selected Packages in Germany

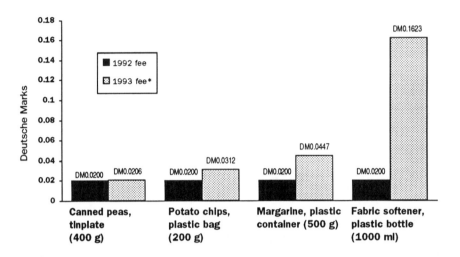

* Based on plastics fee of 2.61 DM/kg.

Source: Duales System Deutschland, "Comparison of License Fees" ("Lizenzgebühren im Vergleich").

Applying for the Green Dot

To determine the amount a company must pay DSD in green dot fees, the company must estimate the number of packaging units it expects to sell on the German market in the following year. Adjustments for over- or under-payments are made at the end of the year.[35] Applications for the green dot are usually made by consumer product companies. For imported goods, applications may be made by the importer or the manufacturer. DSD originally intended to monitor the accuracy of company reporting through spot checks. Following the financial crisis of September 1993, a new monitoring system was established, as described in the Epilogue.

In the case of products sold in individual packages within a box, the 1992 fee schedule required separate dots for each of the packages. For example, the Wild Company, which manufacturers a juice drink sold in boxes of 10 individual servings, each in its own aluminum pouch, had to pay for 11 green dots: one for each pouch and one for the large box. Under the 1993 fee schedule, the number of packages per box will no longer be relevant, as the fee will be assessed on the total weight of the packaging.

Packages Outside the Green Dot System

The green dot system was designed primarily for the kinds of packages sold in supermarkets that contain foods and small household items. Supermarkets and department stores are requiring green dots, and the suppliers are applying for them. However, primary packaging in some other industries, particularly for large items such as computers, appliances, and furniture, is sometimes being handled differently.

A computer manufacturer, Apple Computer, for example, found that many of the small computer retailers want to take the packages back because this brings the customers back to the store. Even before the new 1993 green dot fees were announced, Apple was not getting the green dot for its packages sold by small retailers and was paying retailers directly to take back the packages. Apple was getting the green dot for its computer packages sold through major department stores, because the department stores required it.

The 1993 green dot fee schedule gave computer manufacturers an added reason to find alternatives to the green dot because shifting to fees based on weight and material resulted in substantial cost increases for large containers. According to Apple Computer, the new schedule will increase the average green dot fees for its packages six to eight times. Under the 1992 fee schedule, the maximum fee for containers larger than 30 liters was DM0.25 ($0.15) — DSD's DM0.20 fee plus a surcharge for plastics recycling. Thus the fee for the 277-liter package on Apple's 21-inch monitor, for example, would have been DM0.25. Under the new schedule based on weight and material, the fee on the package, which consists of corrugated cardboard and plastic weighing more than five kilograms, increased more than 16 times.[36] Although Apple does not expect to redesign existing packages, it does plan to design packages for its new products that contain more cardboard and less plastic, thereby minimizing the need to pay the higher fees for plastics.[37]

Alternative systems for handling primary packages are permitted under the ordinance, provided the manufacturer pays for taking back the packages and for their reuse or recycling, independent of the public waste management system.

Harmonization of DSD and the Waste Management System

The relationship between DSD and the localities is at the heart of the Dual System. The provision allowing for an exemption from the primary packaging regulations requires that the Dual System "be harmonized with existing collection, recycling, and reuse systems run by the authorities for waste disposal in whose area it is set up."[38] This requirement was intended to ensure that existing systems and facilities be properly utilized and integrated into the new system, and to prevent the development of an entirely new waste management system.

True to its name, the Dual System will in fact constitute a packaging waste management system that literally operates parallel to existing municipal waste management systems. DSD has signed separate contracts with local waste management authorities throughout Germany. As of April 1, 1993, almost all localities had signed — 534 out of 549 — and negotiations were under way with the remaining communities.[39] The contracts specify how packaging waste will be managed, who will do the managing, and what fees DSD will pay the localities.

Revenue for Municipalities

The Dual System can be lucrative for local solid waste management authorities. As communities negotiate their own contracts with DSD, some get better terms than others. DSD may agree to manage all packaging waste, in which case the locality is relieved of the responsibility and can save the money it normally would spend on managing this portion of its waste stream — one-third, by weight. Alternatively, DSD may pay the locality as a subcontractor to manage some or all of the packaging waste.

For example, the city of Wuppertal, with a population of 390,000, had an annual municipal solid waste budget of DM35 million ($21 million) per year and was to receive DM10 million ($6 million) per year under its contract with DSD. Wuppertal negotiated a contract that enables it to manage waste as it did before, using municipal sanitation workers who will now be paid in part by DSD. The city sees this arrangement as protecting its interests: if DSD fails, Wuppertal will have its sanitation system intact. The city has arranged to retain control over the glass and paper drop-off bins, because collections from these facilities in residential neighborhoods can be noisy, and Wuppertal wants to maintain local control over this procedure. DSD will share the costs, however. It will pay all the costs of the glass bins because all of the glass brought to these bins is packaging waste. It will pay 25 percent of the cost of the paper bins, because 25 percent of the paper deposited in them is estimated to be packaging; the remainder is newspapers and other printed materials. City workers will collect recyclable materials from the drop-off and curbside (DSD) bins and direct them to sorting and recycling facilities.

DSD will pay Wuppertal based on the tonnage of packaging waste the city collects and sorts. The city will also receive the standard payments that DSD makes to all localities of DM1 ($0.60) per person per year for public education advertising and DM0.5 ($0.30) per person per year to fund local waste advisers who provide information to the public. Wuppertal will receive a total of DM585,000 ($351,000) per year for these purposes.

Shifting Financial Responsibility

Prior to the advent of the Dual System, municipalities had often funded solid waste management by charging households based on the amount of waste they generated (per-bin charges), and also partly through general tax revenues. In effect, the Dual System shifts the financing of managing packaging waste from the municipal solid waste budgets to the green dot fees, which are like a sales tax in that companies pass the fees on to consumers through higher prices. At the same time, many localities are running out of disposal capacity, and DSD relieves them of responsibility for about one-third of their municipal solid waste, reducing the pressure to site additional waste disposal facilities.

To the extent that DSD expenditures represent a shifting of costs from localities to the Dual System, the money spent by consumers in green dot fees should be offset by savings in the local solid waste budgets. These local budgets had been slated for huge increases, so the savings may be in the form of smaller increases rather than actual reductions. To some extent, however, the green dot fees represent a real increase in costs, and these will not be offset locally. Estimates are not available on the incremental costs of the Dual System compared with the former costs of managing primary packaging waste.

Ultimately, the public pays for managing packaging waste one way or another. The shift from taxpayers to industry means costs are passed on in higher product prices; thus the individual ends up paying as a consumer, rather than through local taxes or garbage collection fees. With DSD costs of about DM4 billion ($2.4 billion) per year and a German population of 80 million, the green dot fees average DM50 ($30) per person per year or DM200 per year ($120) for a family of four. However, this DM4 billion was not the full cost of the system, given that recycling costs are born by industry and also passed on in higher prices. Polls have shown that 76 percent of German consumers believe the costs of managing packaging waste should be included in the price of products.[40]

Packaging Changes in Germany: The Impact of the Ordinance

Assessing the ordinance's impact on the use of primary packaging in Germany is difficult because the primary packaging provisions of the Packaging Ordinance have been in effect only since January 1993; thus as of mid-1993, when this report was being completed, results were just beginning to emerge. In some cases, when packaging changes can be documented, it is not clear whether they occurred in response to or in anticipation of the ordinance, or if they would have occurred anyway, without the legislation.

One consequence, however, seems certain: the political debate and publicity surrounding the ordinance have heightened public awareness of the impact of packaging on the environment. According to Dr. Jan Bongaerts, Director of the Institute for European Environmental Policy (Institut für Europäische Umweltpolitik, or IEUP), "The Packaging Ordinance has drastically changed the attitudes of consumers and — even more so — the

Strategies for 'greening' packaging materials and packaging systems are increasingly considered as marketing instruments that have a promising future. As things stand, a return to the past is out of the question."[41] Bongaerts concludes that the ordinance is leading to source reduction and the use of more recyclable materials; he specifically cites reduced use of polyvinyl chloride (PVC), blister packs, and polystyrene cushioning, as well as increased use of lighter packages and a trend to "avoid" packaging for many appliances.[42] (Many German environmentalists want to ban the use of PVC, as discussed in Chapter 8.)

Reduced Packaging

The first official report on packaging changes was prepared by the Group for Packaging Market Research (Gesellschaft für Verpackungsmarktforschung, or GVM), for the Federal Environment Ministry and released in July 1993. It found that packaging consumption of materials with quotas in the ordinance was reduced by 514,000 metric tons from 1991 to 1992, as shown in Table 6-6.

The total packaging reduction was 661,000 metric tons. The data is for all packaging, as shown in Table 3-4. No separate data were released for primary packaging; however, this is the largest packaging category. Composite drink cartons were the only type of packaging that increased; they may increase even more under the new green dot fee schedule, because they are light and will have lower fees per container relative to other materials.

GVM says its 1995 projections are conservative and do not include major packaging changes that may occur, such as a big shift from corrugated containers to reusable plastic shipping containers. Still, the forecast puts total 1995 packaging, by weight, below the 1991 total. GVM assumes a decrease in packaging weight, particularly with the new fee schedule, but expects the number of containers to increase by 1995 because of economic growth.[43] DSD has noted that the reported decrease in packaging between 1991 and 1992 occurred in a period when Gross Domestic Product increased in Germany, before the onset of the recession.

Environment Minister Klaus Töpfer expressed satisfaction with the GVM study results: "The fact that the amount of packaging used has al-

Table 6-6: Changes in Total Packaging Consumption* in Germany, 1991-92
(thousands of metric tons)

Materials		Actual Packaging Consumption 1991		Actual Packaging Consumption 1992
Glass		4636.8		4426.3
Tinplate**		793.1		752.2
Aluminum		124.0		114.8
Plastic		1606.5		1542.1
Paper/paperboard		5209.3		5035.3
Composite				
a. Beverage cartons	198.2		201.6	
b. Paper-based	177.9		168.1	
c. Plastic-based	28.0		26.8	
d. Aluminum-based	6.8		6.4	
Composite total		410.9		402.9
Subtotal (quota materials)		*12,780.6*		*12,273.6*
Steel***		293.4		259.0
Wood, cork		2249.9		2131.6
Other		14.0		12.5
Subtotal (non-quota materials)		*2557.3*		*2403.1*
TOTAL		15,337.9		14,676.7

Note: INFORM has confirmed with GVM that the slight difference in the 1991 figure for paper in this table as compared with Tables 3-4 and 3-5 is due to a correction GVM made after the baseline data was published in January 1993.

*   As discussed in Chapter 1, Germany classifies discarded materials as waste (Abfall) or valuable materials (Wertstoffe). The total amount of packaging consumption includes both Abfall and Wertstoffe, and corresponds to the US term "packaging waste."
**   Coated steel cans for consumer goods, mostly food and beverages.
***   Steel barrels, drums, transport containers, pallets, and straps.

Source: *Entwicklung des Verpackungsverbrauchs 1992/1995: Vorausschätzung/Prognose (Development of the Use of Packaging 1992/1995: Estimate/Forecast)*, prepared by Gesellschaft für Verpackungsmarktforschung (GVM), for the Federal Environment Ministry (BMU), July 1993.

Change 1991-1992	Percent change	Projected Packaging Consumption 1995
-210	-5	3980.5
-41	-5	722.6
-9	-7	105.6
-64	-4	1498.5
-174	-3	5107.7
(+3)	(+2)	205.4
-10	-6	164.5
-1	-4	23.9
0	-0	6.1
-8	-2	399.8
_-514_	_-4_	_11,814.7_
-34	-12	269.6
-118	-5	2064.9
-2	-14	12.1
_-154_	_-6_	_2346.6_
-661	-4	14,161.3

ready been reduced two years after the introduction of the Packaging Ordinance proves that we are following the right course," he said.[44] DSD points out that, prior to 1992, the quantity of packaging used in Germany rose steadily each year, increasing 11.7 percent in 1990 and 3.5 percent in 1991; DSD also believes the data demonstrate the success of the Packaging Ordinance and the Dual System.[45]

DSD has also conducted several surveys to document packaging reductions. As those cited here were conducted before January 1993, any company actions in response to the ordinance were taken either to comply with the provisions on transport and secondary packaging or in anticipation of the Dual System for primary packaging. The surveys do not distinguish among the three packaging categories.

Between August and November 1992, DSD surveyed 8,689 companies that had obtained green dots for their packages; 1,062 responded.[46] Respondents included many large companies that produce more than 21 billion packages a year, more than one-tenth of all German packages.

Four of five companies reported "optimizing" their packages in the last two years by 1.) reducing the materials, 2.) making them reusable or returnable, and 3.) changing materials to make them more recyclable or to use recycled content. When asked their plans for 1992-1994 with respect to reusable packaging, 12 percent expected to increase reusables, 73 percent to use the same amount, and 1 percent to decrease reusable packaging; the remaining 14 percent did not respond. The companies reported a decrease in the use of plastics, blister packs, and composites. In response to questions on blister packs, 77 percent reported not using any, 8 percent planned to decrease their use, 11 percent planned to use the same, and 4 percent to increase use.

Following are the responses of the companies in the DSD survey reporting on their plans for 1992-1994. (Some companies reported multiple plans, so the percentages do not add up to 100.)

- Use less material – 38%
- Reduce the number of materials – 18%
- Replace composites – 12%
- Replace blister packs – 9%
- No plans – 25%

The motives for "optimizing" packaging were reported as follows:

- Packaging Ordinance – 55%
- Environment – 49%
- Pressure from retailers – 42%
- Technical – 30%
- Pressure from consumers - 20%
- Cheaper – 20%
- Design – 11%
- Use more recyclable materials – 7%
- Increase shelf life and stability – 5%

These responses indicated that the Packaging Ordinance was having a significant impact. Not only was it cited as the top motive, but the next two categories, environment and pressure from retailers, are driven by the ordinance.

DSD has published before-and-after photographs of primary packages that have been reduced. Some of these appear on page 76.

Some companies say their packaging changes were not affected by the Packaging Ordinance. Procter & Gamble GmbH (P&G) says it has always worked to minimize packaging and reduce the weight of packaging materials, and that its policies are not based on reactions to legislation.[47] P&G cites its initiatives in developing the refill pouch for fabric softener and in selling soap powders in concentrated form as examples of policies to reduce packaging that predated the Packaging Ordinance. At the same time, P&G says toothpaste tubes sold without the carton meet consumer demand, which is, to a degree, influenced by the ordinance and the accompanying public discussion.[48]

Case Study: Tengelmann Supermarkets

Large retailers can exert great influence on consumer product companies to make packaging changes. Tengelmann is a large, privately held company that operates more than 4,400 supermarkets in Germany.[49] It owns a controlling 53 percent of the common stock in the Great Atlantic and Pacific Tea Company in the United States, which operates such supermarket

Before and After Photographs of Primary Packaging Changes

Lever GmbH "Sunil"
laundry detergent:
concentrated formula,
reduced size of box,
used recycled plastic
for handle.

Procter & Gamble
GmbH "Ariel" laundry
detergent: developed
light-weight refill bag.

L&L Feinkist Handels
GmbH salmon: re-
placed composite con-
tainer with glass jar
and metal lid.

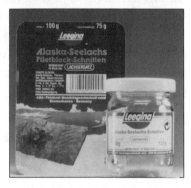

Source: Duales System Deutschland, "Daten und Fakten zum Grünen Punkt: Der
Ökologische Wandel bei Verpackungen" ("Data and Facts about the Green Dot: The
Ecological Change in Packaging"), November 1992.

Hans Maier flower bulbs: reduced size of box by almost 50 percent.

Henkel KGaA "Pril" dishwashing liquid: developed bottle with 30 percent recycled content.

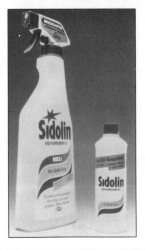

Thompson GmbH "Sidolin" glass cleaner: concentrated formula and developed refill bottle.

chains as A&P, Food Emporium, Waldbaum's, and Borman's, and also produces food products. Tengelmann's sales, including its foreign subsidiaries, are estimated at $24 billion per year.

Because Tengelmann claims to have had an active environmental program since 1984, it is difficult to determine which activities were initiated in Germany in response to the Packaging Ordinance. However, Tengelmann says the ordinance has made its suppliers more responsive to the company's long-standing appeals to reduce packaging.[50]

Besides working with Schoeller to develop a reusable shipping container (as described in Chapter 4), Tengelmann says its environmental efforts have included these packaging initiatives:
- Technical assistance to suppliers on reducing packaging – 1988
- Withdrawal of PVC bottles – 1989
- Press advertisements to promote packaging reductions – 1990
- Pilot project to recycle yogurt containers – 1990
- Placement of recycling containers in stores – 1990
- Making available, for a fee, reusable shopping bags – 1990
- Use of Chep brand wooden reusable shipping pallets – 1991

Tengelmann says its environmental policies for packaging between 1989 and 1991 have had these results:
- Reduced 6,800 metric tons of cardboard and 486 metric tons of foil through packaging modifications in cooperation with industry
- Directed that 200,000 one-way pallets be replaced by reusables
- Sent to recycling: 168,000 metric tons of paper and paperboard, 380 metric tons of foil, about 5 million wooden vegetable and fruit boxes, and 67,000 one-way pallets
- Returned about 6.1 million wine bottles to wine growers for refilling
- Eliminated 400,000 fruit and vegetable boxes by shifting to reusables

Tengelmann supermarkets were also test-marketing reusable containers for detergents, with deposits, and testing detergent-refilling machines that allow consumers to refill and reuse their own bottles. Tengelmann-owned Wissoll Chocolates was even experimenting with a packaging material made of starch and sugar.[51]

Notes

1. Thomas Rummler and Wolfgang Schutt, *The German Packaging Ordinance: A Practical Guide with Commentary,* Hamburg: B. Behr's Verlag GmbH & Co., 1990, p. 102. The Packaging Ordinance targets detergents because many are sold in bulky plastic containers that cause disposal problems. The mandatory deposit does not apply to the soft refill pouches many companies now offer for these products. Among paints, only emulsion (water-based) paints are targeted because other paints are considered hazardous and will be covered under a different ordinance.

2. Ines Siegler (Information Officer, Duales System Deutschland), written communication, April 23, 1993.

3. DSD, "The Green Dot: Don't Let Packaging Go to Waste," Bonn, p. 1.

4. Siegler (DSD), written communication, *op. cit.*

5. *Ibid.*

6. DSD, "Packaging Materials are Raw Materials," Bonn, August 31, 1992, p. 10.

7. *Ibid.,* p. 19.

8. Cynthia Pollock Shea (Bureau of National Affairs), "Packaging Ordinance Leads Most Firms to Reduce Packaging, Improve Recyclability," *International Environment Reporter,* Washington, DC, March 24, 1993, p. 231-232.

9. Siegler (DSD), written communication, August 10, 1993.

10. DSD, "Beverage Cartons," Bonn, April 1, 1993.

11. Siegler (DSD), written communication, August, 10, 1993.

12. DSD, "Report Regarding Quantity and Reprocessing of Secondary Raw Materials Anticipated for 1993," Bonn.

13. *Ibid.*

14. *Ibid.*

15. DSD, "Stand der Verwertung" (State of Recycling), (Graph), *DSD Business Report 1992,* Bonn.

16. Jan C. Bongaerts (Institut für Europäische Umweltpolitik e.V., [Institute for European Environmental Policy (IEUP)], Bonn), written communication, September 13, 1993.

17. DSD, "Problems in Rhineland-Palatinate Being Solved," press release, Bonn, June 16, 1993.

18. Siegler (DSD), written communication, *op. cit.*

19. Technische Fachhochschule Berlin, (Dr. Dieter Berndt, *et. al.*), *Abschätzung der gegenwärtigen und zukünftigen Kosten für das Sammeln und Sortieren von Verkaufsverpackungen im dualen System (Transparente Modellrechnung) (Estimate of Present and Future Costs for Collection and Sorting of Sales Packaging in the Dual System)*, Berlin, August 1992, p. 18.

20. Hubert Gehring, (BMU), interview, Baltimore, MD, July 15, 1993.

21. Siegler (DSD), written communication, August 10, 1993.

22. DSD, "Business Sector Strengthens Duales System," press release, Bonn, May 27, 1993.

23. *Ibid.*

24. DSD, "Drastic Reorganization at Duales System," press release, Bonn, June 25, 1993, p. 2.

25. DSD, "Duales System Finances Assured in the Long Term," press release, Bonn, June 20, 1993, p. 1.

26. DSD, "Drastic Reorganization at Duales System," *op. cit.*, p. 2.

27. *Ibid.*

28. DSD, "Duales System Presents Consolidation Concept," press release, Bonn, August 28, 1993.

29. DSD, "Drastic Reorganization at Duales System," *op. cit.*, p. 3.

30. DSD, "Informationen zur neuen Gebührenordnung" (Information about the New Fee Schedule), April 1993.

31. *Ibid.*

32. Technische Fachhochschule Berlin, (Dr. Dieter Berndt, *et. al.*) *op. cit.*, p. 14.

33. Harry Teasley (Coca-Cola), "Presentation to Implementation Subcommittee/ Packaging Standards Committee," Source Reduction Council of the Coalition of Northeastern Governors, Boston, MA, April 24, 1990.

34. Eberhard Kraft (Rudolph Wild Company, Heidelberg), telephone interview, July 1, 1993.

35. Rummler and Schutt, *op. cit.*, p. 27.

36. Joachim Tabler (Apple Computer GmbH, Germany), panel discussion at IN-FORM-US EPA: "Seeing Green: A Workshop in Business Waste Prevention," Los Angeles, CA, June 8, 1993.

37. Joachim Tabler (Apple Computer GmbH, Germany), written communication, September 8, 1993.

38. Ordinance on the Avoidance of Packaging Waste (*Verpackungsverordnung*), Article 6 (3), June 12, 1991.

39. Siegler (DSD), written communication, April 23, 1993.

40. Pollock Shea (Bureau of National Affairs), *op. cit.*, p. 231-232.

41. Jan C. Bongaerts (Institut für Europäische Umweltpolitik e.V., [Institute for European Environmental Policy (IEUP)], Bonn), "The Packaging Ordinance in Germany and its Implementation, First Experiences," Report for European Congress: Packaging and Environmental Strategies, Brussels, November 26-27, 1992, p. 12.

42. *Ibid.*, p. 13-14.

43. Gesellschaft für Verpackungsmarktforschung (GVM) (Association for Packaging Market Research), *Entwicklung des Verpackungsverbrauchs 1992/1995: Vorausschätzung/Prognose* (*Development of the Use of Packaging 1992/1995: Estimate/Forecast*), Wiesbaden, July 1993, p.3.

44. DSD, "Two Years of the Packaging Ordinance," press release, Bonn, July 21, 1993

45. *Ibid.*

46. DSD, "Daten und Fakten zum Grünen Punkt: Der Ökologische Wandel bei Verpackungen" ("Data and Facts about the Green Dot: The Ecological Change in Packaging"), Bonn, November, 1992.

47. Klaus Draeger (Procter & Gamble GmbH, Germany), telephone interview, April 15, 1993.

48. Klaus Draeger (Procter & Gamble GmbH, Germany), written communication, September 27, 1993.

49. Rosemary Baumeister (Tengelmann, Mülheim), written communication, April 30, 1993.

50. Anja Raffalsky (Tengelmann, Mülheim), interview, October 27, 1992.

51. "Recycling ist nur der zweitbeste Weg" ("Recycling is the Second Best Choice"), *Der Spiegel*, 25/1993, p. 50.

Chapter 7

Maintaining the Refillable Beverage Container System

INFORM observed in Germany that refilling bottles is a way of life for residents: the tradition of refilling is long-standing and enjoys strong public support. Before passage of the Packaging Ordinance, Germany already had one of the most extensive refilling systems in the world. Maintaining the existing refilling system while promoting recycling of one-way packaging materials is a major element of the ordinance. The Bundesrat, the upper house of Parliament, has even sought to increase the use of refillables.

But the beverage market is changing. The introduction of plastic refillable bottles has led to shifts away from glass. And the number of one-way beverage containers sold is increasing because, even though refillables are increasing their share of the market, the overall consumption of beverages is increasing. The result: a highly charged controversy over the relative environmental impact of one-way and refillable containers. This chapter explores the use of refillables in Germany, the impact of the ordinance on refilling, and recent trends and innovations.

Refilling and the Packaging Ordinance

The Packaging Ordinance requires that refill rates be maintained if industry is to be exempt from the mandated deposits on one-way containers and the requirement to take back primary packaging. That is, the ordinance specifies that, as a condition of industry's exemption, the refill rate for milk must not fall below 17 percent and the refill rate for all other beverages combined (beer, bottled water, soft drinks, juices, wine) must not fall below 72 percent. These were the average refill rates in West Germany in 1990. The ordinance also specifies that the refill rate in each state must not fall below the 1991 rate in that state.

The threat of mandatory deposits is a strong incentive to prevent the refill rates from falling. If DSD loses its exemption for beverage containers, the federal government will impose a DM0.50 ($0.30) minimum deposit on all one-way containers, increasing to DM1.00 ($0.60) for a 1.5-liter bottle. With deposits of this magnitude, one-way containers would lose the advantage of convenience over refillables, as consumers would have to return them to redeem the deposits.

The DM0.50 mandatory deposit on one-way plastic beverage containers that Germany imposed in 1988 was dropped January 1, 1993, when the provisions for primary packaging went into effect. Under the ordinance, plastic beverage containers are treated no differently from containers made of any other material. A major reason for removing the deposit on plastic beverage containers was to prevent retaliatory action by the European Community (EC). As described in Chapter 12, the EC has been battling Germany for years on the issue of restrictive trade policies; the European Community opposed the earlier mandatory deposits on plastic beverage containers. Germany has crafted its Packaging Ordinance to avoid future EC challenges and has set no material-specific refilling quotas. The ordinance further protects Germany's position by seeking to maintain the status quo rather than seeking an increase in refillables, which might be viewed in the European Community as a restrictive trade policy. The ordinance supports refillable systems without prohibiting one-way containers.

In their guide to the ordinance, Rummler and Schutt point out that it contains no legally binding provision to maintain the 72 percent refill rate. Protecting this rate is a condition for exemption from the primary packaging take-back and deposit regulations, and industry decides whether to seek that exemption.[1]

The Environmental Debate

The relative environmental impact of one-way vs. refillable beverage containers remains controversial. The Federal Environmental Agency (Umweltbundesamt, or UBA) commissioned an "eco-balance," or life-cycle analysis, to determine the environmental impact of different types of packaging. (UBA is the government agency responsible for implementing environmental policy.) The study was conducted by the Fraunhofer Institute for Food Technology and Packaging in Munich (Fraunhofer-Institut für Lebensmitteltechnologie und Verpackung) in conjunction with the Institute for Energy and Environmental Research in Heidelberg (Institut für Energie- und Umweltforschung, or IFEU) and the Group for Packaging Market Research in Wiesbaden (Gesellschaft für Verpackungsmarktforschung, or GVM). Using a computer model, the study group compared packaging systems for fresh milk, such as refillable glass, gable-top cartons, aseptic brick-shaped cartons, and polyethylene pouches. Similar analysis was done for beer packaged in steel cans, aluminum cans, one-way glass, and refillable glass.

The Fraunhofer group published its data in September 1993, showing the packages' environmental impact, including air and water emissions and raw materials consumption. More than 200 measurements — for example, the amounts of carbon monoxide and nitrogen oxides released to the air — were made for each packaging system. However, the Fraunhofer study draws no conclusions as to which packaging system is best for the environment, or whether refillables are better than one-way containers. The Fraunhofer Institute has said the study was not intended to find whether refillables are better than one-way containers, but under which circumstances each system is preferable. The institute noted the importance of transport distances for all containers and the number of trips made by refillable bottles in assessing environmental impact. It further noted that the study data may be used to identify opportunities for improving the environmental performance of current packaging systems — both refillable and one-way.[2]

As Environment Minister Klaus Töpfer pointed out, life-cycle analysis does not end but rather begins with such a study.[3] The Federal Environmental Agency (Umweltbundesamt, or UBA) faces the difficult task of evaluating the data. As there are no objective standards for comparing different environmental effects, UBA must determine the criteria — partly based on political judgments.

The Rummler-Schutt guide to the ordinance cites previous studies indicating that refillable containers "promise very positive eco-balances" where trippage rates are at least 20.[4] The trippage rate is the number of times a container is refilled. Rummler and Schutt assert that the refill systems — particularly those for beer and bottled water, which constitute the largest share of the beverage market and the highest refill rates — "make an impressive contribution to waste avoidance." [5]

When the Packaging Ordinance was first circulated, environmentalists expressed concern that its emphasis on recycling would undermine the existing system for refilling beverage containers: consumers might think a recyclable can with a green dot was as good for the environment or even better than a refillable bottle. So environmentalists who support refilling — as do many German consumers — succeeded in getting the refillables quota inserted in the ordinance.

Developments in the former East Germany provided another impetus to include a refill provision in the ordinance. After the unification of East and West Germany, the local refill systems in the former East Germany collapsed. The number of one-way beverage containers increased, causing a 1 - 2 percent decline in the national refill rate. The refill provision was intended to counter that trend in eastern Germany, as well as to protect refillables throughout Germany.[6]

Pressure for More Refillables

Table 7-1 shows the refill rates compiled for the government by Gesellschaft für Verpackungsmarktforschung (GVM) and published in September 1992. They indicate that the refill rate increased from 72.60 percent in the first half of 1991 to 74.61 percent in the first half of 1992 for beverages other than milk. Most one-way containers in Germany are glass, and only about 7 percent of beverages were sold in cans. Refill rates were highest for bottled water and beer — 91.66 and 83.61 percent, respectively. Refill rates for noncarbonated drinks, primarily juices, were lower but rose to 37.12 percent in the first half of 1992, from 35.14 a year earlier.

Table 7-1: Volume of Beverages In One-Way and Refillable Containers In Germany

	1991 (Jan.–June) percent	1992 (Jan.–June) percent
All Drinks	100.00	100.00
Refillable	**72.60**	**74.61**
One Way	**27.40**	**25.39**
glass	11.65	11.16
cans	7.83	7.00
composites	7.92	7.23
Mineral Water	100.00	100.00
Refillable	**91.73**	**91.66**
glass	91.38	90.83
plastic	0.34	0.83
One Way	**8.27**	**8.34**
glass	7.25	7.28
cans	0.53	0.45
composites	0.50	0.61
Noncarbonated Drinks	100.00	100.00
Refillable	**35.14**	**37.12**
One Way	**64.86**	**62.88**
glass	19.22	18.95
cans	0.09	0.08
composites	45.55	43.85
Carbonated Soft Drinks	100.00	100.00
Refillable	**73.91**	**75.90**
glass	64.35	61.92
PET	9.56	13.98
One Way	**26.09**	**24.10**
glass	10.24	9.98
cans	15.85	14.13
Beer	100.00	100.00
Refillable	**82.32**	**83.61**
One Way	**17.68**	**16.39**
glass	5.28	4.87
cans	12.40	11.52
Wine	100.00	100.00
Refillable	**39.26**	**39.65**
One Way	**60.74**	**60.35**
glass	56.97	56.32
composites	3.77	4.03
Milk	Not available	

Source: Gesellschaft für Verpackungsmarktforschung (GVM), Wiesbaden, 1992.

As a condition of passing the Packaging Ordinance, the Bundesrat insisted that the Federal Environment Ministry (the Bundesministerium für Umwelt, Naturschutz und Reaktorsicherheit, or BMU) draft a separate ordinance to increase the refill quotas to 76 percent by 1996, 78 percent by 1998, and 81 percent by 2000.[7] The government's draft in response to this demand specifies refill quotas as shown in Table 7-2.

Despite refill quotas that seem high from the US perspective, environmentalists in Germany remain concerned about the growing number of one-way containers. As noted earlier, beverage consumption is increasing in Germany, so even though the refill rate has held steady, the number of one-way containers is increasing.

The German Federation for the Environment and the Protection of Nature (Bund für Umwelt und Naturschutz Deutschland e.V., or BUND), the largest environmental organization in Germany, with over 200,000 members, notes that West German consumers used approximately four million one-way glass bottles in 1966. At that time the glass industry, organized in the Bundesverband Glas, launched an advertising campaign with the slogan "Ex und Hopp" (drink and chuck), which BUND describes as "the most disastrous attack on the environment ever launched by the packaging industry."[8] The ad campaign increased the popularity of the "modern" one-way glass bottles, which rose to 4 billion in 1985 and 5 billion in 1990.[9] Figure 7-1 shows the increase in one-way glass bottles (in filling volume), rising to more than 2 billion liters by 1990.

Even though the market share of refillables has increased recently, BUND focuses on the increased number of throwaway packages, and specifically the 10 billion throwaway drink containers in 1991. BUND, dissatisfied with the provisions on refillables in the Packaging Ordinance, wants to limit or ban one-way containers.

As can be calculated from the GVM data (Table 7-1), about 44 percent of the volume of beverages sold in one-way containers in 1992 was packaged in glass. Cans and composites like Tetra Pak each accounted for about 28 percent. There were no one-way plastic beverage containers, such as those used widely in the United States. After one-way polyethylene terephthalate (PET) bottles were put on the market, the German government, in 1988, imposed high mandatory deposits on one-way plastic bottles. This

Table 7-2: Refill Quotas for Beverage Containers – Draft Ordinance on Refillables

	1992 (actual)	1997 (quota)	1999 (quota)	2002 (quota)
Mineral Water	91.66	92	93	94
Noncarbonated Drinks	37.12	45	50	
Carbonated Soft Drinks	75.90	78	82	
Beer	83.61	87	91	94
Wine	39.65	45	50	
Milk	N/A	26	31	

Source: Die Verbraucher Initiative (DVI), Bonn, 1992.

requirement resulted in removal of the bottles from the market. The Coca-Cola Company withdrew its one-way PET bottle and introduced a refillable PET bottle. Coke now sells 74 percent of its drinks in refillable bottles — glass and PET — which the company says are cheaper than one-way containers.[10]

Table 7-3 illustrates the relative costs of one-way and refillable packages. BUND cites such studies as evidence that refillable bottles are no more expensive than one-way packaging.

The data in Table 7-3 are based on the assumption that the refillable glass bottles make 15 trips. BUND concludes that a returnable bottle system creates jobs because it requires labor-intensive services, whereas one-way packaging mostly involves consumption of energy and raw materials. Packaging materials account for only 36 percent of the cost for refillable bottles, compared with about 87 percent for one-way containers.[11] Washing the bottles accounts for about 20 percent of the packaging cost of refillable bottles.

BUND proposes five key strategies to optimize the use of refillable bottles:

1. Minimize transport distances to save energy and avoid emissions.
2. Reduce throwaway components, e.g., lids and labels.
3. Make all materials completely recyclable when they can no longer be refilled.

Figure 7-1: Use of One-Way Glass Bottles In West Germany, 1966-1990

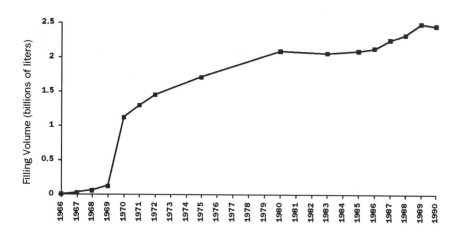

Source: BUND, "The Returnables Roundabout – Requirements for an Environmentally Friendly System of Returnable Drink Containers," Bonn.

4. Achieve highest possible trippage.
5. Standardize shapes, sizes, and materials to allow companies to refill and recycle bottles that are not necessarily their own.

Costs and Deposits

Germany has an established system for refilling water, beer, and soft drink containers, and the retail prices of these beverages are usually cheaper in refillable bottles. As for milk, however, the systems are not as established, and milk in a refillable bottle often costs more at retail than milk in a one-way container. One liter of milk in a refillable bottle typically costs about DM1.89, including the DM0.30 deposit; one liter of milk in Tetra Pak (aseptic) typically costs DM1.19. When consumers bring their own bottles to the store and fill them at a dispenser, called a "steel cow," the cost is generally the same as the purchase price of milk in a refillable bottle.

Deposits on refillable bottles in Germany are high relative to the price of the product — undoubtedly a factor in achieving the high trippage rates.

Table 7-3: Costs of One-Way and Refillable Packages for Beverages In Germany (based on 1 liter of beverage)

	Refillable Glass Bottles (15 fillings)	One-Way Glass Bottles	Beverage Carton	2 x 0.5 liter Aluminum Cans
	(costs in Pfennigs*)			
Packaging Costs				
1-liter beverage container	2.1	23	18.5	28
twist-off cap	4.5	4.5	0	0
label	1.5	1.5	0	0
racks/box/films, 300 reuses	0.3	3.9	1.2	1.8
Recycling Costs				
green dot price 1992	0	2	2	4
reprocessing costs primary packaging	0.1	2	2	4
reprocessing costs transport packaging	0	1	0.3	0.5
Bottle Cleaning	5	0	0	0
Additional costs for handling				
for retailers (taking back empties)	7	0	0	0
for wholesale (redistribution)	3	0	0	0
Total Packaging Costs	23.5	37.9	24	38.3

* 100 Pfennigs = DM1.00. All costs are based on 1992 prices.

Source: BUND, "The Returnables Roundabout – Requirements for an Environmentally Friendly System of Returnable Drink Containers," Bonn.

Table 7-4 shows prices and deposits for selected beverages by container type, based on data collected by INFORM in supermarkets in Bonn and Hanover. The data illustrate the relationship of deposits to prices.

German consumers frequently buy beverages by the crate, paying a single deposit to cover all of the bottles and the plastic reusable crate. A typical deposit for a case of 12 one-liter bottles of Coke is DM6.60 — 41 percent of the DM15.99 price. A case of twelve 1.5-liter bottles of mineral

Table 7-4: Selected German Supermarket Beverage Prices and Deposits by Product and Container Type

Product	Container	Volume (liters)	Price* (DM)	Deposit (DM)	Price per liter (DM)	Price per liter incl. deposit (DM)	Deposit (% of price)
Becks Beer	can	6 × 0.33L	5.99	0	2.99	–	–
Becks Beer	RFG	20 × 0.5L	21.99	6.00	2.20	2.80	27%
Becks Beer	1-way G	6 × 0.33L	4.99	0	2.50	–	–
Löwenbräu Beer	RFG	0.5L	1.25	0.15	2.50	2.80	12%
Coke	can	0.33L	0.69	0	2.07	–	–
Coke	RFG	12 × 1L	15.99	6.60	1.33	1.88	41%
Coke	1-way G	6 × 0.33L	4.49	0	2.50	–	–
Coke	RFPET	1.5L	2.09	0.70	1.39	1.86	33%
Mineral water	RFG	12 × 0.7L	9.99	6.60	0.83	1.38	66%
Melkland milk	RFG	1L	1.59	0.30	1.59	1.89	19%
Melkland milk	Tetra Pak	1L	1.19	0	1.19	–	–

Note: 1) 6 × 0.33 liters means 6 cans of 0.33 liter each. In cases of multi-packs, the deposit is for the containers and the crate; for single containers the deposit is for the container only. 2) Price relationships may fluctuate with special sales promotions.

Key: RFG = refillable glass. 1-way G = one-way glass. RFPET = refillable PET.

* Price not including deposit.

Source: INFORM, supermarket prices recorded October 1992 in Bonn and May 1993 in Hanover.

water also carries a DM6.60 deposit. As the mineral water is cheaper than Coke, the deposit amounts to 66 percent of the price. Deposit as a percentage of beverage price drops for beverages sold without a case, such as individual bottles of beer, and for more expensive beverages. The predominance of refillables in Germany indicates that the deposits do not discourage their use. In fact, the hefty deposits encourage a high rate of return, and thus many refilling trips, which increase the environmental benefits of refillables.

Retailers and Refillables

For retailers, the refill system is more costly than a one-way system because they must handle deposit redemptions and provide space for storing returned bottles. Some large supermarkets have separate beverage stores in their parking lots, where customers can drive up, drop off empties, and pick up new crates of beverages. Inner-city retailers, however, must provide bottle storage space in the store.

Refill systems work best and are most economical when each type of drink is sold in a standardized bottle. In Germany, for each type of beverage there is a standard container that companies may choose to use. Using the standard container reduces costs because a company need not get its own bottles back for refilling, but simply the same number of standard bottles it shipped.

Despite the inconveniences and costs to retailers, most cooperate with the refillable system — even very small local shops. Retailers cooperate because German consumers have demonstrated a dedication to refillables, because many store owners believe in the environmental value of the system, and because refilling has a long tradition in Germany. Small retailers may also like refillables because they bring customers back to the store to return the bottles. However, two of the major discount supermarket chains, Aldi and Lidl, have refused to carry any refillables. These stores discount heavily, have a high-volume business, and claim that they lack the space to handle refillable bottles.

For some consumers, home delivery is a more convenient way of participating in the refill system. Residents may receive weekly deliveries of crates of water, beer, and soft drinks and have the empty bottles collected.

Given that most refillable bottles are of heavy glass, and that many German apartments have no elevators, the service is extremely convenient, but it comes at a price: home-delivered beverages may cost twice as much as those bought in the store.

Refillable Plastic PET Containers

Refillable polyethylene terephthalate (PET) bottles have been a great success in Germany since their introduction in 1988. Their share of the carbonated soft-drink market has grown from 1.3 percent in 1988 to 14 percent in 1992, mainly replacing refillable glass.[12] This is the fastest growing material for beverage containers in Germany and has already captured half the soft drink markets in the Netherlands and Norway.[13] Refillable PET bottles are not used in the United States. (INFORM's new report, *Case Reopened: Reassessing Refillable Bottles,* presents a detailed study of refillable beverage containers in the United States.)

Refillable PET's advantages are that it is light in weight, nonbreakable and, according to the beverage industry, can make 25 trips. It is easier to carry and transport than glass, and it can be made in larger sizes, such as the popular 1.5-liter size.

However, some environmental groups in Germany strongly prefer glass to PET. BUND, for example, opposes the use of refillable PET bottles for the following reasons:

- *Low trip rate.* BUND estimates that refillable PET bottles are making on average four or five trips, not the 25 trips claimed by the Coca-Cola and PepsiCo companies.[14] Others in the beverage industry estimate the trippage at six to eight but say it will increase, since the technology is improving rapidly.[15]
- *Recycling isn't a closed loop.* BUND notes that there is closed-loop recycling for glass but not for PET. In other words, refillable glass bottles are recycled into new glass bottles at the end of their lifecycle, whereas PET bottles are recycled into different products, such as plastic lumber. Recycled PET is not allowed to be used for packaging that comes directly into contact with food or beverages for human consumption, because of the possibility of contamination.

- *Use of additives.* BUND is concerned that various additives are used in PET, making standardization difficult. The additives have properties, such as heat tolerance, that react differently during washing and refilling. BUND claims the variety of additives could create problems in washing and refilling if one company gets back another company's bottles.
- *Long-distance transport.* BUND is concerned about the energy and environmental consequences of shipping refillable PET bottles over long distances. For example, while Coke had 20 filling plants for glass, it has only five for its PET bottles in all of Germany. Coke says the large investment needed for PET filling plants requires it to consolidate its operations for economic reasons and run the plants on three shifts.[16]

Case Study: Development of a Refillable PET Bottle for Juices

While Germany has a strong tradition of using refillable bottles for mineral water, beer, and carbonated soft drinks, this is not true for noncarbonated drinks, such as juices. As shown in Table 7-1, only 37 percent of noncarbonated soft drinks are sold in refillable bottles. The following section describes the Rudolph Wild Company's development of a refillable plastic bottle for hot-filled juices. The case study is based on interviews INFORM conducted with Wild representatives in Germany, and on information from Schoeller Plast GmbH, one of the companies in the partnership that ultimately bought the bottling equipment from Wild. (Schoeller Plast is affiliated with Schoeller International, the company that developed the MTS returnable shipping containers described in Chapter 4.)

The Rudolph Wild company in Heidelberg developed the refillable plastic polyethylene (PET) bottle for its Capri-Sonne brand of juices. The company is part of Wild International, a private group of companies involved in manufacturing fruit juices, fruit flavorings, and other fruit products for the food industry; filling equipment; and refillable bottles and pouches. Besides making bottles and pouches for its own fruit products, the company makes refill pouches for other products, including detergents, shampoos, and cosmetics.

Wild usually sells its Capri-Sonne juice in lightweight aluminum pouches, which it markets in 42 countries, including the United States, where the licensee is Kraft-General Foods. Wild got the green dot — that is, the recycling guarantee — from the aluminum industry, which recycles the pouches.[17] Capri-Sonne juice has been a highly successful product for Wild, and the company intended to continue marketing it in the pouches as well as the refillable bottles. Wild says both refillable and one-way containers have a place on the market. For the latter, Wild cites the convenience of using them in school lunches, on trips, and at the beach.

Green Dot Fees as an Incentive

DSD's 1992 green dot fees provided an incentive to develop refillable bottles. Wild packages Capri-Sonne juice in boxes of 10 pouches, so 11 green dots were required for the complete box (one for each of the 10 pouches and one for the outer box), for a total per-box fee of DM0.22 ($0.13). The fees represented a 5.5 percent addition to the previous DM3.99 ($2.40) retail price. After implementation of the green dot system, the retail price rose 11 percent to DM4.50 ($2.70). Although green dot fees do not account for all of this increase, they do account for a large portion: an increase of 5.5 percent at the manufacturer's level leads to a greater increase in the consumer price because distributors and retailers mark up from a higher base. Wild reports that 1992 was the first year sales of Capri-Sonne did not increase, possibly due to the large price increase.

Under the 1993 schedule, the green dot fees for Capri-Sonne decreased substantially because they are based on weight, rather than the number of packages in the box. The fee for a box of 10 is about DM0.06 ($0.04) for the 10 pouches and DM0.06 for the box, for a total of DM0.12 ($0.07) — about half of the former green dot fee.[18]

Technical Problems and Costs

Technical problems arise in designing a refillable plastic bottle for juices because they are not carbonated and must be filled at high temperatures.

The design of a plastic bottle is different for carbonated and noncarbonated beverages. The pressure within the carbonated drink bottle maintains its shape and prevents shrinkage. Because of this pressure, a one-way bottle can be thin and light in weight, and is thus easily collapsed and discarded when empty. Refillable plastic bottles for carbonated drinks must be mechanically stable when empty; therefore, they are heavier than one-way bottles. A refillable bottle for noncarbonated beverages is heavier still, as it also must hold its shape without the carbonation. A bottle for hot-filled juices must also be able to withstand high temperatures for filling.

Wild fills its juices at 83°C. According to the company, a round bottle would not have the required mechanical stability for filling at this temperature, so the Wild bottle is square, with a design that allows for contraction and expansion as the temperature of the juice changes. These one-liter bottles can make up to 20 trips: shrinkage — from washing and refilling — prevents greater trippage. Shrinkage could be reduced if the bottles were made at a higher temperature, but the higher temperatures make the bottles cloudy, raising problems of consumer acceptance.

The bottles are laser-coded on a rim around the neck each time they are refilled, so they can be pulled from the line after the 20th trip. To assure that plastic bottles are not contaminated, Wild placed "snifters" on the filling lines. The snifters, which cost DM1-2 million ($600,000 - 1.2 million) each, can detect if the bottle has been contaminated by a foreign substance and should be removed.

The Wild refillable one-liter bottle cost DM1 ($0.60) to make, more than three times the cost of a one-way PET bottle. It had a deposit fee of DM0.70 ($0.42), refunded upon return of the bottle. Wild estimated the cost of washing and inspecting a six-bottle case at about DM0.20 ($0.12) and put transportation costs at DM0.30 ($0.18) per case, twice the cost for the lighter one-way bottles. Yet, Wild estimated that the refillable is cheaper than the one-way if it makes more than five trips and is shipped less than 300km (about 180 miles). Wild said a standard truck could carry approximately 18 metric tons of liquid in pouches, compared with 12 tons in refillable one-liter plastic bottles, and nine tons in refillable glass bottles.

Use of the PET Bottle

The success of the refillable PET bottle used by Coca-Cola and PepsiCo clearly encouraged Wild to develop the new plastic refillable container for juices. According to Wild, consumers like them because they are light and do not break. Wild notes PET is the fastest growing material for beverage containers in Germany, and all PET beverage containers in Germany are refillable.[19]

Although Wild developed the refillable PET bottle for its own juice products sold under the Capri-Sonne label, it hoped to sell the bottle to and do the filling for other companies. If the separate Ordinance on Refillables is passed, mandated refill rates for noncarbonated juices and soft drinks could reach 45 percent in 1997 and 50 percent in 1999. In response to the Packaging Ordinance, two of the largest juice companies, namely Granini and Eckes, have increased their use of refillables. Wild hoped its bottle would become the standard for noncarbonated drinks, but the decision will ultimately be made by the large juice producers.

Wild's plastic refillable went on the market in July 1991; it was still the only plastic refillable for hot-filled beverages in Germany in 1992. As of INFORM's October 1992 visit, it had not been very successful, perhaps because of the way new products are marketed in Germany. To get space on retail shelves, Wild had to pay retailers a high "entrance fee." The refillable bottle was in only 12.5 percent of stores at that time, as Wild was not prepared to pay greater entrance fees to increase its market penetration.

At the end of 1992 Wild sold the equipment for the production of the refillable PET bottles to a company called REF-PET SYSTEMS — a partnership between Schoeller Plast GmbH and Franz Delbrouck GmbH. REF-PET intends to produce and sell refillable PET bottles for both noncarbonated and carbonated soft drinks, and milk. As of mid-October 1993, it was running tests on the hot-filled juice bottles to resolve technical problems of filling at high temperatures and extending shelf life. It expected to begin marketing these bottles in the second half of 1994. Schoeller said two other companies in Germany and France are also developing refillable plastic bottles for hot-filled juices.[20]

Notes

1. Thomas Rummler and Wolfgang Schutt, *The German Packaging Ordinance: A Practical Guide with Commentary,* Hamburg: B. Behr's Verlag GmbH & Co., 1990, p. 59.

2. Fraunhofer-Institut, "Ökobilanzen zu Einweg- und Mehrwegverpackungssystemen am Beispiel von Frischmilch und Bier" ("Ecobalances for One-way and Refillable Packaging Systems Using the Examples of Fresh Milk and Beer"), press release, Munich, September 8, 1993.

3. Federal Environment Ministry (BMU), "Ökobilanz für Gertränkeverpackungen" ("Ecobalance for Beverage Packages"), press release, Bonn, September 21, 1993.

4. Rummler and Schutt, *op. cit.,* p. 58.

5. Rummler and Schutt, *ibid.*

6. Rummler and Schutt, *ibid.,* p. 106.

7. Rummler and Schutt, *ibid.,* p. 59.

8. BUND, "The Returnables Roundabout – Requirements for an Environmentally-Friendly System of Returnable Drink Containers," Bonn, p. 11.

9. BUND, *ibid.*

10. Bernd Hader (Coca-Cola, Essen), telephone interview, October 23, 1992.

11. BUND, *op. cit.,* p. 9.

12. Gesellschaft für Verpackungsmarktforschung (GVM) (Association for Packaging Market Research), Wiesbaden, 1992.

13. Robert C. Levandoski, "Europe Eyes 90% Recovery Rate for all Beverage Packaging," *Beverage Industry,* April 1993, p. 47.

14. Olaf Bandt (BUND, Bonn), interview, October 21, 1992; and "PET-Mehrweg- (k)eine ökologische Alternative?" ("PET – Refill-(no) Ecological Alternative?"), BUND, 1992.

15. Eberhard Kraft (Rudolf Wild Co., Heidelberg), interview, October 14, 1992.

16. Bernd Hader (Coca-Cola, Essen), telephone interview, October 23, 1992.

17. Eberhard Kraft (Rudolf Wild Co., Heidelberg), telephone interview, July 1, 1993.

18. Kraft, *ibid.*

19. Kraft, interview, October 14, 1992.

20. Claus Trube (Schoeller Plast GmbH, Düsseldorf), written communication, October 25 and November 4, 1993.

Chapter 8
Plastics and the Packaging Ordinance

Meeting the Packaging Ordinance's recycling quota for plastics has become the Achilles' heel of the Dual System: the broad consensus is that the system will fail, and industry will lose its exemption unless this problem is solved. Duales System Deutschland (DSD), facing a crisis in mid-1993, completely restructured the system for recycling plastics. It created a new company to manage plastic recycling and replace the original one, and it increased the green dot fees for plastics. This chapter examines the issue of plastics recycling in Germany — how problems evolved and what is being done to solve them.

The Plastics Industry Resists

Most of the materials industries responsible for recycling packaging waste — glass, metals, paper, and composites — have cooperated with DSD and have worked to improve recycling technologies and increase recycling capacities. The plastics industry has not. The giant chemical companies that make plastics — Bayer, BASF, and Hoechst, for example — have claimed they cannot meet the recycling quotas in the Packaging Ordinance and need more time.

Three approaches to handling used plastics that the plastics industry considers recycling are: 1.) mechanical recycling, in which plastics are ground up and reused in a variety of products, such as carpet fiber, bottles, and pipe, 2.) chemical recycling, in which plastics are broken down into smaller chemical compounds, such as synthetic crude oil used as fuel, or chemicals that may be used to create new products, and 3.) incineration with energy recovery. The big chemical companies continue to argue that incineration with energy recovery, which they call "thermal recycling," should count toward the recycling quotas, but the government has rejected this contention because it does not consider this technology recycling.

The Packaging Ordinance undeniably poses a major challenge for the plastics industry. Of the 1.4 million metric tons of German plastic packaging waste covered by the ordinance in 1992 (shown in Table 3-5), only 50,000 metric tons, or 3.8 percent, was recycled.[1] The Packaging Ordinance mandates 9 percent recycling of plastic primary packaging in 1993 and 64 percent by 1995, raising serious questions of whether and how these rates can be attained.

The plastics industry has resisted making a major investment in recycling because of the expense, and perhaps also the fear that recycled resins may undermine the market for virgin resins. The Berlin Technical College (Technische Fachhochschule Berlin, or TFB) study of DSD's costs cited in Chapter 6 estimated the costs of bins and collection for the "light fraction" of packaging (plastics, metals, and composites) at DM480-880 ($288-528) per ton. This study estimated that the cost of sorting plastics ranges from DM898 to DM4,256 ($539-2,554) per ton, and that the total cost of recycling plastics, including collecting and sorting, ranges from DM2,540-6,610 ($1,524-3,966) per ton — about 20 times the cost of collecting and burning plastics.[2]

The plastics industry has waged an intensive campaign for government recognition of incineration with energy recovery as a legitimate recycling technology. According to Dr. Karl-Geert Malle of BASF, one of the world's biggest chemical producers, "It is a lot more difficult to recycle plastics than paper or glass....It costs more to recycle plastics than to make new plastics and incinerate used plastics."[3] On the other hand, Gerhard Rüschen, chairman of Nestlé Deutschland and former chairman of DSD's advisory board, says the plastics industry took the wrong approach initially: "For too long a period they relied on thermal recycling, which is rejected by public opinion."[4]

DSD and the Federal Environment Ministry (Bundesministerium für Umwelt, Naturschutz und Reaktorsicherheit, or BMU) have rebuffed the plastics industry's pleas to count "thermal recycling" toward the mandated recycling quotas. According to Michael Scriba, general counsel of DSD in 1992, "the chemical industry needs to realize that the burning of plastics is politically unacceptable."[5] Rejecting industry's request to delay implementation of the 64 percent recycling quota from 1995 to 1999, Environment Minister Töpfer said, "No exceptions involving an extension of the deadlines will be made for any type of material."[6]

A Plastics Glut

In the spring of 1993, a plastics crisis erupted: DSD was collecting more plastics than planned — and far more than could be recycled. Of the roughly 1 million metric tons of primary plastic packaging, DSD was required to collect 30 percent in 1993 and recycle 30 percent of what it collected, for an effective mandated recycling rate of 9 percent. In other words, the quota specified the collection of about 300,000 metric tons and the recycling of about 90,000 metric tons. DSD announced in May that it would collect 400,000 tons in 1993 — more than four times as much as it was mandated to recycle. A major conflict developed over what DSD should do with the plastics it collected but was not required to recycle.

The ordinance itself failed to deal with the issue, even though it might have been anticipated that a public that had conscientiously sorted packaging waste and paid green dot fees to have it collected separately would not be happy to learn that DSD was sending much of the material collected to landfills and incinerators. Timing was part of the problem, as DSD was required simultaneously to coordinate the establishment of a new collection system with the creation of new recycling capacity. While the collection quotas for all materials are higher than their respective recycling quotas, in practice the disparities became a significant problem only for plastics; DSD claimed it was able to recycle all of the other materials collected.[7]

As of June 1993, DSD reported that the Technical Inspection Agency (Technische Überwachungsverein, or TÜV) working group had identified

276,000 metric tons of plastics recycling capacity for 1993: 124,000 metric tons in Germany and 152,000 tons abroad.[8] By July 1993, DSD had signed contracts for recycling 161,000 metric tons: 60,000 metric tons in Germany and 77,000 metric tons abroad were slated for mechanical recycling. Another 24,000 metric tons were designated for chemical recycling at a plant in Bottrop, Germany.[9] The DSD contracts for recycling 161,000 metric tons of plastics in 1993 gave DSD a capacity almost double the amount it was mandated to recycle, but this capacity equaled only 40 percent of the amount of plastics DSD would collect in 1993.

The States Protest

As stockpiles of plastics grew in 1993, public concern also rose, leading a number of the states, including Lower Saxony, Hamburg, Baden-Württemberg, and Rhineland-Palatinate, to protest. Monika Griefahn, the environment minister of Lower Saxony, threatened to revoke industry's exemption from the ordinance's mandatory deposits and from the requirement that stores take back primary packages. She was one of the three state environment ministers who had granted the exemption conditionally, as described in Chapter 9. DSD contended that, as it would exceed the collection quota for 1993, there was no legal basis for this action. It warned, "The environmental minister of Lower Saxony is in grave danger of letting herself be swayed by environmentally political reactionaries."[10] According to Griefahn, if stores must take back packages, they will pressure their suppliers to use more refillable containers, thereby reducing packaging waste.[11]

Klaudia Martini, the environment minister of Rhineland-Palatinate, complained, "We are suffocating under mountains of DSD waste and we have no more storage for it."[12] Martini, too, threatened to withdraw industry's exemption. After negotiations, DSD agreed to transport the plastics collected in Rhineland-Palatinate either to recycling facilities or intermediate storage facilities.

Wolfram Brück, chairman of DSD's board of directors, contended that DSD should not be held responsible for the large amount of non-packaging plastic materials it was collecting. As described in Chapter 6, DSD claims 40 percent of the materials in its bins — much of it plastic products — is not packaging. Brück argues that, "The problems with which we are currently being confronted in Rhineland-Palatinate are due to the success of the Dual System. Far more plastics are being collected, sorted, and recycled at present than actually required by the Packaging Ordinance. The federal states and municipalities are the first to benefit from this. It is ridiculous to try to use this success against the Dual System."[13] The municipalities would have to collect and dispose of these materials if DSD did not collect them. According to DSD, the amount of waste going to landfills has declined by up to 30 percent in many localities, saving local authorities about DM1 billion ($600 million).[14]

DSD tried to alleviate the plastics crisis by proposing to reduce the amount of plastics it sorted until the recycling capacity could be increased. Under this plan, only the plastics more easily recycled, such as bottles, would be sorted, and the remainder of plastics collected but not sorted would be disposed of as waste — sent to incinerators or landfills. "We know this is an unpopular decision," said Brück.[15] He was correct: the decision led to widespread press reports that DSD had approved the burning of plastics, and the plan was withdrawn. Environment Minister Klaus Töpfer acted as the intermediary in a compromise negotiated between DSD and the Association of Local Authorities that was announced July 25, 1993. Under this agreement, DSD would continue to sort all the plastics it collected but would recycle more abroad and put the rest in storage for two or three years until adequate recycling capacity was available. Wolfram Brück claimed that a capacity of 700,000 - 800,000 metric tons would be available by 1996. As part of the compromise, the localities agreed to help solve DSD's financial problems by reducing the amount DSD was to pay them by DM80 million ($48 million).[16]

The Role of Chemical Recycling

Germany must build plastics recycling capacity quickly to meet the 1995 quota, set by the Packaging Ordinance, for recycling more than 600,000 metric tons. Although the government has denied industry's requests to count incineration with energy recovery toward the plastics recycling quota, it has agreed to count "chemical" recycling. DSD believes "that the future of plastic recycling lies in chemical recycling processes, which reconvert used packaging into the starting product oil, into petrochemical products or gases. These robust processes are particularly suitable for the processing of mixed plastics and consequently simple sorting."[17] Chemical recycling provides three major advantages to industry: the sorting process is cheaper, as mixed plastics can be processed with little sorting; large capacity can be developed in a relatively short time using existing oil refineries; and the end product, oil or gas, does not compete with plastics.

Chemical recycling experiments have been conducted at the Kohleöl-Anlage Bottrop (KAB) plant run by Veba Oel AG in Bottrop. The plant's annual plastics recycling capacity was 24,000 metric tons per year in mid-1993 and was expected to increase to 40,000 metric tons per year by 1994.[18] It employs the hydrogenation process, in which the long plastic chains are cracked at high pressure and high temperatures in the absence of oxygen; hydrogen is added to create synthetic crude oil products, which can be used in fuels and lubricants and to manufacture plastics.

DSD expects RWE Entsorgungs AG, Germany's largest waste management company, to chemically recycle 70,000 metric tons of plastic per year starting in 1995, and it expects that another 200,000 metric tons will be chemically recycled at plants in the former East Germany, around Halle, Merseburg, and Bitterfeld.[19] Of the 1995 recycling capacity identified by DSD as of June 1993, chemical recycling accounted for about half.[20]

In response to questions about the environmental effects of chemical recycling, the TÜVs commissioned three universities to conduct a technical study comparing data from two chemical recycling plants — the KAB hydrogenation plant and the Energiewerke Schwarze Pumpe (ESPAG) gasification plant — with data from waste-to-energy plants.[21] The universities computed "energy balances" showing the percentage of energy recovered in the processes studied. The results indicated that only 50-70 percent of the energy present in plastics is recovered in modern waste-to-energy plants, compared with 76-86 percent at the KAB hydrogenation plant and 73-76 percent at the ESPAG gasification plant. Wolfram Brück of DSD concluded, "These energy balances confirm that we are moving in the right direction....We assume that the results obtained will lead to political support for Duales System and to further investments in recycling plants."[22]

However, despite the apparent energy balance advantages of chemical recycling over incineration claimed in the study, INFORM's analysis finds it limited. The study does not consider a key question: what is done with the end product of the gasification or hydrogenation processes? Are the resulting materials burned or used as chemical building blocks? Energy balance studies do not answer comprehensive life-cycle questions regarding the overall environmental consequences of chemical recycling.

Brück claims chemical recycling will be more economical than waste-to-energy incineration. He says the hydrogenation costs are now about DM800 ($480) per ton and that if large-scale hydrogenation plants with capacities of several hundred thousand tons per year were built, the costs of reprocessing plastics could be reduced to about DM300 ($180) per ton.[23] Brück has pointed to average incineration costs of about DM600 ($360) per ton, but he has not made public the basis of his estimate. The figure seems high, compared with the incineration tipping fees in the range of DM100-300 ($60 - $180), reported to INFORM in Heidelberg and Wuppertal — a range that was consistent with the Berlin Technical College (TFB) data.[24] Fees at new waste-to-energy plants are about DM400 ($240) per metric ton.[25]

Who Will Invest in Plastics Recycling?

Should chemical recycling prove economically and environmentally viable, it could enable DSD to meet the plastics recycling quotas. However, building the necessary recycling infrastructure requires a major investment, which industry has not yet made. On June 25, 1993, DSD announced a "drastic" reorganization of plastics recycling. It established a new company, called DEKUR-Kunststoff Recycling (DKR), to take over the tasks of plastics recycling formerly performed by VGK (Verwertungsgesellschaft gebrauchte Kunststoffverpackungen mbH), the company established and funded by the chemical industry. In addition to VGK's failure to make sufficient investment in recycling capacity, its loss of credibility had become damaging to the Dual System. The public prosecutor's office in Frankfurt was investigating it on charges of fraud and deceit: VGK was suspected of illegally shipping used plastic packaging to France and to Bulgaria, as well as other places in Eastern Europe.[26]

DKR will have capital of DM50 million ($30 million), half to be contributed by the public utility and waste management industries and one quarter each to be contributed by DSD and the chemical industry.[27] DKR's operating expenses will be financed by green dot fees for plastics, which DSD raised in June to DM3.00 ($1.80) per kilogram, from DM2.61 ($1.57) per kilogram (announced in March 1993) "to assure the long-term financing of DKR."[28] As discussed in Chapter 6, the green dot fee for plastic packaging is far higher than that for any other material because the fee includes some recycling costs: for all other materials, the respective materials industries bear the recycling costs.

Although the chemical industry has refused to pay the full costs of plastics recycling, the incentives are working as envisioned in the ordinance. Including plastics recycling costs in the green dot fees means these costs will be incorporated into the price of plastic packaging, thereby affecting the competitive position of plastic relative to other packaging materials.

The GVM report on packaging changes released in July 1993 (described in Chapter 6), found that plastic packaging had decreased by more than 60,000 metric tons, or about 4 percent, from 1991 to 1992 — about the average decrease for all packaging materials. Larger decreases in plastic packaging were expected after the new green dot fees took effect in October 1993. The fee per kilogram for plastic is almost 20 times the fee for glass. However, because plastic is lighter, the per package difference in fees is not that great (as shown in Table 6-5).

Despite the many opportunities to substitute other materials for plastics in packaging, their versatility affords many uses for which there are no comparable substitutes. While the ordinance discourages the use of plastic for single-use packaging, it encourages a shift from corrugated cardboard boxes to reusable plastic shipping containers, such as the MTS reusable container system described in Chapter 4.

Large, well-financed companies, such as the utility RWE, have begun investing in chemical recycling facilities for plastics, assuming that when the take-back and recycling of products such as automobiles and electronics are mandated (as discussed in Chapter 10), demand for chemical recycling will increase. Packaging accounts for 21 percent of plastic waste in Germany; the auto industry accounts for 7 percent.[29]

Environmental Concerns
about Polyvinyl Chloride

Polyvinyl chloride (PVC) poses a particular problem that goes beyond the general complexities of recycling plastics. Some politicians and consumer and environmental groups in Germany have demanded a ban on PVC packaging. Greenpeace has waged a major international offensive against PVC, advocating a ban on all chlorine production because of the toxics emitted in the production and use of chlorinated products. A study in the United States by Tellus Institute, a nonprofit consulting firm, found PVC the most environmentally damaging packaging material. A study commissioned by the German Federal Ministry for Research and Technology in 1989 found that "although PVC packaging makes up only 0.5 percent of the volume of waste by weight, it is responsible for 50 percent of the chlorine in the waste stream."[30]

PVC complicates the recycling process. It is difficult to separate PVC from polyethylene terephthalate (PET), commonly used in beverage containers, because the materials look alike, yet one PVC bottle can contaminate 100,000 PET bottles in the recycling process.[31] At the KAB plant, the mixed plastics feedstock can contain only 10 percent PVC because the plant cannot handle a higher percentage of chlorides.

As plastic packaging is not labeled by resin in Germany, the consumer is not informed whether a package contains PVC and therefore cannot choose whether or not to purchase it. PVC is often used to package meats and other food products, including yogurt, jam, and ketchup.

In a survey published in March 1992, DSD contacted a random sample of 400 companies, 315 of which returned useful responses.[32] DSD queried the companies on the materials used to substitute for blister packs, PVC, and composites. As the three pie charts in Figure 8-1 indicate, much of the substitution for these packaging materials was accomplished by actually eliminating the entire package or a layer of packaging. When substitute materials were used, they consisted primarily of paper, polyethylene (PE), and polypropylene (PP).

PVC packaging is being phased out in other countries, including Switzerland, Sweden, the Netherlands, and Australia. In the United States,

Figure 8-1: Packaging Changes Made by Companies in Germany to Eliminate or Substitute for PVC, Composites, and Blister Packs

1. Elimination/Substitutions for PVC

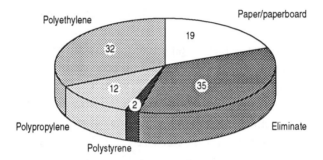

2. Elimination/Substitutions for Composites

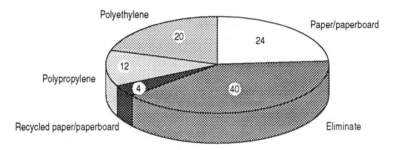

3. Elimination/Substitutions for Blister Packs

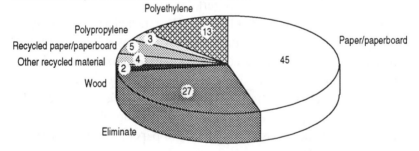

Source: Duales System Deutschland, "Daten und Fakten zum Grünen Punkt: Ökologische Verpackungsoptimierung" ("Data and Facts about the Green Dot: Ecological Packaging Optimization"), Bonn, March 1992.

Procter & Gamble announced that it would phase out PVC by 1994.[33] The large department stores Hertie and Karstadt and the Tengelmann supermarket chain have said they plan to eliminate packages with PVC from their stores.[34] According to the Environment Ministry, "there is no future for PVC in packaging in Germany."[35]

Exporting Used Plastic Packaging

Given the difficulties in building recycling capacity for plastics in Germany, it is not surprising that used plastic packaging is being exported.

Shipments of German plastic packaging waste have turned up as far away as Jakarta and Singapore, and the environment senator of the city of Hamburg, Fritz Vahrenholt, stopped the loading of 1,200 metric tons bound for India. "Without proof of proper recycling, nothing is leaving here," he said. Waste managers in Germany assert that wastes from Europe, shipped to Third World countries, usually end up in landfills.[36] To prevent this, DSD has asked the TÜVs to monitor 110 plastics recyclers worldwide.

The new EC rules on international shipments of waste, discussed in Chapter 12, prohibit the export of recyclable materials destined for landfills or incinerators. The regulations require that materials shipped be actually recycled, but monitoring is likely to remain a problem.

System's Success Hinges on Plastics Recycling

Recycling plastic packaging is clearly key to the Dual System's success — and even its survival. Meeting the recycling quotas of the Packaging Ordinance has been more difficult for plastics than for any other material. The timely development of adequate recycling capacity, using technologies accepted by the German government and DSD, is necessary if industry is not to lose its exemption.

Building adequate recycling capacity for plastics will require an investment of billions of Deutsche Marks. The series of crises that faced DSD in 1993 have left the future of the Dual System in doubt. The chemical industry continues to hope that the crises and stockpiling of plastics will force the government to accept burning plastics, "thermal recycling," as a way of meeting the recycling quotas, even as some of the opposition parties and environmentalists oppose counting chemical recycling toward those quotas. New technologies, such as using plastics as a substitute for coal in steel production, are under consideration. But until there is more certainty on a policy for plastics, it is unlikely that the massive investments required to reach the recycling quotas will be made.[37]

Notes

1. William H. Le Maire, "Germany's Precedent-Setting Dual System, A Model for the Future or a Blueprint for Chaos?" *Packaging Strategies' Green 2000*, Vol. 2, No. 7, West Chester, PA, July 1992, p. 12.

2. Technische Fachhochschule Berlin, (Dr. Dieter Berndt, *et. al.*), *Abschätzung der gegenwärtigen und zukünftigen Kosten für das Sammeln und Sortieren von Verkaufsverpackungen im dualen System (Transparente Modellrechnung) (Estimate of Present and Future Costs for Collection and Sorting of Sales Packaging in the Dual System)*, Berlin, August 1992, p. 18.

3. Samantha Swiss, "Pack up Your Troubles," *Environment Risk,* April 1992.

4. Don Loepp, "German Package Recycling Goals May Be Unattainable," *Plastics News,* November 2, 1992, p. 1.

5. Swiss, *op. cit.*

6. "Germans Heartened by First Test of Chemical Recycling," *Plastics News,* May 18, 1992, p. 15.

7. DSD, "New Sorting Criteria for Plastics: Sorted Material Will Be Recycled," press release, Bonn, July 1, 1993.

8. DSD, "Recycling Capacities for Plastic 1993," press release, Bonn, June 4, 1993.

9. *Ibid.*

10. DSD, "Threats to Revoke Exemption for Plastic Packaging Constitute Totally Wrong Signal," press release, Bonn, June 17, 1993.

11. Monika Griefahn (Environment Minister of Lower Saxony), telephone interview, June 30, 1993.

12. Arian Genillard, "Too Much of a Good Thing," *Financial Times,* London, June 23, 1993, p. 10.

13. DSD, "Problems in Rhineland-Palatinate Being Solved," press release, Bonn, June 16, 1993.

14. DSD, "Reform Proposals from Five Local Government Bodies are Unimaginative," press release, July 21, 1993.

15. DSD, "New Sorting Criteria for Plastics," press release, July 1, 1993.

16. DSD, "Agreement with Local Authorities," press release, July 25, 1993.

17. DSD "New Sorting Criteria for Plastics," *op. cit.*

18. DSD "Recycling Capacities for Plastic 1993," *op. cit.*

19. *Ibid.*

20. *Ibid.*

21. The study commissioned by the TÜVs was conducted under the direction of professors at three universities: Dr. F. Ebert, Universität Kaiserslautern, Department of Mechanical Process Engineering and Fluid Mechanics; Dr. M. Baerns, Ruhr-Universität Bochum, Department of Technical Chemistry; Dr. E. Klose, Technische Universität Bergakademie Freiberg, Institute for Energy Process Engineering and Chemical Engineering.

22. DSD, "Recovery of Raw Materials from Plastic Packaging," press release, July 7, 1993.

23. *Ibid.*

24. Rolf Friedel (Stadt Heidelberg, Amt für Abfallwirtschaft und Stadtreinigung [City of Heidelberg, Department of Sanitation]), interview, October 14, 1992; <u>and</u> Erwin Rothgang (Amtes für Umweltschutz, Stadtverwaltung Wuppertal [Department of Environmental Protection, City Administration Wuppertal]), interview, October 28, 1992.

25. Jan C. Bongaerts (Institut für Europäische Umweltpolitik e.V., [Institute for European Environmental Policy (IEUP)], Bonn), written communication, September 13, 1993.

26. "Recovery Loses Out to Eco-Tax Option," *Europe Environment,* No. 412, Europe Information Service, Brussels, June 22, 1993, p. 17.

27. DSD, "Drastic Reorganization at DSD," press release, June 25, 1993.

28. *Ibid.*

29. BMW, "Recycling of Plastics," 1991.

30. Environmental Action Foundation, Washington, DC, Solid Waste Action Paper #8, "The Real Wrap on Polyvinyl Chloride Packaging," p. 3.

31. *Ibid.*

32. DSD, "Daten und Fakten zum Grünen Punkt: Ökologische Verpackungsoptimierung" ("Data and Facts about the Green Dot: Ecological Packaging Optimization"), Bonn, March 1992, p. 3.

33. Environmental Action Foundation, *op. cit.,* p. 4.

34. Maria Rieping (Die Verbraucher Initiative [DVI] [The Consumer Initiative], Bonn), interview, October 21, 1992.

35. Hubert Gehring (BMU), interview, Baltimore, MD, July 15, 1993.

36. "Kippe in Fernost" (Garbage Dump in Far East), *Der Spiegel,* No. 53, December 28, 1992, p. 48.

37. Joachim H. Spangenberg (The Wuppertal Institute), "The German Waste Policy," September 27, 1993.

Chapter 9
Criticisms of the Packaging Ordinance and the Dual System

Criticism in Germany

INFORM conducted a month-long series of interviews with public and private organizations throughout Germany in the fall of 1992 that revealed widespread support for the underlying principles of the Packaging Ordinance. (Appendix C lists the sources interviewed.) Throughout its interview and research process, INFORM did not find public opposition to the principle of making industry responsible for the waste generated by its packages. INFORM also found that industry favored the market-based approach that allows the private sector to work out the details, rather than subjecting companies to "command and control" government regulations.

Despite generally positive reactions from much of the public and industry, environmentalists, consumer groups, political leaders, and the Green Party criticized the Packaging Ordinance early on for not promoting a program strong enough to reduce packaging waste significantly. Critics have focused on Duales System Deutschland (DSD), charging that the Dual System is "protecting the packaging industry rather than the environment" and that DSD is a "giant tax machine."[1] At the outset, some local officials expressed resentment at sharing their authority and responsibilities with DSD. Some have questioned the effectiveness of DSD while others, like the Munich Department of Environmental Protection, have claimed that the entire system is a "betrayal" and a "sellout to industry."[2] The Bavarian city of Munich vociferously opposed the system before eventually joining it.

Prior to implementation of the Dual System in January 1993, Bavarian Environment Minister Peter Gauweiler was the program's most vocal critic and threatened to withhold DSD's exemption for primary packaging within the Bavarian state. Ultimately, he went along with the rest of the country, and all the states granted the exemption for the Dual System. Had he not granted the exemption, retailers in Bavaria would have had to take primary packages back, and mandatory deposits would have been imposed.

At a press conference in December 1992, shortly before the January 1, 1993 deadline for implementing the regulations for primary packaging, Environment Ministers Peter Gauweiler of Bavaria, Monika Griefahn of Lower Saxony, and Harald Schäfer of Baden-Württemberg cited four principal reasons for their opposition to the Packaging Ordinance and the Dual System:

1. They do not give enough attention to waste avoidance.
2. They do not sufficiently promote refillable bottles.
3. They do not ban environmentally harmful packages.
4. They mislead the public with the green dot symbol.

Despite these objections, the three ministers agreed to comply with the ordinance and grant the exemption to DSD on five conditions:

1. DSD had to be in place in all localities by March 1, 1993.
2. The exemption for plastics was given only until June 1, 1994, because DSD had not demonstrated that the recycling capacity existed for the volume of plastics that would be generated.
3. DSD must prove that the required amount of plastic packaging is being recycled and identify the products made from the recycled material.
4. Independent experts like the Technical Inspection Agencies (Technische Überwachungsvereine or TÜVs) must monitor DSD's sorting and recycling facilities in Germany for plastics and composites, and abroad for all materials.
5. The Dual System must be expanded to reuse and recycle natural materials such as wood, jute, and stoneware.[3]

The three ministers argued that the Packaging Ordinance is unsatisfactory and that other ordinances are needed to compensate for the inadequacies. They urged Environment Minister Töpfer to fulfill his pledge to promote an ordinance on refillable beverage containers and to compile a list of ecologically harmful or questionable packaging that should be prohibited.

The statement by the three ministers includes the major objections of most of the Dual System's critics. INFORM heard many other specific objections to the system through interviews with environmental and consumer organizations, state and local officials, academics, and government and industry representatives. The following sections describe three of the major criticisms voiced by these groups — the ordinance does not promote source reduction, the Dual System undermines refillables, and the green dot is misleading — and other complaints about the system.

The Ordinance Promotes Recycling, Not Source Reduction

The Packaging Ordinance does not specifically address source reduction, called waste avoidance *(Abfallvermeidung)* in Germany, which raises the concern that a program focused on recycling may ultimately undermine reduction efforts. Similarly, DSD's stress on recycling over source reduction in the local public information campaigns that it funds has sometimes created conflict between local officials, who want to stress avoidance, and DSD's focus on recycling. Munich, for example, attempted to enforce waste avoidance through a ban on nonrefillable beverage containers, but the federal court later found the ban unconstitutional. DSD has now agreed to include avoidance in some of its advertisements.

The Dual System Undermines Refillables

Most Germans support the refilling system for beverages and take seriously any perceived threat to this system. Although the ordinance mandates that the refill rate not decline if the Dual System is to retain its exemption, the Bundesrat (upper house of Parliament) does not consider this provision strong enough; it passed the Packaging Ordinance on the condition that the government pass a separate ordinance on refillable containers that mandates higher refill rates. A draft of this ordinance has been circulating since mid-1992 (as discussed in Chapter 7).

Many of the ordinance's critics have called for restrictions or bans on one-way containers and certain packaging materials, particularly the plastic polyvinyl chloride (PVC).[4] Some recommend mandated refill rates for non-beverage products, such as jams and marmalades, and are concerned that the convenience of curbside collection of packaging, provided by DSD, may discourage consumers from returning refillable bottles, thereby undermining the refillable system. The green dot symbol is seen as a threat to refillables, as discussed below.

The Green Dot is Misleading

Critics have argued that the green dot leads consumers to believe that a package is environmentally sound, when the green dot is effectively the symbol of a non-environmentally sound package because it appears only on one-way packaging. For example, consumers may think a one-way beverage can with a green dot is better for the environment than a refillable bottle without the dot, and this perspective might undermine the refill system. An early DSD advertising campaign that claimed the green dot identified packages that are good for the environment faced broad criticism: DSD no longer makes such a claim.

The green dot is supposed to stand for a guarantee that the package on which it is placed will be recycled. However, most packages carry the dots even though sufficient capacity for recycling is not yet in place. With the system still in transition, at best the green dot means only that the package can be recycled, not that it actually will be recycled. In 1993, the number of green dots awarded was greatly outstripping the number of packages being recycled, thereby damaging the credibility of the Dual System.

DSD is Stockpiling Recyclables

Owing to the lack of adequate plastics recycling capacity, DSD has stored large amounts of used plastic packaging. A major fire in October 1992 called attention to the fact that recyclers were stockpiling some plastics rather than recycling them. The fire, at a plastics recycling facility where plastic materials were stored in Lengerich, near Münster, led officials to evacuate the area because of hydrochloric acid emissions from burning PVC. Although DSD says the plastics were residues from plastic production, not packaging materials collected by DSD, the incident is an example of a less frequently considered but nonetheless potentially damaging environmental impact from storing plastics for recycling, which reinforced demands for less plastic packaging. As described in Chapter 8, concern about plastics stockpiling led the environment minister of Rhineland-Palatinate to threaten to withdraw DSD's exemption for plastics in that state.

Recycling is Not Effectively Monitored

Even though the Technical Inspection Agencies (TÜVs) have been appointed to ensure that DSD is meeting its recycling goals, concern remains that materials will be burned, landfilled, or exported to countries that will dispose of them in an environmentally unsafe manner. For even if the TÜVs can document that a firm is recycling, it is difficult to monitor its total input and output. Firms abroad may be importing more used materials than they can recycle and dumping the excess. The DSD system is complex and difficult to monitor. The three environment ministers from Bavaria, Lower Saxony, and Baden-Württemberg have demanded that DSD specify the end products of plastics recycling.

Critics are also concerned that the TÜVs are paid by DSD to monitor, and that they have no authority to close down plants that do not meet standards.

Life-Cycle Analysis is Needed

Some recycling technologies may pose more environmental problems than disposal. The current compromise allowing chemical recycling of plastics has not undergone life-cycle analysis, and the environmental impact of this process has not been determined. If plastic packaging is processed into synthetic crude oil, which is then used as fuel, is this preferable to waste-to-energy incineration, and should it be called "recycling?"

The environment senator in Hamburg, Fritz Vahrenholt, questioned whether recycling is always better for the environment than incineration. He said even environmentalists admit that modern incinerators have lower emissions than older incinerators, and maintains that it is better to incinerate certain materials and separate the ash than to recycle them.[5]

Germany's Federal Environmental Agency (Umweltbundesamt, or

UBA), commissioned three nonprofit organizations to conduct life-cycle analyses of packaging. As described in Chapter 7, the organizations, led by the Fraunhofer Institute, prepared a database to provide life-cycle information on issues raised by the Packaging Ordinance. The Fraunhofer group first used its computer model to evaluate different packaging alternatives for milk and beer, but the programs may also be used to address such questions as the life-cycle consequences of chemical recycling.

The Green Dot System Permits "Free Riders"

In a report titled "Will the Dual System Manage Packaging Waste?" the Kiel Institute for World Economics, a nonprofit think tank in Kiel, Germany, expressed concern over the potential for "free riders" on the green dot system. This report was issued in January 1992, before the Dual System was operative. The institute said that retailers, particularly small ones, have an incentive to carry packages without the green dot because they will be cheaper. Kiel contends this lack of participation could cause the collapse of the Dual System. It has not so far been a major problem, however, because retailers have a strong incentive to make the Dual System work: if it fails, they get the packages back.

But another type of free rider has emerged. Some companies are printing the green dot on their packages without paying the required fees to DSD, or are paying partial fees and placing more packages on the market than they report to DSD.[6]

Incentives Are Not Specific

Given the huge number of packages, it would be virtually impossible to require each company to take back its own packages and recycle them, thereby creating company- and package- specific incentives. Instead, German industry is being made responsible for taking back packaging "collectively." The Kiel report argues that "the advantages of the polluter-pays principle in terms of dynamic effects, however, may be softened through the global reprocessing guarantees as they do not provide enough incentives for the individual companies to improve their products in terms of reprocessing costs."[7] The new 1993 green dot fee schedule (described in Chapter 6) partially addresses this concern: although the new schedule does not make incentives company-specific, it does make them material-specific.

The Ordinance Requires Recycling at Any Cost

In general, German industry has not greatly criticized the Packaging Ordinance because it wants the Dual System, which it is running, to succeed. However, industry has criticized the extension of the Packaging Ordinance to other products, and these criticisms reflect its underlying view of the packaging legislation as well. The Federation of German Industries (Bundesverband der Deutschen Industrie e.V., or BDI), has said, "Recycling at any price is not a rational strategy....Returning materials for recycling is only sensible when markets exist for the collected materials."[8] The plastics industry is particularly vociferous on this point, arguing that the 64 percent recycling quota is too high, and that the cost of recycling plastics is higher than the cost of virgin resins.[9]

DSD Contracts are Too Costly

According to a study by the Wuppertal Institute, the disposal industry's profit margins from its contracts with DSD were as high as 100 percent, supporting charges that DSD's contracts with the waste management industry and the localities were unjustifiably costly.[10] Strategies to control these costs are discussed in the Epilogue.

Localities Lose Authority

Localities are ambivalent toward DSD — appreciating the funding but not liking the loss of control over their waste management programs. Some localities had been working to set up recycling systems, which they did not want DSD to scuttle. Approval of the Dual System required them to negotiate which functions they would carry out and which would be handled by DSD. In some cases where DSD takes over the management of packaging waste (rather than paying localities to do so), municipal solid waste departments have to lay off some workers. Localities have also pointed out that DSD is taking the most politically appealing part of waste management, recycling, and leaving the localities with the unappealing portion, disposal.[11]

Inefficient Separation of Materials

Critics claim that commingling metal and plastic packaging materials in the yellow DSD bins lowers the quality of the recyclable materials and increases sorting costs. These bins are used for foils, cans, films, composites, and all types of plastic packages. In fact, all packaging other than glass bottles and paper brought to drop-off containers are put in the yellow DSD bins. In addition, some local waste managers believe it is inefficient to collect plastic packaging separately from plastic products, and they would prefer to collect plastics together, as ultimately they may be going to the same recyclers.

DSD Violates Antitrust Laws

DSD's dominant role in the management of packaging waste nationwide has put it in conflict with Germany's strict antitrust laws, designed to prohibit unfair restraints on competition. Parties that feel they are injured have brought alleged infractions to the attention of the Federal Cartel Office (Bundeskartellamt). Negotiations have been under way between DSD and the Cartel Office on a series of antitrust-related issues.

For example, small recyclers dependent on DSD for their supply of recyclable materials have complained that DSD is preventing competition in the recycling industry. Companies managing the bottle banks that sell the cullet (crushed glass) complain that DSD is "killing" their markets by offering glass free of charge to recyclers.[12] The nationwide DSD network has led to greater concentration in the waste industry: carters and recyclers not selected as DSD contractors have complained to the Cartel Office, which is investigating the complaints.

Ines Siegler, a spokeswoman for DSD, says that charges that DSD is preventing competition are unjustified — "The law forces us to have a nationwide network and therefore operate as a monopoly."[13] According to Frank Annighofer of the US management consulting firm Arthur D. Little's European environment department, "We cannot say now if the recycling industry will also become monopolistic as a result of DSD activities. But pressure is likely to grow on legislators to ensure that this is not the case."[14]

On January 12, 1993, the Cartel Office filed an action against DSD because of its intention to extend its operations to include the collection of packaging waste from commercial enterprises. The office claimed that "the expansion of DSD's activities, which have been pushed for by the state environmental ministries, would drive out many medium-sized companies." The Cartel Office was concerned about DSD's endangering the livelihood of the hundreds of independent companies that handle commercial waste. Environment Minister Klaus Töpfer supported DSD's contention that the expansion was requested by the states and is backed by the federal government in Bonn.[15] DSD agreed in April 1993 to eliminate the allegedly unfair advantages of its own contractors, and the Cartel Office announced it would drop the charges.[16]

Negotiations continue between DSD and the Cartel Office on how best to minimize restraints of competition. On June 28, 1993, the Cartel Office decided that DSD would not be permitted to collect transport packaging waste.[17]

Another of the Cartel Office's concerns has been the concentration of contractors that collect and process waste for DSD. For example, RWE, a large electric utility also in the waste business, has bought 70 waste management companies in the last four years. The Cartel Office was watching the situation but had not initiated any action as of late 1993.[18]

International Concerns

The Ordinance is a Trade Barrier

Other EC nations have argued that the German Packaging Ordinance is a barrier to free trade in the European Community (as discussed more fully in Chapter 12). The Industry Council for Packaging and the Environment (INCPEN), based in the United Kingdom and composed of 60 major European and international companies, has lodged a formal complaint with the European Commission (the executive branch of the European Community), against the German Packaging Ordinance as has the British Department of Trade and Industry (DTI). The Belgium-based Association of European Plastics Manufacturers is also demanding that the European Community take action against the German Packaging Ordinance.[19]

At the same time, the European Community is working on its own Packaging Directive, which could overrule the German Ordinance. German officials believe this unlikely, however; they say they cannot be expected to water down their environmental policies to the level of poorer EC countries such as Spain, Greece, and Ireland. German Secretary of State for the Environment Clemens Stroetmann says the European Community will have to make its directive similar to Germany's; that each month the German ordinance is in force will strengthen Germany's negotiating position, as it will be able to demonstrate success.[20]

The German Federal Environment Ministry says it would gladly defend its Packaging Ordinance in the European Court. "By the time the court ruled, we would be recycling 70 percent of our waste....Would the judges really order us to cut that to 60 percent?"[21]

Recyclables are Dumped Abroad

A scandal arose when packages with green dots were found in landfills in France in 1992. The media reported the incidents as evidence that the companies that handle DSD's materials are not recycling them but dumping them abroad. Green dot packaging materials are classified as "recyclables" rather than "waste," yet sightings in foreign landfills indicate they are sometimes being disposed of as "waste." Exporting materials for recycling is legal, but tracking these materials to assure they do not end up in incinerators or landfills is difficult. DSD has denied allegations, made on the German television program "Panorama," that 60 percent of plastic packaging waste shipped abroad by VGK (the now-defunct plastics recycling company) was not recycled.[22]

In response to these problems, the TÜVs have compiled a list of approved recyclers worldwide to which DSD shipments will be permitted. The new European Community directive on waste shipments, described in Chapter 12, will also require permitting and tracking of such shipments. As the rules on exporting waste in Germany and the EC are complex and rapidly changing, it remains to be seen whether the new monitoring will solve the problem of dumping.

Markets are Disrupted

The United Kingdom, France, Luxembourg, the Netherlands, Spain, Belgium, and Denmark have complained to the European Commission about the flood of packaging materials exported to their countries from Germany. Germany, in turn, has apologized for any "negative fallout" of its policy and has promised to cooperate in finding a solution.[23]

Companies selling raw materials for recycling in the United Kingdom have claimed that German exports of recyclable packaging materials are killing the UK recycling industry. "The Germans are screwing it up for everyone else," says the British recycling group Recoup.[24] German plastics, paper, and bottles have flooded UK markets, causing prices for secondary materials to collapse. One company reported a drop in the price of plastic film from £120 ($180) per metric ton to zero in 18 months.[25] The British Department of Trade and Industry reported that plastic waste imports to the United Kingdom increased 450 percent from 1991 to 1992 — mostly coming from Germany.[26] Recyclers warned that, "Britain risked building up huge stockpiles of recyclable materials while the Germans continued to pay for other countries to dispose of theirs."[27] The British Plastics Federation feared that UK recycling firms would turn to Germany as a source of materials, which "would impede the development of a domestically driven recycling culture."[28] Linpac and Reprise, the leading British plastics recycling firms, have refused to handle German material unless it is recycled for shipment back to Germany.[29]

British materials manufacturers have also complained that, despite the drop in secondary materials prices, they must still pay relatively high prices for these materials, whereas German manufacturers can get them free. Glass manufacturers in the United Kingdom have pointed out that their German competitors are getting cullet free from DSD and therefore have a competitive advantage, subsidized by the German consumer through the green dot fees. The British Paper and Board Industry has voiced similar complaints. It says German mills are getting used paper free, while British mills must pay £30-40 per ton ($51 to $68) for it.[30] Rowena Mills, head of the UK packaging consulting firm RMA, Ltd., expressed the hope that "Germany does not manage to export its waste problem as successfully as it has managed to export its inflation and interest rate problems."[31]

In April 1993, French paper recycling firms launched demonstrations throughout France, blocking roads and disrupting traffic. The protesters claimed that Germany was selling paper to French mills "at artificially low prices that French recovery and recycling firms cannot match."[32] The flood of imported paper from Germany has led to a major decline in the price of used paper and a 30 percent decrease in the amount of paper waste collected in France since January 1993.[33] The price of old corrugated cardboard fell from 550 francs ($110) in 1989 to 60 francs ($12) in April 1993. According to French industry, "The way things are going, the value of paper waste will soon reach zero, and the amount of waste imported from Germany will exceed the amount produced in France by the end of the decade." This could cause the collapse of the paper recycling industry and a loss of 27,000 jobs.[34] French paper recyclers have asked that the government extend the August 1992 decree that prohibits imports of garbage for disposal from Germany to prohibit waste paper imports as well.[35] The French Environment Minister, Michel Barnier, has said that when recyclables arrive with a negative price they should be considered waste.[36]

Germany has countered that it is a net importer of packaging materials such as paper if both virgin and secondary materials are counted; that is, it imports more paper, overall, than it exports. As long as other countries want to ship paper to Germany, it asserts, they should not complain about Germany's exporting its used paper, because the paper markets are connected. Germany consumes 16 million metric tons of paper per year but produces only 8 million tons. DSD says this means that "a high recycling rate...can only be realized in cooperation with foreign countries."[37]

According to Greenpeace, imports of cheap plastics for recycling from Germany are threatening the livelihood of 200,000 impoverished waste collectors in Indonesia. The Indonesian recycling plants are buying directly from the Germans, instead of from their local collectors. Greenpeace says the income of the local collectors has been cut in half, to $1.50 per day, and that much of the material the Germans send is burned or dumped — not recycled.[38]

In response, DSD has said that the United States, France, and Germany have long shipped plastics to recycling facilities in Indonesia, and that the German plastics shipped there are primarily from industrial and municipal collections, not from DSD.[39]

The amount of German packaging materials shipped to Asia has not been documented, but press reports indicate shipments to many destinations there, including China, the Philippines, and Malaysia. Some of the materials are not shipped directly to Asia by Germany; plastic packaging shipped from Germany to the Netherlands for recycling has been found in Singapore.[40]

The Packaging Industry is a Scapegoat

In addition to complaints about trade barriers and the disruption of markets, critics in the United Kingdom have argued that there is no "packaging problem," and that industry is being "scapegoated" — arguments not voiced in Germany. For example, Jonathan Sims, also of the RMA, Ltd., packaging consulting firm, declared at a July 1992 packaging conference in the United States that the packaging problem has been "identified wrongly and is being tackled by equally wrong means. Policy is being guided by emotion and by political expediency not by reason....Packaging has become a useful scapegoat....If there is a problem, it is with excessive consumption....More resources are being spent transporting waste packaging around Germany, sorting it, recycling it, than are being saved. Repeat this on a European scale and in the name of environmental benefit we will be committing environmental vandalism."[41]

Concerns Raised in the United States

The US Department of Agriculture (USDA) is concerned about health effects, price increases that will be passed along to consumers, and discrimination against US products. The department says leaving secondary packaging in the store can lead to deterioration of the basic package and reduce product safety. It is particularly concerned about the health and safety impact of refillable bottles.

USDA claims discrimination against US products on the grounds that they have longer distances to travel, need more packaging, and will therefore have to pay higher green dot fees.[42] However, US consumer product companies generally package their products in Europe for the European market. USDA has also said it is difficult for US companies to go through the application process for the green dot, but it has not produced evidence of discrimination against non-German companies in granting green dots.

Catherine Vial, an international trade specialist at the US Department of Commerce, has criticized the German law, contending that: the purpose of the Packaging Ordinance is to protect the German beer industry; "polluter pays" means the consumer pays; DSD is a monopoly; and Germany is dumping the packaging materials it collects on foreign markets.[43]

Aside from the specifics of the German legislation, at least one major US business organization has argued against its relevance for the United States. According to Harvey Alter, manager of resources policy for the US Chamber of Commerce, the "dogma" that "there is too much packaging" cannot be substantiated. He argues that "we've had a garbage crisis every fifteen years since 1885," that packaging is not a problem, and that incineration should count toward recycling goals.[44]

In evaluating the German model, US policymakers would do well to consider, in addition to the criticisms described here, a key element lacking in the Packaging Ordinance: consumer incentives. The ordinance depends on voluntary consumer participation. It requires retailers to provide bins for secondary packaging but does not require consumers to leave the packaging in the store. If DSD fails to meet the recycling quotas, retailers must also take back primary packaging, but the ordinance does not require consumers to bring it back.

Shortly after implementation of the Dual System in the winter of 1993, problems began to develop with respect to consumer use of the yellow DSD bins. Many consumers were not sorting their garbage correctly. As households pay by the bin for trash pick-up, but DSD picks up packaging waste in its bins free, households have an incentive to put non-packaging trash into the DSD bins.

The "Polluter Pays" Principle Outside Germany

Undoubtedly, Germany's increased exports of recyclable materials resulting from the Packaging Ordinance have caused serious dislocations in world markets, affecting recycling programs and manufacturing companies that use secondary materials. What remains to be seen is whether these dislocations represent "growing pains" that will diminish as recycling capacity increases in Germany and other countries, or whether they will remain a long-term problem.

The forthcoming EC Packaging Directive will apply to all of its member countries, with a combined population of 341 million, and may affect the implementation of the German legislation and the markets for recyclables. Still, it should be noted that none of the criticisms raised in Europe attacks the basic concept of making industry reponsible for managing packaging waste.

Even as European countries are protesting Germany's exports of used packaging materials, many of them are adopting the "polluter pays" principle as the basis of their own packaging legislation. They differentiate between the exports resulting from the high recycling quotas, which they oppose, and the basic principle of manufacturers' responsibility, which they support. Austria and France have adopted packaging ordinances, based on the German model, that make industry responsible for packaging waste. Austria has hired the US management consulting firm of Arthur D. Little to design a system based on the DSD model. France's "Eco-Emballage" system has adopted the green dot as its symbol, but it differs from the German system in many respects. An important difference is that it puts waste-to-energy incineration on a par with other recycling technologies, so "thermal recycling" can count toward meeting the recycling quotas.

In January 1993, the Swedish government proposed take-back legislation for packages and products. It has ambitious targets, like the German law, and would require 65 percent recycling of plastics by 1997.[45] Moreover, Belgium's new packaging initiative, "FOST PLUS," relies on packaging taxes to make industry responsible for packaging waste, and the Netherlands and Denmark are pressuring the European Community to toughen its Packaging Directive and make it more like Germany's. Closer to the United States, Canada is seriously considering a system of shared responsibility between industry and municipalities for managing packaging waste, modeled in part on the German system.

Notes

1. "Waste: New German Law for Economic Recycling," *Europe Environment*, No. 408, Europe Information Service, Brussels, April 15, 1993, p. II-2.

2. Wigand Kahl (Landeshauptstadt München, Umweltschutzreferat [City of Munich, Environmental Division]), interview, October 9, 1992.

3. Bavarian Environment Ministry, press release, Munich, December 15, 1992.

4. Maria Rieping (Die Verbraucher Initiative [DVI] [The Consumer Initiative], Bonn), interview, October 21, 1992; and Olaf Bandt (BUND, Bonn), interview, October 21, 1992; and Jürgen Maas (Die Grünen, Bonn), interview, October 23, 1992.

5. "Recycling ist nur der zweitbeste Weg" ("Recycling is the Second Best Choice"), *Der Spiegel*, 25/1993, p. 50.

6. *Ibid.*, p. 34.

7. Gernot Klepper and Peter Michaelis, "Will the 'Dual System' Manage Packaging Waste?" Kiel Working Paper No. 503, Kiel Institute of World Economics, Kiel, January 1992, p. 19.

8. Bureau of National Affairs, "Cabinet Approves Amended Waste Law Despite Widespread Industry Objections," *International Environment Daily*, Washington, DC, April 2, 1993.

9. "Plastikbranche macht Druck" ("Plastics Industry Applies Pressure"), *Frankfurter Rundschau*, September 21, 1993, p. 14.

10. Joachim H. Spangenberg, "The German Waste Policy," Wuppertal Institute, September 27, 1993, p. 8.

11. Karl-Heinz Striegel (Landesamt für Wasser und Abfall [Agency for Waster and Waste]), North Rhine-Westphalia, interview, October 27, 1992.

12. "World News: Germany," *Warmer Bulletin*, No. 36, February 1993, p. 9.

13. Ariane Genillard, "Falling Victim to its Own Success," *Financial Times*, London, January 27, 1993, p. 40.

14. *Ibid.*

15. Bureau of National Affairs, "German Cartel Office Will Examine Regulation Scheme for Garbage Collection," *Antitrust and Trade Regulation Report*, Washington, DC, January 1, 1993, p. 62.

16. Bureau of National Affairs, "German Agency Resolves Concerns About Firm's Waste Collection Service Plans," *International Environment Daily*, Washington, DC, April 7, 1993. Clarified by Ines Siegler (DSD), telephone interview, April 26, 1993.

17. "Environment Ministers Reach Consensus on Waste Prevention," *Europe Environment,* No. 413, Europe Information Service, Brussels, July 6, 1993, p. I-5.

18. Quentin Peel, "German Waste Industry Under Fire," *Financial Times,* London, January 18, 1993, p. 2.

19. "German Efforts Seen as a Threat," *Chemical Week,* New York, February 17, 1993, p. 20.

20. Clemens Stroetmann (German Secretary of State for the Environment, Bonn), interview, October 22, 1992.

21. "Environmental Protection in Europe: Abolishing Litter," *The Economist,* London, August 22, 1992, p. 59.

22. DSD, "Verwertung von Kunstoff-Probemengen in Indonesien ordnungsgemäß" ("Trial Quantities of Plastics Properly Recycled in Indonesia"), press release, Bonn, March 29, 1993.

23. "Environment Ministers Reach Consensus on Waste Prevention," *Europe Environment,* No. 413, Europe Information Service, Brussels, July 16, 1993, p. I-4.

24. Sonia Purnell, "Germany's Waste-Size Problem," *The Daily Telegraph,* London, March 26, 1993, p. 23.

25. *Ibid.*

26. Emma Chynoweth, "Germany's Waste Policy Draws More Complaints," *Chemical Week,* New York, May 12, 1993, p. 24.

27. *Ibid.*

28. "German Efforts Seen as a Threat," *op. cit.*

29. *Ibid.*

30. Bureau of National Affairs, "German, EC Packaging Measures Will Hurt U.K. Industry, House of Commons Panel Told," *International Environment Daily,* Washington, DC, March 8, 1993.

31. Rowena Mills, RMA, Ltd. (United Kingdom), "Overview of Approved and Pending Environmental Packaging Legislation within Individual EC Member Countries," Institute of Packaging Professionals Conference: Executive Update on Domestic and International Environmental Packaging Legislation, Alexandria, VA, July 24, 1992.

32. Bureau of National Affairs, "French Paper Recycling Industry Launches Protests Against German Imports," *International Environment Daily,* Washington, DC, April 16, 1993, p. 59.

33. *Ibid.*

34. *Ibid.*

35. *Ibid.*

36. "Environment Ministers Reach Consensus on Waste Prevention," *op. cit.,* p. I-4.

37. DSD, "Two Years of the Packaging Ordinance," press release, July 21, 1992.

38. "German Waste Imports Seen Hurting Indonesian Poor," *The Reuter Library Report,* March 5, 1993.

39. DSD, "Verwertung von Kunstoff-Probemengen in Indonesien ordnungsgemäß" ("Trial Quantities of Plastics Properly Recycled in Indonesia"), *op. cit.*

40. "Kippe in Fernost" ("Garbage Dump in Far East"), *Der Spiegel,* Vol. 53, December 28, 1992, p. 48.

41. Jonathan Sims, RMA, Ltd. (United Kingdom), "Current Status of European Community Environmental Legislation," Institute of Packaging Professionals Conference: Executive Update on Domestic and International Environmental Packaging Legislation, Alexandria, VA, July 24, 1992.

42. Audrey Talley (USDA), "The EC's Directive on Packaging and Solid Waste and Germany's Ordinance on Avoidance of Packaging Waste: Current Status and Likely Impact on the American Packaging Community," Institute of Packaging Professionals Conference: Executive Update on Domestic and International Environmental Packaging Legislation, Alexandria, VA, July 24, 1992.

43. Catherine Vial (US Department of Commerce), "The EC's Directive on Packaging and Solid Waste and Germany's Ordinance on Avoidance of Packaging Waste: Current Status and Likely Impact on the American Packaging Community," Institute of Packaging Professionals Conference: Executive Update on Domestic and International Environmental Packaging Legislation, Alexandria, VA, July 24, 1992.

44. Harvey Alter (US Chamber of Commerce), "The Likely Final Form and Packaging Implications of the Resource Conservation and Recovery Amendments of 1992," Institute of Packaging Professionals Conference: Executive Update on Domestic and International Environmental Packaging Legislation, Alexandria, VA, July 24, 1992.

45. "Status of Proposed Takeback Regulation In Sweden and Germany," *Business and the Environment,* Cutter Information Corp., January 1993, No. 1, Vol. 4.

Chapter 10

Proposed Waste Avoidance and Recycling Legislation for Products

Industry and government in Germany are expanding the "take-back" strategy to encompass not only packaging but many products. A new comprehensive waste act awaiting parliamentary approval in Germany would employ the "polluter pays" principle in a law that would pave the way for sweeping take-back ordinances for products. Proposals for automobiles and electronics have already affected the way in which these products are made. Ordinances have also been proposed to require the take-back of batteries and newspapers. This chapter looks at the proposed legislation for autos and electronics, and at industry's response.

The Closed-Loop Economy and Waste Management Act

On July 17, 1992, the Federal Environment Ministry (Bundesministerium für Umwelt, Naturschutz und Reaktorsicherheit, or BMU) issued a draft of new waste legislation that would supersede the 1986 "Waste Avoidance and Waste Management Act" *(Abfallgesetz),* on which the Packaging Ordinance was based. The new act is called "The Closed-Loop Economy and Waste Management Act" *(Kreislaufwirtschafts-und Abfallgesetz)*; the "closed-loop economy" refers to making industry responsible for collecting and recycling its products after they are discarded by consumers or other end users. Under this legislation, all products, from toys to clothes to furniture, could be subject to take-back ordinances.

"A comprehensive materials policy, as opposed to a waste removal strategy, is the focus of our efforts," said Environment Minister Klaus Töpfer, in describing the new act. He said industry must be made responsible for taking back and recycling its products if it is to practice sound materials policy at the design stage. Töpfer has said that "privatizing" the costs of recycling and disposal puts the burden on the private sector, where it belongs, and that, in the future, managing used products will be as important as supplying consumers with new goods.[1]

The Cabinet approved the act on March 31, 1993, and the Federal Environment Ministry expected parliamentary approval in about one year. The law would take effect two years after passage.[2] Although the new waste act would give the "polluter pays" principle the force of law, applying to products as well as packages, the Cabinet and the Bundesrat, the upper house of Parliament, would still have to pass separate ordinances for specific industries.

According to the Federal Environment Ministry's announcement of the Cabinet's approval of the new law, "The saving of resources and the avoidance of waste are the main priorities of the new law. Industry, trade, and consumers alike must make every effort in the future to avoid waste materials as far as possible and, only where the production of waste is unavoidable, to fall back on recycling — in other words, reintroducing the waste in the form of secondary raw materials into the economic cycle. This principle takes priority over waste disposal. Nothing should be treated as waste that can be recycled as a secondary raw material."[3]

The new act clearly defines a solid waste hierarchy:
1. Avoidance (source reduction)
2. Recycling
3. Waste-to-energy incineration
4. Other processing or landfill

Under the 1986 waste law, the hierarchy was more ambiguous: source reduction was placed before recycling, but recycling could include burning. This new act makes it clear that recycling is preferable to waste-to-energy incineration.

The new act defines "waste" as materials that cannot be recycled.[4] Producers will have to prove that their waste cannot be recycled before they can send it to an incinerator or landfill. Exports of "waste" will be forbidden. At present, materials are defined by their owners as either "waste" *(Abfall)* or "valuable materials" *(Wertstoffe)*. The inconsistent application of these definitions has environmental implications because regulations are stricter for handling the *"Abfall"* than *"Wertstoffe."*[5]

The new act also requires companies to conduct materials audits and to report every three years on the amount of materials recycled and the amount of waste that remains.

The act gives the federal government explicit power to promulgate ordinances requiring industry to take back waste generated by its products. Industry may design its own programs to take back waste; in fact, government bans and regulations are to be kept to a minimum. "The dismantling and recycling of used products is to be made into the main priority…and is to be taken into account in the early stages of production."[6]

Under the act, waste must be disposed of within Germany, except for cooperative arrangements with neighboring countries in border areas. Recyclable materials may be exported, subject to Euorpean Community regulations and international surveillance. The Federal Environment Ministry asserts that the new waste management law is an instrument for adopting the EC waste legislation into national law and notes that the new EC waste transportation ordinance, which will take effect in 1994, requires member states to be self-sufficient in waste management. The ministry concludes, "The step from waste disposal to a future-oriented waste management and product recycling system is an integral component of the ecological and social market economy in an industrial society."[7]

Response to the Waste Management Act

The Federation of German Industries (Bundesverband der Deutschen Industrie e.V., or BDI) claimed in the summer of 1992 that the law was not warranted, as industry had long worked to conserve resources.[8] BDI has taken particular exception to the waste management hierarchy, contending that it makes no sense and that incineration and landfilling, if done locally, can be preferable to reuse or recycling that requires shipping materials long distances, sorting, and cleaning the materials. The organization argues that Germany needs more disposal facilities and that politicians have not done their job in making such facilities acceptable to the German public.[9]

According to BDI, the proposed law will interfere with industry, increase the cost of production, and make German industry less competitive. It finds the reporting requirements excessive, in conflict with the need for confidentiality, and unfair in that they may be administered differently in the different states.

Extending product durability is not always preferable, BDI says, because it conflicts with consumer preferences for new designs and "fashion" and can prevent the introduction of new technological improvements that could benefit the environment, such as products with improved energy efficiency.[10]

To BDI, the "closed-loop economy" with no waste is an illusion. It asserted in April 1993 that "Recycling at any price is not a rational strategy....Returning materials for recycling is only sensible when markets exist for the collected materials." To BDI's objections, Töpfer responded, "Industry always says it can do things better on its own, but without public pressure it doesn't act to develop new systems and technologies."[11] Töpfer also maintained that the law is in the interest of business and would challenge the "creativity of the economy and society."[12]

Secretary of State for the Environment Clemens Stroetmann says, "We know a circulatory economy is not 100 percent possible...but it is indisputable that this is a sensible idea. Germany has no more room for landfills and almost no natural resources left, so we need the increasingly precious resources we have."[13]

The new act's critics are not limited to business. Members of the Green and Social Democratic parties have charged that Töpfer has sold out to the chemical industry and produced a watered-down bill that is "largely inadequate for environmental needs."[14]

Proposed Ordinance on the Reduction and Recycling of Waste from Automobiles

A draft of this ordinance, originally proposed in 1990, was circulated by the Federal Environment Ministry in August 1992. Since the auto industry has been working to design cars that are more recyclable, it has not opposed the ordinance in principle, although it is negotiating with the government over specific items. Some of the provisions, described below, may be changed before the ordinance takes effect.

The challenge posed by the auto ordinance is less than that of the Packaging Ordinance because the former entails fewer companies, fewer units, and far less material in terms of weight or volume. Approximately 2.6 million cars are scrapped each year in Germany, compared with 180 billion packages. Unlike packaging waste, most auto material has long been recycled.

The material composition of a typical car is about 75 percent metal and 10 percent plastic, with the remainder made up of rubber, glass, and other materials.[15] About 75 percent of the materials in the scrapped cars is recycled (mostly ferrous metals), but a residue called "fluff," of about 450,000 metric tons, is landfilled. Fluff is primarily plastic but also contains fluids, fabrics, glass, rubber, and dirt. Recycling the remaining 450,000 metric tons of fluff from autos is a much less daunting task than recycling 12 million metric tons of packaging waste. Discarded auto parts are not included in fluff, but most end up in landfills as well — only 10 percent of old parts the auto industry replaces are reused or recycled.

Objectives of the Auto Ordinance

The ordinance specifies that the auto industry work toward these objectives:

1. To design and manufacture autos and their parts for maximum durability, easy dismantling, reuse, and recycling.
2. To use materials that facilitate recycling, that are labeled uniformly, and that make possible benign disposal of the residues.
3. To reuse parts in the manufacturing of automobiles or as spare parts, and to recycle parts that cannot be reused.

Auto Take-Back Provisions

The draft ordinance would require auto manufacturers and dealers to take back scrap cars of the brand they sell from the car's last owner, free of charge. Auto dealers would also have to take back spare and replacement parts.

In a major new approach to auto recycling based on an EC idea, a "Certificate of Disposal" will be introduced to certify that the auto has been taken to an authorized dismantling and recycling facility. For the owner of a car, the certificate will be a prerequisite for the deregistration of a scrapped vehicle; the owner remains responsible for the vehicle unless this certificate is filed. The goal is to encourage recycling and to prevent illegal dumping.

The draft ordinance requires manufacturers to meet quotas for reusing or recycling the auto materials they take back, as shown in Table 10-1.

Manufacturers and dealers may engage a third party to manage the recycling. They will still have to furnish proof on the use of recycled materials and the method of disposal of the residues.

Auto Industry Objections

The auto industry objects to the provision that cars must be taken back free of charge. It is particularly concerned about the cost of recycling older cars that were not designed for disassembly and recycling. The industry has proposed charging the last owner for the cost of disassembling and recycling, currently estimated at about DM200 per car ($120), but the government wants the industry to "internalize" these costs by including them in the price of new cars.[16] As negotiations continued on this issue, industry was advocating "free pricing," by which the final cost or price would be negotiated between the last owner of the car and the recycling center.[17]

The auto industry also opposed the material-specific recycling quotas in the proposed ordinance (shown in Table 10-1). Manufacturers and recyclers claim it is feasible to recycle 20 percent of the fluff by the year 2000; that is, 20 percent of the 25 percent of auto materials not now recycled, or about 90,000 metric tons per year. They say they can recycle 60 percent of the fluff by 2000 if chemical and "thermal" recycling (incineration with

Table 10-1: Proposed Recycling Quotas for Materials in Automobiles, from Draft Ordinance

Material	1996 (% by weight)	2000 (% by weight)
Steel	100	100
Nonferrous metals	85	90
Tires	40	50
Glass	30	50
Plastics	20	50
Other elastomers*	20	30

* *Synthetic compounds with the elasticity characteristic of rubber.*

Source: BMW of North America, March 1993.

energy recovery) are allowed to count toward the recycling goals.[18] The government has considered declaring "fluff" a hazardous material, which would increase the cost of disposing of it and the pressure to recycle it.

The question of who is to dismantle scrapped cars is also at issue. The auto manufacturers prefer to authorize some of Germany's 4,000 "dismantlers" to handle used cars, but may need only several hundred. The fate of the remaining dismantling operations has become a political issue. Manufacturers' authorization of the dismantlers raises antitrust issues. According to BMW, if manufacturers are required to meet specified quotas, they should be able to control the dismantling process because they will be responsible for assuring that the materials get recycled; they also want to control the costs.[19] In October 1991, BMW named Preimesser, in Munich, to be its first authorized dismantler. BMW said it intends to authorize an additional 100 dismantlers in Germany within the next three years.[20]

Some of industry's criticisms of the ordinance are similar to those raised against the new waste act: recycling and incineration should be ranked equally; the administrative burden is excessive; and extending product durability will prevent the introduction of new, more environmentally sound technologies. Some concerns, however, are specific to the auto industry: reuse must be limited by the demands for quality and safety; it is unfair to make the take-back requirement retroactive to cars not designed for recycling; and industry cannot recycle imported parts, as it does not know their material composition.[21]

Auto Industry Initiatives

With these reservations, the auto industry is responding positively to the proposed ordinance. Led by Volkswagen, two US-owned companies in Germany, Ford and Opel, have announced they will take back some of their models free of charge at the end of their useful lives. The guarantee is an effective marketing tool, relieving consumers of the fear that they may have to pay to dispose of their cars. Most of the actual take-backs will not occur for at least 10 years, when current models will begin to be scrapped, with the exception of cars damaged in accidents.

Although it is not clear whether the companies will ultimately take back and disassemble their own cars or whether they will arrange for others to do so, the auto makers are conducting pilot studies to determine the most efficient and cost-effective disassembly systems and ways of linking disassembly with new design. If third parties handle disassembly, the auto manufacturers will be able to advise on the best, most cost-effective system for their cars. The German automobile manufacturers association (Verband der Automobilindustrie, or VDA) has formed an organization called PRAVDA, to develop a recycling strategy for the industry.

The major initiatives already taken to make autos more recyclable include:

1. Designing for disassembly: reducing the number of fasteners and types of fasteners to make the disassembly process quicker and cheaper; developing special equipment and techniques for disassembly; and developing efficient systems for draining auto fluids to avoid contaminating other materials.
2. Reducing the number of different plastic resins used.
3. Replacing plastics that are difficult to recycle with thermoplastics, such as polypropylene and polyurethane, that are easier to recycle.
4. Coding all plastic resins for rapid identification.
5. Increasing recycled content.
6. Recycling parts, e.g., bumpers and the precious metals in catalytic converters.

Volkswagen

Volkswagen started a pilot project for disassembly and recycling in April 1990. It recycles its bumpers in a closed-loop system: old bumpers are used in new bumpers that have 20-30 percent recycled content. Higher levels of recycled content could be achieved if more used bumpers were available. The bumpers are generally made of polypropylene. The company has decreased the use of polyvinyl chloride (PVC) and eliminated chlorofluorocarbons (CFCs), cadmium, and asbestos in all components it produces.[22]

Volkswagen's newly designed fuel tank, with 11 fewer parts, is both easier to disassemble and cheaper to make. Volkswagen says making fuel tanks from recycled plastics is one of the first successes of its recycling project; it describes the tanks as "visually as well as functionally perfect."[23] As of May 1993, these fuel tanks were still in the testing stage and had not gone into production.[24] The company believes the economics of auto recycling will improve because cars will be designed for recyclability.[25]

BMW (Bayerische Motoren Werke A.G.)

BMW has developed new systems and cost estimates for disassembly, evaluated the recyclability of materials, and transferred this information back to its designers. The company has been operating a pilot recycling project at its dismantling plant in Landshut, near Munich, since 1990. It began to establish authorized recycling centers in 1991 and expected to have 20 such centers nationwide by the end of 1993. BMW is also setting up such centers in the United Kingdom, France, and the Netherlands. A parallel pilot project involves 30 BMW dealers in taking back old BMWs. The company estimates that by the year 2000, 20 million vehicles will be taken off the road in Europe each year, and about 250,000 of these will be BMWs.[26]

In 1992, BMW launched a two-year pilot recycling project in the United States with the Automotive Dismantlers and Recyclers Association (ADRA), based on experience in Germany. The project is taking place in the Bronx, NY; Los Angeles; and Orlando, FL. Owners of used BMWs may exchange their cars for cash. The authorized project centers will take back any used BMW, regardless of the production year, but will deduct the costs of dismantling and recycling from the price the center pays the car owner for the used vehicle. (Older models are more expensive to dismantle and recycle.) As an incentive to customers, BMW gives a $500 certificate toward the purchase of a new or dealer-certified used BMW.[27]

Identification of used plastic materials is key to the efficient dismantling and recycling of cars. BMW has developed a color coding system for plastics that has been adopted by the German automotive industry, to be used along with labeling. It has also developed color coding for auto fluids to enable them to be more easily separated and recycled.

Like other auto companies, BMW is aiming to reduce the number of plastic resins used, avoid composites, and eliminate toxic, nonrecyclable materials. The company regrinds bumpers and uses them to line luggage compartments; seating foam is reused for noise insulation; and engines, transmission housings, and alternators are reconditioned and sold as spare parts with BMW warranties. In its new Series-3 cars, 81 percent of the materials, by weight, can be reused or recycled.[28]

BMW says, "Although BMW does not support many of the requirements proposed [in the ordinance], including the recycling quotas, BMW in general is supportive of the legislation which would provide the economic incentives for manufacturers and consumers alike to achieve a greater re-utilization of the automobile materials once it [sic] reaches the end of its life cycle."[29]

In an October 1992 speech, Karl H. Gerlinger, President and CEO of BMW of North America, Inc., noted that firms that pursue product life-cycle management will have an advantage over those that do not.[30] The "Big Three" US auto manufacturers (General Motors, Chrysler, and Ford) seem to concur. According to *Plastics News,* "Because of Germany's actions, the Big Three believe BMW, Volkswagen and Daimler-Benz of Germany have a strategic lead as the time approaches when vehicles will have to meet any country's recycling standards."[31] Soon there will be other standards to meet outside of Germany: Austria, France, and the United Kingdom, as well as the European Community, are planning to enact legislation that shifts the responsibility for reduction and recycling of auto waste to industry.

Proposed Ordinance on the Reduction and Recycling of Used Electric and Electronic Equipment

This proposed ordinance, originally circulated in July 1991 and later revised, covers a heterogeneous group of products that contain electric or electronic parts, including large household appliances (e.g., washing machines and stoves); small household appliances (e.g., hair dryers, toasters, electric razors, and clocks); entertainment systems (e.g., stereos and televisions); office equipment (e.g., computers, copy machines, and telephones); medical equipment; electronic tools; and large office information and communications equipment (e.g., data processing machines and telephone exchanges).[32] The July 1991 draft called for the ordinance to take effect in January 1994, but the ordinance had not been adopted when this report was prepared for publication. The timetable was slowed by the economic recession and the parliamentary elections scheduled for the fall of 1994.

Electronic waste constitutes roughly 4 percent of the German solid waste stream. Electronic waste was estimated at about 1.3 million metric tons for the former West Germany in 1994 and 1.9 million metric tons for all of Germany in 1998, as shown in Table 10-2.

Objectives of the Electronics Ordinance

The objectives of the ordinance are to promote source reduction and recycling by:
1. Using more "environmentally compatible and recyclable materials."
2. Making products easier to repair and disassemble.
3. Establishing collection systems that are easily accessible to end users and that achieve a high return rate.
4. Delivering returned equipment for reuse and recycling.
5. Properly disposing of equipment that cannot be recycled.[33]

Table 10-2: Estimated Quantity of Waste from Used Electric and Electronic Equipment

Product Category	1994* (metric tons)	1998 (metric tons)
Household appliances	600,000	823,000
Entertainment systems	234,000	444,000
Information technology	98,000	104,000
Medical	7,000	15,000
Other	353,000	487,000
TOTAL	1,292,000	1,873,000

* "West" Germany only

Source: Deutscher Bundestag-12.Wahlperiode (Lower House of Parliament, 12th legislative period), 12/4820, p. 4.

Electronics Take-back Provisions

Under the electronics ordinance, sellers would be required to take back used equipment from end users; manufacturers would have to take it back from the sellers. Both sellers and manufacturers are responsible for delivering the equipment for reuse, recycling, and/or disposal, although third parties could be contracted to fulfill these obligations. Complex provisions specify who must take back what equipment, but the take-back will basically be limited to equipment that the manufacturer or seller carries in its product line.[34] Unlike the Packaging Ordinance, the requirement for companies to take back only their own products provides company-specific incentives for source reduction and recycling.

Electronics Industry Negotiations

The electronics industry is actively negotiating the provisions of the electronics ordinance with the government through the association of tool makers (Verband Deutscher Maschinen- und Anlagenbau e.V., or VDMA) and the association of the electronics industry (Zentralverband Elektrotechnik-und Elektronikindustrie e.V., or ZVEI). Industry is pressing the government not to require the free take-back of electronic equipment. If companies cannot charge for taking back products, they will have to include these costs in product prices, in keeping with the Federal Environment Ministry's support of the "polluter pays" principle. But ZVEI has voiced concern about the expense of taking back products that were not designed for disassembly or take-back. Its members are willing to start taking back 1993 equipment in 1998, but they do not want to take back the older products still in use. Proposed revisions would allow industry to charge for taking back older equipment, provided the fees charged do not exceed the costs of collecting, recycling, or disposing of the particular equipment.[35] The issue will not be finally resolved until the ordinance is passed.

Another area of contention relates to small retailers. According to the Association of Bavarian Retailers (Landesverband des Bayerischen Einzelhandels e.V.), small retailers are concerned that the ordinance will put them at a disadvantage because they do not have sufficient space to store the equipment they must take back. The proposed revisions allow sellers with less than 100 square meters (1076 square feet) of space to limit the take-back to the specific number of new pieces of equipment bought by the end user. In other words, a purchaser of one television may bring only one TV back to a small retailer but could bring several back to a larger retailer, provided that retailer carries that brand.[36]

While serious negotiations proceed over specific provisions of the ordinance, and problems with the logistics of a take-back system persist, ZVEI is in general agreement with the objectives of the ordinance, and its members are working to make their products less wasteful and more easily recyclable.[37]

Computer Industry Initiatives

In the computer industry, a number of companies — anticipating passage of the ordinance — are already taking back their products voluntarily and designing them for return and disassembly. Some, such as Compaq, Dell, and Zenith, typically charge consumers between DM30 and DM100 ($18-$60) to take back personal computers, but Apple, NEC, and Siemens take theirs back free of charge.[38] Consumers are concerned that localities will refuse to collect electronic waste once the ordinance is passed; they want an assurance that when they purchase electronic equipment they will be able to get rid of it. The industry also sees the profit potential in taking back some equipment, particularly if it contains a lot of valuable metal. Smaller electronics companies are using third parties to take back their products, and a new industry for recycling electronics has developed.

IBM

IBM has been taking back its products voluntarily in Germany since 1990, and it sees design for reuse and recycling as a top priority. IBM reuses many of the parts and directs the remainder to recycling and disposal. There is a nominal charge for take-back to cover transportation and handling. In 1991, IBM Germany took back 438 tons of old equipment.[39]

Based on the experience in Germany, IBM characterizes the waste in the average computer product, by weight, as follows:

Scrap iron	67.0%
Packaging materials	9.5%
Plastics	8.0%
Cathode ray tubes	6.8%
Precious metals	3.3%
Reusable parts	2.6%
Aluminum	1.8%
Nonferrous metals	0.5%
Hazardous waste	0.5%
	100.0%

IBM notes that "today, environmental restrictions are moving into the very heart of product development and design."[40] The company is considering environmental questions in the initial stages of product design, including:

- What components and materials can be reused and recycled?
- How can product packaging be recycled?
- Will any components or materials be considered hazardous waste at the end of the product's useful life?
- What are the ultimate disposal options for the product?

At IBM, product developers are now responsible for a product's entire lifespan — not just its design and manufacture. The company has devised an environmental impact assessment (EIA) to help product managers compile environmental information. The company says the EIA "provides data on the materials contained within and used by the product, technical data on energy usage, transportation, storage, recyclability, reuse and disposal options for the product, its consumables and packaging."[41]

An example of the new design for recycling and disassembly is the Personal System/2 Models 40 and 57. These computers are designed with a new "snap technology" in which many fasteners have been eliminated to facilitate disassembly. The new models use only one plastic resin instead of the dozens that were formerly used. The change simplifies manufacturing and recycling and saves the company money in purchasing, as the resin chosen can be bought in much larger quantities than before.[42]

IBM now requires coding to identify plastics, based on the codes used by the German automobile industry, discussed in the previous section. The codes are molded into the parts so that materials may be separated for recycling. Coding can increase the material's value over that of mixed plastic scrap.

IBM has established the Engineering Center for Environmentally Conscious Products in Research Triangle Park, North Carolina, to maximize reuse and recycling and minimize the volume of materials requiring disposal. The results of the research from this center are shared by IBM facilities worldwide. As many IBM products have a standard design for the global market, the changes will be felt around the world. IBM also voluntarily takes back its products in the United Kingdom, Switzerland, and Austria and planned to do so in France and Italy in 1993. IBM says its voluntary take-back program in Germany is in response to customer demand, not to the proposed German electronic ordinance, and that the company policy is to be pro-active.[43]

Xerox

Xerox, another large US company, says it began taking back products in the late 1960s, long before Germany proposed such legislation; the company says the German initiatives have accelerated industry movement in this direction. Xerox says it designs its products for global rather than national markets and that its designs are driven by the market with the most stringent standards; in environmental terms, that market is Germany. The company also expects the trends set in Germany to spread throughout Europe.[44] According to Jack Azar, manager of environmental design and resource conservation, Xerox and many electronic and business equipment companies are treating "take-back" and "product stewardship" as a "given."[45]

While Xerox has been taking back some of its products since the late 1960s, it did not develop a "design-for-the-environment" strategy until 1991. An asset management organization set up within the company now prepares designer guidelines that are applied at the product's "concept development stage." The guidelines are similar to those used by the auto industry and IBM. Xerox policy follows a hierarchy for the equipment it takes back:

1. Redistribution to new customers if it is in working order.
2. Restoration through remanufacturing.
3. Conversion into another product.
4. Salvaging of parts.
5. Recycling of materials.

Xerox says it "wants to develop new products that, at end of [their] life, will contribute virtually nothing to landfills."[46]

To deal with the problems posed by plastics, the company aims to use 100 percent recyclable thermoplastic resins, 25 percent post-consumer recycled materials by 1995, and 50 percent by 2000. Xerox is reducing the number of plastic resins it uses from more than 500 to fewer than 50: fewer than 10 resins may satisfy 80 percent of the resin applications.[47]

In the first year of its "Asset Recycling Program," Xerox not only reduced its waste but saved $50 million. It contends that its efforts are hindered by government procurement guidelines in the United States and abroad that require products purchased to be "new." The guidelines categorize products using recycled content, particularly reused parts and components, as "used." As government is such a major purchaser, these guidelines create a significant disincentive for companies to use secondary materials and recycled parts. According to Xerox, the growing interest in recycling durable goods "reflects a recognition that most of our planet's resources are finite and should not be squandered by discarding material that is still useful...the industrial community has come to the realization that such waste represents a significant — and avoidable — business cost."[48]

Other Electronics Companies

Apple Computer, a US company with no manufacturing facilities in Germany, began taking back its products in August 1992 at its Munich service center. Apple, too, is trying to maximize the reuse of parts and to keep its equipment running longer through refurbishing and upgrading. The company takes back equipment free, but the customer must pay for shipping. Germany is the only country in which Apple takes back its products.

Take-back of electronic equipment in Germany is not limited to computers and office machines. Grundig, a German television manufacturer, is offering "green TVs" that it promises to take back. By developing experience in designing and manufacturing products with take-back considerations in mind, the company can enhance its competitive position when the ordinance goes into effect.[49]

Siemens, the large German electronics manufacturer, is studying the life cycle of its products with particular attention to the impact of taking its products back. It is developing a program, called "design for upgrade," under which machines are designed to be easily upgraded so that only obsolete parts must be discarded.[50] Siemens Nixdorf, which makes computers, is working on "re-commercializing" its machines: that is, taking them back, refurbishing them, and reselling them.[51]

A Revolution in Thinking

In sum, the changes made by automobile and electronics companies in Germany will likely have an impact around the world. Five years ago, electronics companies were developing new models of products with little attention to what would be done with the older ones they replaced. This thinking has changed dramatically, and companies are taking a new look at how they can optimize their use of materials for the long term. Reusing and upgrading are new objectives in the computer industry. Germany now has two associations for electronic waste recycling, and many more firms entering the business. Both take-back legislation and voluntary take-back programs are more advanced in Germany than in any other country in the world.

The German government's drive for take-back legislation has increased worldwide awareness and concern about industry's responsibility for its products, and created pressures that brought about these changes even before specific legislation was passed. The take-back strategy may lead to more leasing of equipment, which has long been a practice in the auto and electronics industries. As companies design for disassembly and recycling, they may want to have complete responsibility for their products from cradle to grave. Not only can taking back and servicing their own equipment protect companies' proprietary design features, but recycling cars and some equipment offers the potential for profitability.

Notes

1. Bureau of National Affairs, "Waste Law Proposal Will Require Industry to Recycle All Products," *International Environment Daily,* Washington, DC, July 28, 1992.

2. Bureau of National Affairs, "Cabinet Approves Amended Waste Law Despite Widespread Industry Objections," *International Environment Daily,* Washington, DC, April 2, 1993.

3. Federal Environment Ministry (BMU), "The Federal Government Passes New Waste Management Act," press release, Bonn, March 31, 1993.

4. Federal Environment Ministry (BMU), "Töpfer legt neues Abfallgesetz vor: Kreislaufwirtschaft statt Abfallbeseitigung" ("Töpfer Presents New Waste Legislation: Closed-Loop Economy Instead of Waste Disposal), press release, July 17, 1992, p. 3.

5. Jürgen Maas (Die Grünen, Bonn), interview, October 23, 1992.

6. Federal Environment Ministry (BMU), "The Federal Government Passes New Waste Management Act," *op. cit.*

7. *Ibid.*

8. Bundesverband der Deutschen Industrie e.V., (BDI) (Association of German Industry), "Grundsatzstellungnahme" ("Position Paper"), Cologne: June/July 1992.

9. *Ibid.*

10. *Ibid.*

11. Bureau of National Affaris, "Cabinet Approves Amended Waste Law," *op. cit.*

12. "Waste: New German Plan for Economic Recycling," *Europe Environment,* No. 408, Europe Information Service, Brussels, April 15, 1993, p. II-2.

13. Ferdinand Protzman, "Germany's Push to Expand the Scope of Recycling," *The New York Times,* July 4, 1993, p. F-8.

14. "Waste: New German Plan for Economic Recycling," *op. cit.,* p. II-2.

15. Volkswagen, "Recycling at Volkswagen," 1991, p. 15 and 18.

16. Karl-Heinz Ziwica (BMW of North America), "Lessons from the German Experience with Vehicle Recycling," Massachusetts Institute of Technology: Design and Disposal of Durable Products Conference, Cambridge, MA, March 24-25, 1993.

17. Ziwica, written communication, September 3, 1993.

18. Ziwica, "Lessons from the German Experience with Vehicle Recycling," *op. cit.*

19. Ziwica, written communication, September 3, 1993.

20. Ziwica, "Lessons from the German Experience with Vehicle Recycling," *op. cit.*

21. BDI, "Stellungnahme zur AltautoV" ("Response Position Paper on Automobile Take-back Ordinance"), Cologne, October 1992.

22. Gunnar Larsson (Volkswagen AG), "Automotive Recycling in Germany Today and in the Future," Massachusetts Institute of Technology: Design and Disposal of Durable Products Conference, Cambridge, MA, March 24-25, 1993.

23. Volkswagen, "Recycling at Volkswagen," *op. cit.,* p. 16.

24. Rolf Buchheim (Volkswagen, Wolfsburg, Germany) telephone interview, May 6, 1993.

25. Volkswagen, "Recycling at Volkswagen," *op. cit.,* p. 19.

26. BMW, "A Consistent Initiative to Protect the Environment: BMW Car Recycling," July 1992, p. 2.

27. Ziwica, "Lessons from the German Experience with Vehicle Recycling," *op. cit.*

28. *Ibid.*

29. *Ibid.*

30. Karl H. Gerlinger (BMW), "Market Incentives and the Environment," October 15, 1992, p. 3.

31. "Saturn Working Toward Auto Recycling," *Plastics News,* April 5, 1993, p. 19.

32. Federal Environment Ministry (BMU), WA II 3-30 114/7, Working Paper of 15 October 1992, "Regulation Regarding the Avoidance, Reduction and Recycling of the Waste of Used Electric and Electronic Equipment - Electronic Scrap Regulation," p. 3-4.

33. *Ibid.* p. 1-2.

34. Latham & Watkins, International Environment Network, *IEN Client Alert,* "German Electronic Waste Regulation," November 20, 1992.

35. Federal Environment Ministry (BMU), working paper of 15 October 1992, *op. cit.,* p. 5-7.

36. *Ibid.*

37. Zentralverband Elektrotechnik-und Electronikindustrie e.V. (ZVEI) (Association of Electrotechnical and Electronic Industries), "Elektronik-Schrott-Verordnung: ZVEI diskutiert offene Probleme mit BMU-Staatssekretär Stroetmann" ("Scrap Electronics Ordinance: ZVEI Discusses Open Problems with Environmental Secretary of State Stroetmann), April 29, 1993.

38. "Welche Computer Strom sparen und leise arbeiten" ("Computers that Save Electricity and Run Quietly"), *Impulse,* March 1993, p. 184.

39. Barbara Hill (IBM), "Integrating Environmental Attributes into Product Development," at Faredisfare lo scenario del produttore riproduttore, Politecnico di Milano, Italy, October 23, 1992, p. 3 and 5.

40. Hill, *ibid.,* p. 1.

41. Hill, *ibid.,* p. 3.

42. Ed Grimm (IBM), "Update on Safety, Energy and the Environment," 1992.

43. Barbara Hill (IBM), written communication, September 1, 1993.

44. Jack Azar (Xerox), telephone interview, June 16, 1993.

45. Jack Azar, "Recycling Initiatives in the American Electronics Industry," Massachusetts Institute of Technology: Design and Disposal of Durable Products Conference, Cambridge, MA, March 24-25, 1993.

46. Jack C. Azar, James C. MacKenzie and Richard S. Morabito, "Environmental Life-Cycle Design at Xerox," draft for *EPA Journal,* July 1993.

47. Azar, MacKenzie, and Morabito, *ibid.*

48. *Ibid.*

49. Dr. Braden Allenby (National Academy of Engineering), "Europe Trip Report, Oct. 14-23, 1992," November 1992, in papers from Massachusetts Institute of Technology: Design and Disposal of Durable Products Conference, Cambridge, MA, March 24-25, 1993, p. 18.

50. *Ibid.,* p. 19.

51. *Ibid.,* p. 20.

Chapter 11
Local Waste Management Initiatives

German policymakers have been so focused on promoting changes in the production process as a means of reducing waste that less attention has so far been given to changes in product use on the municipal, institutional, and individual levels. But, despite the prevalent philosophy that source reduction should be accomplished through changes in industrial design and production, some local governments have developed programs to reduce the amount of municipal solid waste generated. Some states, for example, North Rhine-Westphalia, already require their localities to submit recycling and source reduction plans, and new federal technical guidelines will require localities to submit municipal solid waste plans to their states.

INFORM did not conduct a survey of municipal solid waste policies throughout Germany, but did identify, during a month of travel, some local initiatives that provide examples of strategies for US planners and policymakers to consider.

Local Source Reduction Strategies

The mechanisms for waste avoidance German localities employ include:
- Bans and taxes on disposables
- Source reduction education

- Repair and reuse programs
- Charging households for the amount of waste they generate (quantity-based user fees)
- Promoting backyard composting

Banning Disposables at Events Held on Public Property

A number of cities, including Munich and Heidelberg, have banned the use of disposable beverage containers at events on public property. Cities can impose such bans because they issue permits for the use of public land. Mobile dishwashers are available for the events. At the two-week-long 1992 Oktoberfest in Munich, the exclusive use of reusable glasses and mugs cut the waste generated from 915 to 400 metric tons.[1] At Heidelberg's annual fair, which attracted more than 100,000 people, waste was reduced by 40 percent.[2]

Munich also bans disposables at publicly owned sports arenas and swimming pools; vendors sell beverages in refillable plastic cups and charge customers a deposit. The publicly owned beer gardens in Munich use only washable mugs and tableware. The private beer gardens are now adopting the same policy, owing to consumer pressure.

Munich is working to ban disposables in public facilities, including schools and government offices. Although Munich's general ban on one-way beverage containers was found by the federal courts to be unconstitutional, Munich still hopes to persuade McDonald's to eliminate disposable containers voluntarily.

Under the Heidelberg waste management law of December 1, 1991, government cafeterias must use reusable dishes, glasses, and utensils.

Taxing Disposables

The City of Kassel taxes disposable cutlery, crockery, and beverage containers used in local fast-food restaurants, roadside and market stalls, and hospitals. The tax, which ranges from DM0.1 - 0.5 ($0.06 - 0.30), is designed to discourage use of these disposable products and reduce waste volumes by 500 metric tons per year.[3]

Subsidized Workers to Promote Source Reduction

Cologne started a program using unemployed people to educate the public on source reduction. These workers, many of them academics, were paid by the federal government to teach source reduction in the schools and the community, with the understanding that after two years the city might hire them. However, as source reduction outreach is now federally mandated, these workers can no longer be used for this purpose. To avoid conflicts with the labor unions, "subsidized" workers cannot be used for any mandated activity.

The Cologne city government and the federal unemployment office also fund the "Umweltzentrum West" (Environment Center West) pilot project. Founded by a church, the project employs "disadvantaged" people (e.g., high school dropouts and the long-term unemployed) to repair used appliances. The center then sells the appliances cheaply to the poor — and, increasingly, to "green" consumers. In a similar private program called EMMAUS, which started in France and now operates in several German cities, homeless and mentally ill people recycle, repair, and resell used appliances and furniture.[4]

In a program in Wuppertal, former prisoners collect appliances, such as refrigerators, freezers, and washing machines, that would otherwise be disposed of, then repair them or separate their materials for recycling. The federal government also pays unemployed workers to repair and resell unclaimed furniture after someone dies. However, the Wuppertal municipal solid waste department has expressed skepticism over whether the mixing of social and waste management goals results in satisfactory results for either.[5]

Quantity-Based User Fees (QBUFs)

Charging citizens for waste collection based on the amount they generate is an important local policy in Germany — unlike the United States, where waste management is usually funded by general tax revenues. In Germany, cities and towns generally set a basic charge for once-a-week collection of a waste container. Citizens may reduce their costs by opting for a smaller container or less frequent collection.

The rates vary considerably by locality, but many are in the range of DM200 to DM600 ($120 - $360) per year for weekly collection of a container of about 120 liters. In light of declining disposal capacity and more stringent environmental regulations for landfills and incinerators, many localities planned major increases in their waste fees in 1993 — often about 50 percent. While in theory the total amount residents pay to localities for waste management should decrease as a result of the shift of materials from municipal to DSD bins, many residents may in fact experience only smaller municipal increases.

The Dual System complicates local waste collection. As noted in Chapter 6, when Duales System Deutschland (DSD) signs a contract with a locality, DSD may agree to manage the packaging waste, pay the locality to do so, or arrange a combination of DSD and local management. In all cases, the costs of managing packaging waste — one third of the waste stream — are transferred from the locality to DSD. Even if the per-bin charges increase, households may pay less to the localities because they can put packaging waste in DSD's yellow bins. The citizen pays regardless — either through green dot fees or local collection charges.

Evidence shows that quantity-based fees are an effective incentive that can substantially reduce the waste going to incinerators or landfills. In Esslingen, near Stuttgart, flat rates were replaced by a charge of DM3.75 ($2.25) per bin starting in January 1991. Esslingen residents put bins out for collection only when full. As a result of this change, waste declined from 300 kilograms per household per year to 155 kilograms per household per year — a reduction of 48 percent. Another community, Billigheim, began charging a flat rate of DM7 ($4.20) per month for each bin, plus DM0.15 ($0.09) per kilogram of garbage. This led to a 50 percent reduction in waste. The high-tech Billigheim system incorporates microchips in the bins and scales in the trucks, enabling collectors to identify automatically the household and the weight of the waste.[6]

The reported waste reductions in these towns can be attributed to both source reduction and recycling. The former is achieved primarily through backyard composting, the latter primarily by bringing more glass and paper to drop-off bins.

Preparing Municipal Solid Waste Plans

Source reduction initiatives at the local level usually begin with solid waste planning and the setting of source reduction goals. As in the United States, many states and localities in Germany are preparing long-term solid waste plans for the first time. These plans may include analysis of the waste stream, source reduction and recycling goals, and estimates of future disposal capacity needs. The state of North Rhine-Westphalia, for example, where Cologne is located, has set a source reduction goal of 15 percent and a recycling goal of 30 percent, both to be achieved in 10 years.

Case Studies: Heidelberg and Wuppertal

These case studies illustrate the costs of waste management in two German cities, how this relates to the Dual System, and how some local source reduction strategies are being implemented. Because there is no standardized reporting system for waste in Germany, the following descriptions are intended for illustration only, and not for direct comparisons of waste generation or budgets. For example, Heidelberg includes sewage treatment in its waste budget, Wuppertal does not.

Heidelberg

Heidelberg, a city of 140,000 people in southwest Germany, has become a leader in waste reduction because of its serious municipal solid waste problem. The city used to dump one-third of its waste, about 25,000 metric tons per year, in France, where tipping fees were much lower than those in Germany. In August 1992, France closed its borders to German waste destined for disposal. This left Heidelberg and other cities in the state of Baden-Württemberg searching for disposal options. Heidelberg now ships waste to Mannheim at a cost of DM486 per ton ($292), almost double the DM250 ($150) per ton it cost to dump in France.[7]

Heidelberg generated about 86,000 metric tons of municipal solid waste in 1992, about 54,000 metric tons of which was household waste. (The 86,000 metric tons includes commercial waste but not the commercial waste that is recycled.) The city has an incinerator that burns 40,000 metric tons per year, but it does not have a landfill. Heidelberg recycles about 46 percent of its household waste, some through municipal composting of yard and food waste. The city distributes the mulch from composting leaves free of charge. It aims to recycle 55 percent of the household waste stream (about 30,000 metric tons) by 1994 but expects to eliminate only 2,000 metric tons through source reduction. The municipal solid waste department asserts that the highest recycling rate it can realistically achieve is 60 - 70 percent.

Heidelberg's waste budget rose about 40 percent in 1993, to about DM50 - 55 million ($30 - 33 million). Annual per-bin charges for household garbage increased about 30 percent, to DM486 ($292) for weekly collection of a 120-liter bin. This is the basic bin for an 8-12 person multi-family residence. A family of four would generally fill a 120-liter can each week, but Heidelberg's separate collection and municipal composting of organic waste lowers its per-person output of garbage. Heidelberg cuts the fees in half for those who opt for pickup once every two weeks. Citizens may also arrange to have pickups only when their bins are full. They do so by buying stickers that they place on the full bins. Each sticker costs DM9.40 ($5.60): the yearly charge divided by 52. Unused stickers may be redeemed for cash at the end of the year. Of the 21,500 bins used to serve Heidelberg's population, 2,100 are picked up every two weeks, and residents use stickers on 5,500. Local officials cite this as evidence that one-third of the population is reducing its waste.

One way to "reduce" the waste in the household bin is to bring more material to the drop-off bins for paper and glass — actually a requirement since recyclables are banned from disposal in Heidelberg. Backyard composting is another reduction strategy. The city has already distributed 2,000 free composting bins and expects to distribute more.

Heidelberg estimated that green dot fees would cost its citizens DM200 - 500 ($120 - 249) per family per year under the 1993 fee schedule. The city will get about DM6 million ($3.6 million) per year from DSD, about 12.5 percent of its annual waste budget. The average three-person family pays about DM120 ($72) annually in per-bin fees. If this is added to the average green dot fee of DM350 ($210), the typical family will pay DM470 ($282) per year for waste management. The Dual System, however, should reduce the waste put out for regular collection because DSD provides special yellow bins for collecting packaging waste.

In response to the Packaging Ordinance, Heidelberg has banned transport packaging from disposal. This has reduced the commercial waste going to disposal by 20 percent. The city imposes fines of DM100-10,000 ($60 - $6,000) for stores that do not provide bins for secondary packaging as the Packaging Ordinance requires.

Wuppertal

Wuppertal is an industrial city of 390,000 people, east of Düsseldorf and northeast of Cologne in the state of North Rhine-Westphalia. It generates 200,000 metric tons of municipal solid waste per year, half from households and half from commercial sources. The city shares an incinerator that has the capacity to burn 330,000 metric tons per year with a nearby community, Remscheid. Built in the 1970s, the incinerator has been refurbished and was to have three upgraded furnaces by 1997. Debate surrounds the proposed retrofitting of a fourth furnace: the Wuppertal waste department wants to reduce waste, not increase burning.[8]

In 1992, Wuppertal charged DM83 ($50) per person per year to pick up 40 liters of waste a week. A family of three would thus incur costs of DM249 ($150) per year for weekly collection of a 120-liter bin. In 1993, the fee for a 120-liter bin rose 35 percent to DM335 per year ($201). However, Wuppertal estimated that this bin size would service a four-person household, because 10 liters per person would be diverted to the DSD bins. Thus the amount paid to Wuppertal per person remained about the same.

Wuppertal's novel program to encourage waste reduction began in January 1992, when the city mailed residential property owners cards listing options for waste reduction. If households reduce their waste by 50 percent, their bill is reduced by 35 percent; if they reduce waste by 25 percent, the bill is reduced by 17.5 percent. Households that participate can request smaller bins or fewer pickups. What is unusual about the Wuppertal scheme is that every household must post a large sticker on its bin indicating the reduction option it has chosen. Besides providing information to waste collectors, the sticker also creates pressure to reduce waste, as the neighbors can see which families are "good citizens."

Wuppertal estimates the new system has reduced waste by 10,000 -

20,000 metric tons — 10 to 20 percent of household waste. Of its 50,000 residential buildings, 13,000 chose, through the sticker system, to reduce waste by 50 percent; 9,600 by 25 percent. Much of this waste, however, is deposited in drop-off recycling bins for paper and glass. The city has increased the distribution of these bins from 200 to 400, as required by DSD, almost doubling the amount of paper and glass collected.

Residents in single-family homes may substantially reduce waste by composting food and yard waste. Wuppertal planned to reduce the standard waste allotment from 40 to 30 liters per person in 1993, and perhaps to 20 liters in 1994. The reduction would not necessarily reflect a real cut in total waste generation, as packaging waste would be shifted to the DSD bins.

As noted in Chapter 6, Wuppertal was to receive DM10 million ($6 million) under its contract with DSD — almost one third of its former solid waste budget of DM35 million ($21 million). Wuppertal continues to use municipal sanitation workers to collect household waste, including the waste from the yellow DSD bins. The glass and paper from the drop-off bins is collected by municipal workers, who take it to transfer points for pickup by recyclers. Wuppertal's rationale in negotiating a contract with DSD was to preserve its sanitation system, in the event DSD should fail. Also, by continuing to use its own municipal workers, noise levels and schedules can be controlled locally.

Besides banning disposables for events held on public property, as in Heidelberg and Munich, the Wuppertal waste department meets regularly with one teacher in each of the 200 schools to coordinate environmental policies. The department also helps schools obtain reusable supplies by buying bulk quantities for groups of schools. The University of Wuppertal no longer provides disposable cups for beverages in campus lounges and cafeterias. Anyone wishing to drink must bring a cup or buy a reusable one at the University store.

Notes

1. Helmut Paschlau (Landeshauptstadt München, Amt für Abfallwirtschaft [City of Munich, Department of Sanitation]), interview, October 9, 1992.

2. Rolf Friedel (Stadt Heidelberg, Amt für Abfallwirtschaft und Stadtreinigung [City of Heidelberg, Department of Sanitation]), interview, October 14, 1992.

3. "World News: Germany," *Warmer Bulletin,* No. 36, February 1993, p. 9.

4. Renate Fries (Presse- und Informationsdienst für Politik, Wirtschaft und Kultur GbR [Information and Press Service for Policy, Economy and Culture], Cologne), interview, October 24, 1992. Also, written communication, September 2, 1993.

5. Erwin Rothgang (Amtes für Umweltschutz, Stadtverwaltung Wuppertal [Department of Environmental Protection, City Administration Wuppertal]), interview, October 28, 1992.

6. "World News: Germany," *op. cit.,* p. 9.

7. Case study based on Rolf Friedel (Stadt Heidelberg, Amt für Abfallwirtschaft und Stadtreinigung [City of Heidelberg, Department of Sanitation]), interview, October 14, 1992. Also, written communication, September 14, 1993.

8. Case study based on Erwin Rothgang (Amtes für Umweltschutz, Stadverwaltung Wuppertal [Department of Environmental Protection, City Administration Wuppertal]), interview, October 28, 1992. Also, written communication, September 21, 1993.

Chapter 12

The German Packaging Ordinance and the European Community

Germany exercised great care in crafting its Packaging Ordinance to avoid conflicts with European Community (EC) law, but the European Community could still pass legislation that overrides the German ordinance. The relationship of German law to EC law is somewhat analogous to that of state law to federal law in the United States (although the US government's authority in relation to the states is more established than the European Community's) —raising common questions for the United States and Europe. Can states limit waste shipments from other states, or is free trade in waste protected? How should conflicts between free trade and environmental protection be resolved? Should there be a common environmental policy? If so, may individual states enact more stringent legislation? To what degree should waste prevention be emphasized over waste management (particularly recycling), and how might such an emphasis affect economic growth?

Passage of EC packaging legislation could affect implementation of Germany's Packaging Ordinance. It could also affect US companies doing business overseas, possibly forcing producers to modify their packaging and accept financial responsibility for recovering packaging waste in all 12 member states. Moreover, the issue of balancing free trade and environmental protection across international boundaries is likely to become increasingly important for the United States with respect to the North American Free Trade Agreement (NAFTA).

Waste Policy in the European Community

The European Community consists of 12 member states: Germany, Italy, the United Kingdom, France, Spain, the Netherlands, Portugal, Greece, Belgium, Denmark, Ireland, and Luxembourg. Negotiations are under way to admit Austria, Sweden, Finland, and Norway, and the Community is discussing membership for eastern European countries.[1] The movement toward a unified Europe with a common market, common defense, and even a common currency has slowed as sentiments swing between this goal and the need to protect the sovereignty of EC member states.

The European Community government consists of the Council of Ministers, which makes the major policy decisions, and is comprised of ministers from each of the member states; the European Commission (the executive branch); the European Parliament (an advisory body directly elected by EC citizens); and the European Court of Justice.

Two issues currently before the European Community could have substantial impact on the success and continued implementation of the German Packaging Ordinance: 1.) the regulations on the transboundary shipments of waste and 2.) the proposed EC Directive on Packaging Waste.

Environmental standards among the EC member states vary widely. Harmonizing these disparities can avert barriers to trade and ease the difficulty of dealing with diverse national laws. But should the environmental standards of countries as different as Germany and Greece be harmonized? And, more specifically, should a country be required to reduce its environmental standards in the interests of harmonization?

"Subsidiarity" or "Member States' Rights"

The debate on member-state versus central authority in the European Community is centered on what is called the "subsidiarity" principle, under which the European Community will act only in instances when objectives cannot be achieved by member states or can be better achieved at the Community level.[2] Subsidiarity is similar to what is known in the United States as "states' rights" and, in the environmental arena, it relates to how authority over environmental policies is to be allocated between member states and the central EC government in Brussels. While subsidiarity is intended to increase the authority of member states vis-à-vis the central government, the members agree little on specifics. For example, what are the respective roles of the EC government and the member states regarding environmental protection, including regulating packaging waste and waste shipments? The answer is crucial for German waste policies, for it could determine whether Germany is permitted to maintain its more stringent environmental policies. Former EC Environmental Commissioner Karel van Miert has stated that the environment could become "the sacrificial lamb" in the power struggle between Brussels and the member states over limiting EC decision making.[3]

Free Trade vs. Environmental Protection

The legal basis for waste legislation continues to be debated within the European Community: is the primary interest free trade or environmental protection? The dispute is not merely technical or procedural; it has important substantive implications. If waste legislation is authorized under the environmental protection provision of the EC treaty (article 130S), member states may keep or adopt stronger environmental protection measures than the European Community. If the legislation is authorized under the free trade provision of the treaty (article 100 A), environmental protection measures in member states are largely limited by the interests of free trade and cannot be more stringent than those of the European Community, without prior approval by the EC Commission. Resolution of this issue is critical to Germany, which has stricter environmental protection policies than most EC countries.

EC Regulation of Waste Shipments

In October 1992, after two years of deliberations, the EC Council of Ministers agreed on new regulations for the transboundary shipment of waste. The measures — an application of the "subsidiarity" principle — are of great importance to Germany, a major exporter of waste. Formally adopted in February 1993, they were intended to take effect in 1994. They regulate the supervision and control of waste shipments within, into, and out of the European Community.[4]

The new regulations reversed a prior policy that protected free trade in waste. Under the new regulations, "member states may take measures in accordance with the Treaty to prohibit generally or partially or to object systematically to shipments of waste."[5] The regulations distinguish between waste for disposal and waste for recovery (which includes recycling and waste-to-energy incineration) and allow a country to close its borders to waste for disposal. The European debate on this issue has a direct parallel in the United States, where free trade in waste has been protected by the Interstate Commerce clause of the Constitution. Legislation has been proposed in the US Congress that would permit states to limit imports of waste for disposal as the new EC regulations do. As of mid-1993, the United States had not adopted the proposed legislation. The issue is not completely resolved in the European Community either, as the European Parliament has sued to have the waste shipment regulations annulled on the grounds that the Council of Ministers should have based them on free trade (article 100A), not environmental protection (article 130S).[6] The lawsuit is partly political, as the Parliament has greater power under article 100A.

Implications of EC Regulations for German Waste Policy

The details of the waste regulations, including the complicated requirements for advance notification and consent, are beyond the scope of this report, but some implications for Germany, as a major waste exporter, should be noted. The new regulations allowing EC countries to close their borders to waste destined for disposal will put added pressure on Germany to reduce and recycle its waste. For shipments of waste for disposal among EC members, the new regulations require prior notification to the importing country and a certificate of disposal to document that the waste was legally disposed of; these regulations are intended to curtail illegal dumping.

The regulations legalize France's August 1992 ban on imports of waste for disposal, which caused serious problems in southwestern Germany. Communities there had legally been shipping 700,000 tons of waste per year to French landfills at a cost of about one-third of disposal costs in Germany.[7]

Exports of waste for disposal outside of the European Community will be virtually banned with a few exceptions for European countries that are members of the European Free Trade Association shown in Table 12-1.

The impact on shipments of waste for recovery will be less severe, although additional tracking documents and, in some cases, agreements with receiving countries will be required. Shipments of recyclables to 69 African, Caribbean, and Pacific countries will be forbidden.

The new regulations alone will not restrict Duales System Deutschland's (DSD) exports of used packaging materials from Germany to other EC countries, as these are "waste for recovery." However, receiving countries, including the United Kingdom, France, and Belgium (as described in Chapter 9), are becoming increasingly troubled by the flood of materials from Germany and may take other actions.

EC Directive on Packaging Waste

The European Community has been developing a Packaging Directive since 1990, but it had not been adopted by the time this report was prepared for publication. (Refer to the Epilogue for a description of the political agreement reached on the directive in December 1993.) The EC directive could have a range of implications for the future of the German Packaging Ordinance, from no impact (if Germany is permitted to follow its own regulations, irrespective of what the European Community adopts), to overruling the German ordinance and requiring Germany to conform to the EC directive. Most likely, the impact will fall somewhere between these extremes, with some of the issues to be resolved by the European Court. However, as Germany is the most powerful country in the European Community, with the largest population and the dominant economy, it may play an important role in shaping the EC directive.

As in Germany, packaging is a major component of municipal solid waste generated in the European Community, accounting for 25-30 percent of the total. The European Community reports that its 341 million inhabitants generate about 50 million tons of packaging waste per year: 25 million tons from households, 15 million tons from the service sector, and 10 million tons from industry.[8] About 20 percent of this waste is recycled, 60 percent landfilled, and 20 percent incinerated.[9]

Table 12-1: Organization for Economic Cooperation and Development (OECD), European Community (EC), and European Free Trade Association (EFTA) Member Countries

	OECD	EC	EFTA
Australia	■		
Austria	■		■
Belgium	■	■	
Canada	■		
Denmark	■	■	
Finland	■		■
France	■	■	
Germany	■	■	
Greece	■	■	
Iceland	■		■
Ireland	■	■	
Italy	■	■	
Japan	■		
Liechtenstein			■
Luxembourg	■	■	
Netherlands	■	■	
New Zealand	■		
Norway	■		■
Portugal	■	■	
Spain	■	■	
Sweden	■		■
Switzerland	■		■
Turkey	■		
United Kingdom	■	■	
United States	■		

Sources: *OECD Environmental Data, 1991*, Paris, 1991; and *The New York Times*, December 9, 1991.

The EC Packaging Directive aims primarily to reduce packaging waste going to final disposal (landfills or incinerators without energy recovery), and to adopt a common policy for member states to avoid distortions in competition, restraints of trade, and the need for companies to contend with different regulations in each of the 12 member states. However, the member states differ substantially on what that common policy should be. Germany, Denmark, and the Netherlands have pushed for the strongest legislation by promoting, for example, waste prevention and refilling. But other EC member states (particularly the United Kingdom), along with private industry, have pressured for more lenient measures, including a lower recycling rate, recycling rates that are not material-specific, and greater acceptance of incineration.

A key provision of the draft Packaging Directive circulated in 1993 states that within 10 years of its effective date, 90 percent, by weight, of all packaging must be recovered (by recycling, composting, or waste-to-energy burning) and 60 percent, by weight, of each packaging material must be recycled or composted. Final disposal (landfilling or incineration without energy recovery) of packaging will be limited to the residues of the sorting and collecting processes and must not exceed 10 percent of packaging consumption. Moreover, this draft of the directive would require companies to meet standards for heavy metals in packaging, measured in parts per million, no later than five years after the directive takes effect.[10]

In June 1993, the European Parliament adopted the Commission's proposed Packaging Directive, with amendments, clearing the way for redrafting by the Commission and consideration by the Council of Ministers. The parliamentary environment committee's report on this directive was described as "the most lobbied report in the history of the European Parliament,"[11] even though its role is only advisory.

The Debate Over Prevention

The concept of waste prevention, or source reduction, continues to be hotly debated. Early drafts of the EC Packaging Directive included a "standstill" provision specifying that per-capita consumption of packaging in 10 years could not exceed the EC average in 1990, estimated at 150 kilograms (330 pounds) per capita per year.[12] Industry, which views the standstill principle as a hindrance to economic growth, succeeded in getting the provision removed. But environmental groups such as the European Environmental Bureau and the Greens in the European Parliament continue to press for its inclusion on the grounds that prevention at the source should be the top priority. Parliament adopted an amendment specifying a hierarchy of waste policy options from prevention as the highest option through reuse, recycling, incineration with energy recovery, incineration without energy recovery, and, last, landfilling.

However, the EC Commission has made it clear that it will not accept the hierarchy and favors a more flexible approach. The Commission objects to policies that favor reuse over recycling. It argues that all the waste processing methods should be equivalent: in other words, recycling should not be preferred over waste-to-energy incineration.[13]

The Economic and Social Committee (ESC) of the European Community, which has advisory powers only, has joined the environmental organizations and the member states' delegations in the Council of Ministers in calling for more emphasis on prevention.[14] Denmark, Belgium, and the

Netherlands, in particular, advocate reusing or refilling. Moreover, 55 European non-governmental organizations (NGOs) have established a common agenda on packaging issues in which they emphasize prevention, support the reintroduction of refill systems in Western Europe, and oppose the introduction of one-way packaging in Eastern Europe. The groups are concerned about the gradual weakening of the Packaging Directive. "Every new draft has shown further watering down and confusion and would lead to lower standards in many member states."[15]

All 12 member states agreed at the Council of Environmental Ministers meeting in June 1993 that prevention should receive greater emphasis. They are considering guidelines on eliminating secondary and unnecessary packaging and encouraging the reuse of packaging. These guidelines could be implemented by the member states.[16]

Setting Recycling Targets

The European Commission has accepted Parliament's amendment to the Packaging Directive, which sets intermediate, five-year targets of 60 percent recovery and 40 percent recycling of each packaging material by weight. The European Community seems to be moving toward greater flexibility in the directive, as specific goals may be impossible to achieve in rural, sparsely populated areas. Discussion continues as to whether the goals should be set by material or whether there should be global goals for all packaging. As of mid-1993, there was no agreement on whether a clause would be introduced allowing member states to adopt more stringent goals. Moreover, the issue of unequal financial hardship had not been resolved.[17] Greece and Ireland, the two poorest members of the European Community, claim they could not handle the directive's financial burden, nor its quantitative objectives.[18]

Allowing EC Packaging Taxes

Parliament voted to allow the European Community to create "economic instruments," such as packaging taxes, to promote the Packaging Directive's objectives. The Commission's initial proposal would allow only individual member states to adopt economic instruments. Which version would be included in the final directive was unresolved as of mid-1993.

The Directive and the Member States

The United Kingdom and Germany oppose each other on most of the issues under debate. A British study of the proposed EC Packaging Directive estimated the additional cost of compliance for British industry at about £2.6 billion ($4.42 billion) per year — more than half attributable to the cost of recycling plastics.[19] The United Kingdom opposes material-specific recovery and recycling targets and supports a single target for diverting all packaging materials collectively from landfills, enabling member states to decide how much of each material should be reused, recycled, or incinerated. The United Kingdom argues that the reporting requirements will constitute an excessive burden and says member states should be restrained from going "further or faster" than the EC directive.[20] The Netherlands, on the other hand, has said it would not take a single step backward to comply with weaker EC legislation.[21]

The German ordinance and the EC directive could conflict in several areas. The initiatives are based on different definitions of the waste management hierarchy, with Germany giving greater preference to refillable packaging than the European Community and the latter allowing more incineration than Germany. Germany also places greater responsibility for waste on industry (the producers) than does the European Community, which has favored shared responsibility between the private and public sectors, although the matter is still being debated. Germany has deferred to the European Community and has waited to pass regulations on package labeling, reducing toxics, and the banning of specific materials such as PVC. However, the recycling quotas set by Germany are higher than those of the European Community and must be met much sooner. The European Court of Justice may ultimately have to rule on whether the more stringent measures taken by Germany are primarily protecting the environment or are a form of green protectionism.

Notes

1. Alan Riding, "Europeans Try to Revive a Faded Dream of Unity," *The New York Times,* June 20, 1993, p. 8.

2. "EC Environmental Policies and the Subsidiarity Debate," *The ENDS Report,* No. 215, December 1992, p. 19.

3. David Gardner, "Brussels Green Sprouts," *Financial Times,* London, October 21, 1992, p. 22.

4. "Environment Ministers Approve Waste Shipments Regulation," *Europe Environment,* No. 397, Europe Information Service, Brussels, November 5, 1992, p. I-4.

5. The European Community, Council Regulation #259/93, on the "Supervision and Control of Shipments of Waste within, into, and out of the European Community," Article 4.3(a), Brussels, February 1, 1993.

6. "Court Refuses to Annul Framework Directive," *Europe Environment,* No. 407, Europe Information Service, Brussels, March 30,1993, p. I-6.

7. Bureau of National Affairs, "Illegal Exports from Germany to France Spur Ministers to Form Interim Trade Plan," *International Environment Daily,* Washington, DC, August 25, 1992.

8. The European Community, "Draft Council Directive on Packaging and Packaging Waste," Commission of the European Communities, com(92)278 final-Syn436, Brussels, July 15, 1992, p. 2-3.

9. The European Community, "Discussion Document on Packaging Waste," October 1990, p. 28.

10. The European Community, "Draft Council Directive," July 15, 1992, *op. cit.* The September 1993 draft of the directive specifies the following limits for heavy metals in packaging: Lead 150 ppm, Cadmium 1.5 ppm, Hexavalent chromium 100 ppm, and Mercury 1 ppm.

11. "European Parliament Committee Adopts Much Amended Report," *Europe Environment,* No. 411, Europe Information Service, Brussels, June 8, 1993, p. I-20.

12. The European Community, "Draft Proposal for a Council Directive on Packaging and Packaging Waste, DGXI-A4," Draft No. 2, September 30, 1991.

13. "Negotiations Start Up Again on New Foundations," *Europe Environment,* No. 414, Europe Information Service, Brussels, July 20, 1993, p. I-21.

14. "ESC Calls for More Preventive Action," *Europe Environment,* No. 408, Europe Information Service, Brussels, April 15,1993, p. I-1; <u>and</u> "Packaging Waste: National Experts Call for More Emphasis on Prevention," *Multinational Service: The National and Regional Contexts,* Section III, No. 0330, March 12, 1993, Europe Information Service, Brussels.

15. "European Environmentalists Agree on Packaging Agenda," *The ENDS Report,* Environmental Data Services Ltd., No. 215, December 1992, p. 23.

16. "Negotiations Start Up Again on New Foundations," *Europe Environment,* No. 414, Europe Information Service, Brussels, July 20, 1993, p. I-21.

17. *Ibid.,* p. I-22.

18. "European Parliament Mends Draft Directive," *Europe Environment,* No. 413, Europe Information Service, Brussels, July 6, p. I-11, 12.

19. "DTI Assessment of EC Packaging Rules," *The ENDS Report,* No. 217, February 1993, p. 14.

20. "U.K. to Oppose EC Targets for Packaging Waste," *The ENDS Report,* p. 40-41.

21. "Packaging Waste: National Experts Call for More Emphasis on Prevention," *op. cit.*

Chapter 13

Implications of the
German Approach for US Waste Policy

Some Lessons from Germany

In evaluating potential applications of the German approach for US waste policy, it is useful to consider some of the problems Germany has encountered, so they can be avoided in the United States. A number of related factors led to the crisis the Dual System faced in 1993: consumers put more materials in the DSD bins than DSD had planned to collect; Germany lacked adequate recycling capacity for the collected materials; the Packaging Ordinance did not require DSD to recycle all of the materials it collected; and many companies failed to pay their green dot fees in full and on time.

The reasons for these shortcomings are instructive. Instead of gradually phasing in the Dual System, political pressures forced DSD to move quickly and make the system nationwide shortly after its implementation in January 1993. The government had intended to phase in the amount of packaging collected from an average of 50 percent in 1993 to 80 percent in 1995; however, there was no way to control these amounts, and DSD ended up collecting more used packaging than anticipated. DSD provided curbside bins for the "light fraction" of packaging waste — specifically, plastic and metallic materials. It intended to collect only 30 percent of plastic packaging, but consumers put much more of it in the yellow bins. They also discarded plastic products, which DSD never intended to collect, in the yellow bins. DSD might have anticipated this result, given the strong incentive for households to put materials in the DSD bins. Households pay steep fees based on the amount of garbage they put in their regular garbage bins and can reduce those fees by placing more in the DSD containers, which are picked up free.

The Packaging Ordinance's requirement that only a portion of the materials DSD collected be recycled in 1993 also created problems. German citizens who were separating their waste and paying for DSD collections through the green dot fees were outraged by DSD's suggestion of sending used packaging to incinerators and landfills after it had been collected separately at additional cost and effort. To take the most visible example, 30 percent of plastic packaging was to be collected, and only 30 percent of the amount collected was to be recycled. The ordinance did not specify what was to be done with the 70 percent of plastics collected that was not required to be recycled. Collection and sorting quotas were set lower in 1993 to allow time to build up recycling capacity, but the level of collections could not be controlled, and the discrepancy between the amount collected and recycling capacity emerged as a major issue.

Recognizing that incinerating or landfilling materials collected separately for recycling is not politically viable, policymakers might avoid such problems in the future by phasing in collections geographically, so that the total collected does not exceed recycling capacity.

The failure of many in industry to pay the required green dot fees also contributed to DSD's financial crisis. In the summer of 1993, 90 percent of the packages on the German market carried the green dot symbol, but fees were paid for only 50-60 percent of the packages. By the time DSD began to develop compliance mechanisms and monitoring procedures, the Dual System was running colossal deficits. To avoid this, future programs modeled on the Dual System would need to focus on financial compliance and articulate strong enforcement measures — before commencing operations.

The German experience also provides positive lessons. DSD imposed dynamic, not static, fees. In other words, fees can change as costs change. If, due to new technologies or greater efficiency, the costs of recycling certain materials were to decrease, the green dot fees would also decrease. This policy differs from some advanced disposal fees considered in the United States that define a fixed rate per package, such as the Florida fee of one cent per container.

The German Packaging Ordinance is an ambitious plan to mandate recycling and reuse which, by making industry responsible for the cost of collecting, sorting, and recycling packaging waste, includes economic incentives to reduce the amount and toxicity of waste generated. Duales System Deutschland's decision to make the green dot fees weight-based and material-specific further increases the source reduction incentive by charging companies more for packages that are heavier or more difficult and expensive to recycle. In the larger context of resource management, the German initiative addresses the issue of materials use by internalizing costs. This provides a powerful impetus for industry to incorporate end-use considerations into the design and development of packages and products, particularly when selecting materials.

One of the most positive aspects of the German system is the consistency between objectives and incentives for industry. For example, the costs of recycling plastic were internalized as the ordinance intended, even though DSD, not the plastics industry, ended up financing the recycling: when the plastics industry failed to build enough recycling capacity, DSD assumed some of this responsibility itself, and it incorporated the costs in the green dot fee for plastics.

The issue for US policymakers is not whether the German system, particularly the Dual System, will succeed or even survive. Modifications of the German policies might avoid many of the problems that have been encountered. The issue, instead, is whether the ideas or strategies implemented in Germany could be productively used in the United States to move this country toward a sound materials policy.

Eleven Questions For US Solid Waste Policymakers

1. How should responsibility for waste be allocated between industry and the public sector?

This is the most important question raised by the German policies. In the United States, residential waste is primarily the responsibility of local government, and its management is funded by taxpayers. Senator Max Baucus (D, Montana), chairman of the Senate Environment and Public Works Committee, has said this use of public money for waste means "taxpayers are subsidizing wastefulness."[1]

In Germany, the "polluter pays" principle shifts the financial responsibility for residential waste from the public sector (funded by user fees and taxes) to industry, thereby providing an incentive for industry to produce less wasteful packages and products. Even though industry can pass the costs on to consumers, companies have an incentive to keep the costs down so their products can be priced competitively. Shifting responsibility does not mean that manufacturers are being made into garbage collectors in Germany; waste continues to be collected by waste management companies and municipalities, but producers must assume the financial responsibility.

"Polluter-pays" municipal solid waste legislation is new in Germany, but there is evidence that it is beginning to have an impact. The first official reports on packaging waste generation, described in Chapter 6, show a 4 percent decline in packaging of 661,000 metric tons from 1991 to 1992, a time when the economy was growing. As discussed in Chapter 10, the auto and electronics industries have made significant changes in selecting materials and designing products.

Shifting responsibility for waste management to industry is synonymous with "internalizing" the costs of waste management. Instead of being funded by public monies, waste management costs are reflected in the prices consumers pay for products. Failure to internalize costs can skew industry's decision-making process in favor of short-lived and disposable products. For example, a beverage company that refills its bottles bears the cost of collecting, storing, and washing those bottles. If the company shifts to one-way containers, the costs of collecting, recycling, or disposing of the containers are not part of the company's accounting equation — these costs become the responsibility of the public sector, the taxpayer. Without internalization of costs, this uneven playing field between refillable and disposable containers is likely to affect the company's choices. Similarly, when companies make decisions on the durability of their products, if costs are not internalized the additional cost of disposing of the shorter-lived products is not taken into account and becomes a problem for local solid waste departments, not for the companies making the design decisions.

Germany has also shifted responsibility for waste within the business sector. The Packaging Ordinance relieves retailers of the financial responsibility for shipping container waste and makes those with greater control of the design stage — manufacturers and distributors — pay for managing the waste.

Some countries that are basing their policies on the "polluter pays" principle, such as France and Canada, have opted for shared responsibility between private industry and the public sector.

2. What should be the consumer's role in reducing and recycling waste?

Germany's shifting of responsibility for waste management has provided incentives for industry to reduce packaging, but what incentives to reduce waste does this strategy give consumers? And how important is the consumer's role?

Individuals always pay for waste management, whether as taxpayers, as users of the system, or as consumers — or some combination of these three (as shown in Table 13-1). Funding waste management through general tax revenues provides little incentive for individuals or industry to reduce waste, although this is the typical funding mechanism in the United States. Funding through user fees, such as per-bin charges for garbage, provides a strong incentive for consumers to reduce waste and to increase recycling, since there is usually no charge for picking up recyclables.

Making people pay by the bag for their trash is common in Germany, and in the United States an increasing number of communities are adopting quantity-based user fees (QBUFs); that is, charging households based on

Table 13-1: Waste Management Funding Mechanisms and Incentives

How the Individual Pays	Funding Mechanism	Source Reduction and Recycling Incentives
Taxpayer	General tax revenues	Almost nonexistent.
System user	Per-bin garbage fees	Individuals: Strong incentive to reduce costs by purchasing less wasteful and more recyclable packages and products. Industry: Weak, indirect incentive to respond to consumer preferences.
Consumer	Waste management costs incorporated in product prices (internalizing costs)	Individuals: Weak incentive to change purchase patterns as fee is a small percentage of purchase price. Industry: Strong incentive to save by reducing materials and using more easily recycled materials.

the amount of waste they generate. More than 1,000 communities in 25 US states planned to have such charges in place by the end of 1993.[2] Besides providing a direct incentive for consumers to reduce waste, a policy based on user fees affects industry indirectly by giving the consumer an incentive to buy less wasteful packages and products; presumably, industry would then respond to the new consumer preferences.

In Germany, the per-bin charges, based on the amount of waste generated, have increased rapidly, providing a strong incentive for households to reduce waste and to put as much as possible in the free recycling bins. On the other hand, the Dual System's shift of the financing for managing packaging waste from per-bin charges to an increase in consumer prices may actually lessen incentives for consumers to reduce waste in Germany. Under the Dual System, the individual still pays, but now as a consumer: in a hidden tax that is just a few cents per package — one less likely to provide an incentive to reduce waste.

The corollary to the German focus on industry as the producer of waste is that less attention is being paid to consumers, who can influence the amount of waste generated by their choice and use of products. As producers are more able than consumers to influence packaging changes, the German policies are designed to affect industry directly, at the design stage, rather than to bring about changes in consumer purchasing habits that might have an indirect affect on packaging decisions.

3. How can markets be created for secondary materials?

The biggest problem facing recycling programs in industrialized countries around the world has been lack of markets for the materials collected. In the United States, municipalities must meet higher and higher recycling targets due to public pressure for recycling, yet often they cannot find markets for the resulting secondary materials. As the amount of recyclables collected grows, the gap between supply and demand for these materials threatens to widen.

Industry Incentives

Germany's policies do not specifically address markets for the materials to be collected, but they do engage industry in the effort to develop markets by changing the rules of the marketplace and increasing industry's responsibility for waste. In theory, requiring industry to take back and reuse or recycle its packages and products gives it strong incentives to create markets for secondary materials by using more recycled content, and by reducing the use of materials that are difficult or expensive to recycle. Presumably, materials that are costly to recycle, like plastics, will become more expensive and will be used less.

To date, however, Germany is flooding world markets for secondary materials with packaging waste, particularly plastics. It is too soon to know to what extent these dislocations may be merely a transitional effect that will dissipate as Germany increases its recycling capacity. Shifting from the use of virgin materials to secondary materials throughout the world will cause substantial dislocations for industry. It is not yet known what costs and benefits would be derived from such a shift and if and how secondary materials markets can be developed to absorb the increase in the quantity of materials.

The proposed ordinances for autos and electronics in Germany make incentives to reduce and recycle company-specific, and manufacturers are already reflecting this in their product design. Under the Packaging Ordinance the incentives apply to industry collectively, because companies do not take back their own packages, and the incentives for industry to create secondary materials markets are less direct.

State and local governments across the United States have sought market development strategies. These often address local situations — for example, by providing incentives for investment in recycling industries — and they often focus on particular materials, such as improving the market for old newsprint by mandating minimum recycled content. Despite market development efforts in every state in the nation, the market problem has persisted in the United States, and there is no coherent national policy.

Government Procurement Policy
As government in the United States accounts for about 20 percent of the Gross Domestic Product — employing one in six workers at the federal, state, or local level and constituting the nation's largest customer — government procurement policies can have substantial impact on markets for secondary materials. Every state has legislation encouraging its agencies to procure products with recycled content — 35 of them offer price preferences for paper with recycled content.[3]

After months of lobbying and negotiating on the federal level, President Bill Clinton issued an executive order in October 1993 requiring federal agencies and the military to buy paper with 20 percent recycled content by the end of 1994 and 30 percent by the end of 1998. The order was intended to encourage paper companies' investment in recycling equipment by guaranteeing a market for recycled paper and also to aid localities in securing markets for the used paper they collect.[4]

While procurement policy has been used in the United States to promote recycling, it has not been used to promote source reduction in general, or packaging reduction in particular. Source reduction affects the markets for secondary materials by limiting the supply, thereby potentially alleviating the dislocations that may result from a flood of materials. Some government procurement policies have actually discouraged source reduction. For example, the computer industry has been hampered in its efforts to reuse parts by government procurement policies that require equipment to be "new."

The competitive bidding required by many procurement policies favors disposables over reusables because disposable products generally have a cheaper initial purchase price, even though they tend to be more expensive over their lifetime. One remedy would be to institute a system of "life-cycle costing," as the state of Wisconsin has done. Instead of comparing products based on purchase price, Wisconsin assesses the annual cost of products over their useful life.[5]

4. What is recycling? What's in a name?

There is an urgent need both within the United States and internationally to establish standard definitions for recycling and waste generation: recycling rates are expressed as a percentage of the waste stream. The lack of standard terminology often makes comparisons of data impossible. INFORM has found that published recycling rates are misleading because they are commonly based on materials collected for recycling, rather than the amounts actually recycled.[6] Failure to recycle materials collected may be the result of contamination of materials, damage caused during collection, improper sorting, lack of markets, and processing losses in recycling facilities.

The German Packaging Ordinance avoids the definition issue by not setting recycling quotas. The ordinance sets collection and sorting quotas and states that all sorted materials should be delivered to recyclers, thereby implying the recycling quota. It is not known to what extent recyclers actually recycle the materials, and what portion is dumped or lost in the process. Still, the German rates are a better measure of recycling than the rates often published in the United States based solely on collections.

In the face of high mandated recycling rates, policy can become hostage to semantics. An example is the pressure from some industry spokespersons to call waste-to-energy incineration "thermal recycling" and to have this count toward meeting recycling quotas. The German government has not permitted burning to count, but it does call plastics hydrogenation processes "chemical recycling." If recycling policies are to succeed, it is important that they define recycling when setting quotas. Further, policymakers need to ask the right questions. For example, if mixed plastic packaging is "chemically recycled" into synthetic crude oil that is then burned, does this harm the environment less than burning these materials in a waste-to-energy plant? And what are the relative costs? Clearly, the chemical recycling option should not be chosen simply because it is called "recycling."

It is interesting to note that, in response to mandates to achieve high recycling rates, "chemical recycling" is being promoted in Germany and also in the US state of Washington.[7]

5. What recycling rates can realistically be achieved?

Great difference of opinion exists regarding what recycling rates can realistically be achieved. These rates vary by material and even within material classifications. For example, in the United States in 1990, the overall recycling rate for plastic packaging materials was less than 4 percent, yet within the plastics category, 31.5 percent of polyethylene (PET) soft drink bottles was recycled. Aluminum had the highest recycling rate of any packaging material — more than 50 percent— yet most of this was attributable to aluminum cans' recycling rate of 63 percent: all other types of aluminum packaging have recycling rates of less than 10 percent.

To put Germany's recycling rates in context, Table 13-2 shows the actual US recycling rates for packaging materials in 1990 and the German Packaging Ordinance's quotas for the same materials. Although the US figures are for all packages and the German quotas are for primary packages only, this discrepancy has a significant affect only on the paper category: the high US rate reflects the recycling of corrugated shipping containers, classified as transport packaging under the German Ordinance.

No consensus currently exists as to what recycling rates are practical, or even what "practical" means. When J. Winston Porter was an assistant administrator of the US Environmental Protection Agency in 1988, he set the national recycling goal at 25 percent by 1992. The US recycled about 21 percent of its municipal solid waste in 1992. Porter now says that "a practical ceiling for a national recycling rate is about 33 percent."[8] In contrast, Barry Commoner, director of the Center for the Biology of Natural Systems (CBNS) at Queens College in New York City, argues that much higher rates are feasible. A CBNS project in East Hampton, New York,

Table 13-2: Recycling Rates for Packaging Materials

Materials	US actual* 1990	German quota** 1993	German quota** 1995
Glass	22.0	42	72
Tinplate	22.1	26	72
Aluminum	53.3	18	72
Paper/paperboard	36.9	18	64
Plastic	3.7	9	64
Composite	NA	6	64

*   *For all packaging*
** *For primary packaging*

Source: US data from *Characterization of Municipal Solid Waste in the United States 1992 Update,* prepared by Franklin Associates Ltd., for the US Environmental Protection Agency, July 1992.

demonstrated that more than 84 percent of household garbage could be recycled.[9] CBNS has also identified almost 30 buildings in the Park Slope neighborhood of Brooklyn, New York, that achieved household recycling rates of 50 percent or more.[10]

Almost any material can be recycled at high rates if cost is not a concern. Setting recycling goals depends on how much society is willing to pay for added collection costs, building recycling facilities, and reprocessing materials, and how it quantifies the benefits of recycling. A recycling policy raises such economic issues as the comparison of recycling costs to disposal costs, and the price of secondary materials compared to virgin materials of the same quality. Even consumer participation is an economic issue. To take an extreme example, a $10 deposit on packages would lead most consumers to bring them back to the store for redemption and recycling.

Moreover, determining a "practical" recycling rate changes over time. Technological changes create new opportunities to recycle: 10 years ago there was virtually no recycling of aseptic beverage containers anywhere in the world, yet DSD now estimates substantial capacity in Germany by 1994.

6. How much should a society spend on a recycling policy? And how should the costs be allocated?

A policy that mandates internalization of recycling costs raises questions about the investment industry must make to establish recycling, and about the effect of these internalized costs on both materials markets and consumer prices.

Some within industry charge that the German system's high recycling quotas mandate recycling "at any cost." On one hand, the incremental cost of recycling may rise as recycling rates increase, because industry typically recycles materials that are easier and most economical first, leaving the more marginal materials for later. On the other hand, recycling on such a massive scale, as attempted by Germany, could lead to economies of scale and development of new technologies that ultimately reduce per-unit costs. Germany is serving as a laboratory that, through implementing its policies and conducting life-cycle analyses, will provide information on the economic and environmental viability of achieving the mandated quotas.

The German policy is intended to apply pressure on industry to reuse and recycle materials. The policy anticipates that the recycling costs will be high for some materials, that these costs will be reflected in higher prices, and that ultimately materials that are costly to recycle will be used less. The plastics crisis in Germany is a manifestation of the application of this pressure. Germany has chosen not to ban any materials, but rather to internalize the costs of managing the waste and to let market forces determine the demand for the materials. The struggle underway in Germany will determine whether the use of plastic packaging is substantially decreased or whether the government allows more waste-to-energy incineration.

Current costs of the Dual System are high, partly owing to the push to attain the quotas rapidly. There may, however, be a contrast in short-term and long-term costs of recycling. Costs that are initially high during the transition period from an economy based on primary raw materials to one based on secondary materials may decline after the large investments required for the transition are completed and technologies are improved.

Industry in Germany imposes the packaging fees, which are virtually a sales tax, but it is not accountable to the public as elected officials are. This raises the question of how the level of the fees will be controlled. Consumer groups have called DSD "a giant tax machine" (as described in Chapter 9), and some have complained that DSD contracts with the waste management industry are over-generous. Industry, however, clearly has some incentive to keep the fees down, as it would suffer from any decline in consumer spending due to large increases in the fees.

In any case, the German mechanism for raising money to fund the new system — the green dot fees — might have poor political prospects in the United States because it is, in effect, a regressive sales tax, constituting a greater percentage of income for poorer people. Powerful public figures in the United States, such as former Representative Al Ullman (D, Oregon), who was chairman of the House Ways and Means Committee in the 1970s, have been voted out of office after supporting a similarly regressive national sales tax, the Value-Added Tax (VAT). Although regressivity is a major issue in the United States, it does not appear to be an issue in Germany — a country accustomed to raising large amounts of revenue through a national sales tax.

7. How could the United States ensure that recycling targets are met?

The German experience has shown that dumping of recyclables constitutes a serious problem. Even if materials are sent to an authorized recycler, there is no certainty that they will be recycled because recyclers may accept shipments that greatly exceed their capacity. DSD is experiencing difficulty in keeping track of materials shipped for recycling both within Germany's borders and to foreign nations; the United States would probably experience similar problems. Some monitoring will always be required, and its effectiveness will remain problematic.

The most effective way to ensure that materials are actually recycled would be to build the necessary recycling capacity within each country. Government can encourage this by providing tax and other incentives for industry to build additional capacity.

8. Could the take-back strategy work in the United States?

The take-back strategy is an outgrowth of Germany's preference for incentive policy over "command and control" regulations — the market-based approach. The advantage of this approach is that, by allowing industry to set the green dot fees for each packaging material, it avoided the intense lobbying that would have occurred had government set the fees. However, the type of collaboration among competitors required to establish and operate an entity like DSD might run afoul of US antitrust laws, and competing US companies do not traditionally work together as German companies do.

Moreover, the United States is much larger than Germany, so setting up a US "Dual System" that would negotiate contracts with every waste district in the country would be a huge undertaking. Although the take-back strategy for packaging might be difficult to implement in the United States, it might be feasible for larger items such as cars and computers. Many US states already have take-back legislation, in the form of mandatory deposits, that has functioned well for beverage containers.

But shifting responsibility to industry is not contingent on a take-back strategy; it could be accomplished through other mechanisms, such as taxes, fees, or mandated utilization rates, as described in Question 11.

9. How could public policy incorporate positive, not perverse, incentives to reduce and recycle waste?

Incentives are the cornerstone of Germany's market-based approach to reducing and recycling waste. Based on the assumption that industry is more effective than government at tasks such as creating markets for secondary materials, German policy provides the quotas and incentives but allows industry to devise its own implementation system. Presumably, if industry must shoulder responsibility for managing and paying for recycling, it will have a positive incentive to make recycling work and make it cost effective, as well as to reduce the amount of materials it must handle. Yet, as discussed in Question 2, DSD's free recycling bins provide a "perverse" incentive — one that lessens the source reduction incentives for consumers — by shifting their costs from quantity-based fees to an "invisible" increase in product prices.

Some environmentalists, as noted in Chapter 9, have criticized the Packaging Ordinance as emphasizing recycling and seeming to ignore source reduction. However, source reduction of transport and secondary packaging has occurred because the law requires consumer product companies to pay for managing the waste generated by their shipping containers, and provides incentives for retailers to urge suppliers to eliminate packaging. The new industry-developed green dot fee schedule, which took effect in October 1993, clearly contains incentives for source reduction of primary packaging through fees directly related to packaging weight. The German system is coherent in this respect: the incentives for industry are generally consistent with the policy goals.

Some US solid waste policies at present, while not mentioning source reduction, have implicit, perverse incentives that discourage it. For example, tonnage grants paid to communities based on the amount of materials collected for recycling (such as exist in New Jersey) are a disincentive to reduce waste at the source. A reduction in the amount of materials collected for recycling would decrease a community's weight-based grants. By contrast, a policy rewarding communities based on the amount of materials diverted from disposal, such as Westchester County, New York, has adopted, encourages both source reduction and recycling.

Some US policies today actually provide disincentives for both source reduction and recycling. For example, the federal subsidies for virgin materials like timber and oil that lower the prices of these virgin materials provide a disincentive for using secondary materials and for reducing the amount of materials used. The policy of exempting government agencies and public institutions from paying for waste management gives them little incentive to reduce or recycle. Charging them for waste disposal would provide economic incentives for both.

10. Could US policies encouraging the use of refillable beverage containers effectively promote source reduction in this country?

The most striking difference between packaging in Germany and the United States is the extensive use in Germany of refillable beverage containers. In both countries, refillable bottles were widely used prior to the 1960s. Germany maintained its system, and the refill rate for beer and soft drinks in Germany is 80 percent today. In the United States, 84 percent of beer and soft drinks were sold in refillable containers in 1964, but this has now dropped to 5 percent.

Germany did not retain its refillable system through happenstance. Public policy there firmly supports the use of refillable bottles, as demonstrated by the high refill rates specified in the Packaging Ordinance. The government has even taken action against one-way containers, meeting the introduction of the single-use PET bottle in 1988 with a mandatory deposit on one-way plastic bottles. Beverage companies withdrew the single-use PET bottles and replaced them with refillable PET bottles. In contrast, one-way cans currently dominate the US beer and soft drink market, comprising a 70 percent share for beer and a 50 percent share for soft drinks. In Germany, only about 11 percent of these beverages are sold in cans.

The question of whether refillable bottles are better for the environment than one-way containers continues to be controversial in the United States and throughout Europe. A detailed analysis of this issue is beyond the scope of this report, but a forthcoming INFORM publication, *Case Reopened: Reassessing Refillable Bottles* (Spring 1994), will provide a comprehensive study of refillable beverage containers and related policy implications. The report raises the following questions: As an environmental strategy, is refilling, in some or all cases, preferable to the recycling of one-way containers? Is refilling a practical option given today's technology, distribution systems, material and labor costs, marketing practices, and regulatory environment? If refilling is beneficial but is not a practical option under current conditions, how would these conditions need to change in order for refilling to be practical?

Even if Germany and the United States were to agree on the ideal policy regarding refillable versus one-way containers, their policy decisions would likely vary because the countries are starting from very different places. It is far easier and less costly for Germany to maintain its existing refillable structure than for the United States to recreate one. Any environmental benefits from expanding refilling would have to be weighed against the costs entailed in reviving the US refilling system.

The German experience can provide a useful model for US policymakers if the United States decides to promote more refillable bottles. Most Germans agree that their refilling system is worth preserving. Many aspects of the German system, such as standardized bottles, higher bottle deposit fees, the ubiquitous reusable carrying crates, and local beverage distribution patterns could be instructive in designing US refillable policies and programs.

11. What policy mechanisms are available if US policymakers decide to expand manufacturer responsibility for products and packages?

Recycling Advisory Council Policy Options

The Market Development Subcommittee of the Recycling Advisory Council (RAC), a program of the National Recycling Coalition, has listed six policy options as its top priorities.[11] The RAC is made up of high-level representatives from the federal government, municipalities, environmental groups, public interest organizations, community-based recycling groups, the recycling industry, and industry in general. The RAC defines these six policy options as follows:

- **Manufacturers' Responsibility:** Based on the German model, this policy would make manufacturers responsible for financing the recovery of a specified percentage of the materials used in their products. Manufacturers' responsibility could be accomplished by creating an alternative waste management system, such as Germany's Dual System, or by having industry contract out waste management functions or finance existing waste management programs.
- **Shared Responsibility:** Under consideration in Canada, this concept requires industry and the public sector to share responsibility for recycling. Industry may establish an organization to which it would contribute fees for funding recycling. The organization may own and operate sorting and processing facilities, and may pay municipalities for the costs of collecting recyclables, to the extent that these costs exceed those of regular garbage collection.
- **Utilization Requirements:** This strategy would require a manufacturer to recover a percentage of the materials used in its products, either by using the materials in its own manufacturing process or by contracting with third parties to do so.

- **Minimum-content standards:** These standards require the use of a specified quantity of secondary materials in packages and/or products. In the United States, minimum-content legislation began by targeting newspapers and has expanded to include other products. Thirteen states now have minimum-content legislation for newspapers, and 11 more have similar voluntary agreements. These initiatives have contributed to the large increase in use of recycled content by newspaper publishers with circulations over 200,000: from 9 percent in 1989 to 19 percent in 1992.[12]
- **Virgin material taxes:** These taxes can be imposed on the virgin content of products and packages at the manufacturing level as a way of encouraging the use of secondary materials by making them more competitively priced compared to virgin materials. Such taxes could also encourage source reduction by making materials more expensive, thereby creating incentives to use less — for example, by making materials more costly relative to labor. Virgin materials taxes can be a mechanism for internalizing solid waste costs if they are based on the costs of waste management.
- **National materials trust fund:** The RAC list includes a proposal for establishing a national trust fund by imposing fees on packages, based on the materials used. The fund would provide rebates to companies based on the percentage of secondary materials that they use in their products and packages.

Another way to expand manufacturer responsibility that US policymakers have been discussing for almost a decade is the advanced disposal fee (ADF) — charging producers in advance for disposing of their products or packages. The RAC left ADFs off its list because it views them as a mechanism that is a variation on the policy options of a materials trust fund and virgin materials taxes.[13]
- **Advanced Disposal Fees (ADF):** An ADF is a fee levied on a product, based on the cost of waste management. ADFs reflect the approach that these costs should be the responsibility of manufacturers, who pass them on to consumers in product prices. In a 1991 study of ADFs in the United States, the consulting firm Arthur D.

Little found states considering 28 ADF-type bills, with 60 percent of them focusing on packaging.[14]

More than half the states already have ADFs for specific commodities, such as tires, motor oil, appliances, or lead-acid batteries.[15] Only Florida has attempted broader ADF application; its law imposes a one-cent fee on containers that are not recycled at a rate of at least 50 percent, increasing to two cents in October 1995. Early evidence indicates that the Florida ADF, effective October 1993, is leading industry to increase investment in recycling, as this is often cheaper than paying the fees.[16]

In Germany, DSD's 1993 green dot fees are similar to ADFs in that they charge manufacturers in advance for the cost of recycling their packages. However, the green dot fees are imposed by industry rather than government. Nonetheless, the German fees, based on weight and material, could provide US policymakers with an example of how such fees might be set.

US Legislative Initiatives

In the United States, legislation incorporating the concept of expanded manufacturer responsibility has been proposed at the federal, state, and local level, as illustrated by these examples.

- **Responsible entity legislation:** In 1992, a "responsible entity" provision was included in the federal legislation to reauthorize the Resource Conservation and Recovery Act (RCRA). It would have required all brand name manufacturers with annual receipts of $50 million or more to "recover," by themselves or through contracts with others, 50 percent of packaging materials made of glass, paper, metal, or plastic by the year 2000 through source reduction, reuse, or use of recycled content. Although the provision died along with the RCRA reauthorization bill, Senator Max Baucus has said this would be the cornerstone of his solid waste proposals. Speaking at the US Conference of Mayors in April 1993, Senator Baucus cited Germany as a source of his ideas to "internalize" waste management costs and shift them from the taxpayer to industry.[17]
- **Sustainable Manufacturing:** On the state level, the California In-

tegrated Waste Management Board planned to introduce "manufacturers' responsibility" legislation in 1994, which it calls "sustainable manufacturing." The proposed legislation would include a broad range of strategies to change the way businesses deal with the environmental impacts of their products. Paul Relis of the California Waste Management Board has said, "As we look to the future of waste management in California, I believe the German system should receive our closest study."[18]

- **"Rates and dates" packaging legislation:** Ten states have proposed legislation mandating that packaging be reusable, recyclable, or made of recycled content. The actual rates specified and the dates for achieving them have varied among the states. California and Oregon passed such legislation for rigid plastic containers in 1991.[19] In Massachusetts, legislators proposed a "rates and dates" bill that was considered a prototype for the country but went on to defeat in a November 1992 referendum after a massive industry-sponsored lobbying campaign against it.

- **Local initiatives:** In New York City, the Department of Sanitation is applying the German approach of producer responsibility in the development of local legislative proposals that would require retailers to take back dry-cell batteries, white goods (appliances), and tires. The legislation would ban both the collection and disposal of appliances, for example, within the city's waste management system. Consumers purchasing new appliances would be entitled to bring back an old one, of the same type but not necessarily the same brand.[20]

Requiring retailers to provide bins so consumers could leave packaging in the store is another German strategy that could be implemented at the local level — without federal or state action. In Germany this provision has given retailers a strong incentive to pressure their suppliers to reduce packaging.

Pressure from Local Government

Many academics and environmentalists have long supported the concept of internalizing costs, which leads to expanded manufacturers' responsibility. Now local government officials are supporting this idea. Local governments are facing ever-higher recycling mandates as the public clamors for more recycling, but they have not been able to solve the market problem without more help from industry. Costs of recycling programs are rising, competing for funds with much-needed services such as education, law enforcement, fire protection, and health care.

The United States can expect strong pressure from local governments to shift responsibility for managing waste from municipalities to industry. The first action of Mayor Sharpe James of Newark, New Jersey, when he became chairman of the US Conference of Mayors' Solid Waste Task Force, was to commission a study of strategies making recycling the responsibility of manufacturers. "The recycling system in the US would be greatly enhanced if it copied Germany's Dual System," said James. "It would help correct a situation in which municipalities are picking up the tab to recycle huge amounts of waste produced by the private sector.... As it stands right now, a consumer product company can sell a ring in a refrigerator box and taxpayers will subsidize the disposal of the packaging waste. There need to be incentives to minimize waste."[21]

James notes that the US Conference of Mayors is working with Senator Max Baucus on legislation making US industry responsible for recycling what it produces. James says, "Our position is not going to be a popular one with many members of the private sector in this country as companies maintain that it can't be done....And that's just not true — dozens of American companies like IBM, Procter & Gamble, and Colgate Palmolive are already participating successfully in the Dual collection system in Germany....Getting private industry to assume a fair share of the burden in managing our resources and waste is a trend that will only grow stronger across the globe."[22]

Conclusions

Germany's "polluter pays" policies have already succeeded in one important respect: they have helped change the way companies think. Throughout the world, manufacturers of durable goods such as cars and computers are beginning to design for disassembly and to reevaluate their use of materials. The thinking of these companies has changed dramatically from what it was 10 years ago, and Germany's polluter-pays policies certainly deserve significant credit for being a catalyst for much of this change. In the process of materials selection, companies manufacturing packages and products are looking not only at front-end costs but also at ultimate disposal costs, disposal or recycling problems the material may cause, and opportunities for reuse.

Many leaders in the business community are now embracing the concept of a materials policy. Executives at Xerox wrote in 1993: "This growing interest in recycling durable goods goes beyond the problem of landfill capacity. It reflects a recognition that most of our planet's resources are finite and should not be squandered by discarding material that is still useful. In the industrial community we have been coming to the realization that such waste represents a significant — and an avoidable — business cost."[23] And the chairman of Dow Chemical has called for an environmental policy based on full-cost pricing: "What is full-cost pricing? It means that we price goods and services to reflect their true environmental costs, including production, use, recycling and disposal....Our air, water and earth are no longer the 'free goods' our society once believed. They must be redefined as assets, so that they can be efficiently and appropriately allocated. Ideally, we should learn to live off the interest of these assets, rather than by depleting the assets themselves."[24]

The European Commission, in May 1993, commented on resource management in relation to a study of the links between job creation and environmental protection. The Commission said "the high rate of unemployment and the deterioration of the environment could be the symptoms of the same cracks in our current model of economic development: inefficient use of our resources has led to under-use of human resources and over-use of environmental resources."[25] In other words, industrial societies under-use labor and over-use materials.

The biggest questions about Germany's Packaging Ordinance relate to the Dual System itself: Will it reduce the amount of primary packaging? Will the recycling quotas be achieved? Is the system cost-effective? Will it survive financially and politically? It is in the interest of the Kohl government and industry for the Dual System to succeed: both have invested great effort in the system, and industry has invested a lot of money as well. Industry has a major stake in the Dual System's success because it operates and controls the system and would lose this authority if the system were to fail: a likely alternative is more government control. German Environment Minister Klaus Töpfer has already said he is prepared to impose packaging taxes if the Dual System fails, and many environmentalists are calling for packaging bans.

To the extent that packages and products are globally designed or are made by multi-national companies, the United States stands to benefit from industry responses to the German legislation — particularly where source reduction strategies save companies money. Design changes often move quickly around the world — the changes in automobiles and computers are a case in point. Germany has been described as the "California of Europe," and its Packaging Ordinance has been compared to California's pioneering auto emission standards. In both cases, many companies made decisions to produce everything to the world's toughest standards.[26] Some US companies, however, may find themselves at a disadvantage vis-à-vis German competitors who are ahead in developing more environmentally friendly packages and products.

Policymakers in the United States need to resolve the issue of who is responsible for solid waste and to devise a mechanism to transfer responsibility, if that is found desirable. The decision of how individuals should pay for waste — whether as taxpayers, as users of the waste management system, or as consumers — affects source reduction incentives. Responsibility, or lack of it, may be at the heart of our municipal solid waste problem. Historically, those who created waste have not been responsible for paying for its recycling or disposal. Such a system inevitably encourages wastefulness. Environment Minister Töpfer stresses the need to "avoid burdening future generations with the problems of our affluence."[27]

US public policy has already applied the "polluter pays" principle to hazardous waste management and may be able to shift some or all of the responsibility for municipal solid waste as well. Once policymakers resolve the question of responsibility, the United States can begin to evaluate the various strategies, some implemented in Germany and some not, that would constitute the most effective materials management policy. The

United States may look at Germany as providing a laboratory for the study of solid waste policies. The experiences there, along with the statistical data that will be reported, will be of great value to policymakers around the world.

Our ability to learn from the German experience is not contingent upon the Dual System's success. The problems it has faced relate primarily to implementation strategies — the high mandated recycling quotas and the speed at which they must be attained — not to the basic concepts. By understanding what strategies have failed and why, the United States can avoid making similar mistakes. Germany has raised the critical issue of manufacturers' responsibility, and this concept is sweeping the industrial world. Future US policies can be developed within the framework of resource management, taking a broad view of our use of materials and other resources to develop policies that will permit us to live within our environmental means, as well as within our economic means.

Notes

1. Senator Max Baucus, keynote address, U.S. Conference of Mayors: Reality-Based Recycling II Conference, Washington, DC, April 1, 1993.

2. Lisa A. Skumatz and Philip A. Zach, "Community Adoption of Variable Rates: an Update," *Resource Recycling,* June 1993, p. 68.

3. Chaz Miller, "Recycling in the States: 1992 Update," *Waste Age,* March 1993, p. 34.

4. John Holusha, "White House Issues an Order to Bolster Recycling of Paper," *The New York Times,* October 21, 1993, p. A-1.

5. INFORM (Bette K. Fishbein and Caroline Gelb), *Making Less Garbage: A Planning Guide for Communities,* 1992, p. 54.

6. INFORM (Maarten de Kadt), "Evaluating Recycling Programs: Do You Have the Data?" *Resource Recycling,* June 1992.

7. Jerry Powell, "Thermal Plastics Processing: Is it Recycling?" *Resource Recycling,* May 1993, p. 52-55.

8. J. Winston Porter, "Recycling at the Crossroads," Porter & Associates, Sterling, VA, January 1993, p. 4.

9. Barry Commoner, *et. al., Development and Pilot Test of an Intensive Municipal Solid Waste Recycling System for the Town of East Hampton: Final Report,* New York State Energy Research and Development Authority, 982-ERER-ER-87, Albany, NY: December 1988.

10. Barry Commoner *et. al., Development of Innovative Procedures to Achieve High Rates of Recycling in Low Income Neighborhoods,* submitted to the Pew Charitable Trusts and the Aaron Diamond Foundation, April 10, 1992.

11. Clifford Case, "Eliminating Barriers to Recycling in the 90's: The Work of the National Recycling Coalition and the Recycling Advisory Council," New York State Department of Environmental Conservation: Fifth Annual Recycling Conference, Syracuse, September 28, 1993.

12. Chaz Miller, "Recycling in the States, 1992 Update," *op. cit.*

13. Edgar Miller (Recycling Advisory Council), phone interview, November 17, 1993.

14. Arthur D. Little, "A Report on Advanced Disposal Fees," Cambridge, MA, p. 2-3.

15. Russell H. Martin, "ADF Battle in Florida," *Biocycle,* November 1992, p. 59.

16. Edgar Miller, phone interview, *op. cit.*

17. Senator Max Baucus keynote address at U.S. Conference of Mayors, *op. cit.*

18. Paul Relis (California Waste Management Board), written communication to Board members, August 3, 1992.

19. Reid Lifset (Yale University Program on Solid Waste Policy), "Extended Producer Responsibility: Rationales and Practices in North America," Massachusetts Institute of Technology: Design and Disposal of Durable Products Conference, March 1993, p. 42.

20. New York City Department of Sanitation, Bureau of Waste Prevention, Reuse and Recycling, "New York City's Waste Prevention Program," July 12, 1993.

21. Mayor Sharpe James, "Make Private Industry Responsible for Recycling," press release, Newark Public Information Office, August 12, 1993, p. 2.

22. *Ibid.* p. 4, 5.

23. Jack C. Azar, James C. MacKenzie, and Richard S. Morabito, "Environmental Life-Cycle Design at Xerox," draft for *EPA Journal,* July 1993.

24. Frank Popoff, "Life After Rio: Merging Economics and Environmentalism," Chemical Week Conference, Houston, October 15, 1992, p. 4.

25. "European Commission Seeks to Consolidate the Links," *Europe Environment,* No. 410, Europe Information Service, Brussels, May 18, 1993, p. I-10.

26. Frances Cairncross, "How Europe's Companies Reposition to Recycle," *Harvard Business Review,* March-April 1992, p. 40.

27. Bureau of National Affairs, "New Directive Sets Parameters for Incineration, Landfill Disposal," September 22, 1992.

Epilogue

As described in the Notes to the Reader at the beginning of this report, INFORM has been confronted with rapidly changing events throughout the course of this research. The main body of this text went into production in mid-1993. This Epilogue highlights three important events between that time and the end of December 1993, when the book went to press.

DSD Faces Another Financial Crisis

As described in Chapter 6, DSD averted a serious financial crisis in June 1993 when industry agreed to contribute additional funds, and DSD announced plans to control its costs and improve the collection of green dot fees. But the announcement in July that DSD's finances were "assured" turned out to be short-lived. By August, DSD was once again on the brink of insolvency. This time DSD announced a deficit of DM700 million ($420 million) for the remainder of 1993.[1] DSD owed more than DM800 million ($480 million) to waste management firms and localities under the contracts it had signed for the collection and sorting of packaging waste. Waste management firms were threatening to discontinue collections, and Environment Minister Töpfer said the mandatory deposits and retailer take-back of packaging specified in the ordinance would go into effect if the problem was not solved by September 3, 1993. He also said he was considering imposing taxes on packaging.[2]

Representatives of manufacturers, the waste industry, retailers, local authorities, and DSD held a series of crisis meetings the first three days of September. Environment Minister Töpfer chaired the final meeting. The representatives agreed that their three main goals were: to solve DSD's financial problems; to assure that companies pay the required green dot fees; and to control costs. To achieve these goals, the group agreed on a nine-point program and set up a task force to put it into effect. The key points were as follows:

- Conversion of DSD debts (owed to the waste industry and local authorities) to interest bearing loans.
- Assuring payment of green dot fees through auditing, fines, and having retailers withhold amounts due.
- Restructuring DSD, including a major role for the waste management industry.
- Capping DSD payments for waste management at a maximum of DM40 ($24) per person per year through 1994, so there would be no increase in fees before that time.
- Reviewing the Packaging Ordinance and considering amendments.[3]

The waste management companies with which DSD has contracts agreed to convert DSD's DM640 million ($384 million) debt to loans, in exchange for a major role in DSD's management. The contractors will appoint one-fourth of the members of DSD's advisory board and one of DSD's four managing directors.[4] This policy has raised concern among environmentalists and the Federal Cartel Office (Bundeskartellamt) about potential conflicts of interest, because the waste management firms will now sit on the advisory board of the company that determines how much they will be paid. Further, local authorities fear these firms may pressure to get DSD contracts at the expense of using municipal workers for waste collection.[5]

Although representatives of the local authorities at the September meetings agreed to the nine points, many localities balked when asked to implement the arrangement. Major cities such as Frankfurt, Wiesbaden, Darmstadt, Kassel, Mainz, Stuttgart, Hamburg and Hanover resisted converting the debts to loans.[6] Mainz, which DSD owed DM2 million ($1.2 million), threatened to start a debt collection process. The Mayor of Mainz asked why cities should subsidize DSD, when industry was avoiding paying the green dot fees.[7] The localities argued that they were short of funds, that it was not their position to give loans, and that DSD lacked collateral to back them. They requested that Environment Minister Töpfer arrange for the federal government to guarantee the loans, but he refused.[8] Nonetheless, many localities were concerned that they might have to collect used packaging materials if the Dual System were to fail, which would require a big increase in local taxes. Despite their initial resistance, the localities did, according to DSD, ultimately agree to convert the DSD debt to loans.[9]

Major changes have been made to guarantee that manufacturers pay their green dot fees in full and on time. Companies must submit a certified statement from accountants that their fees have been paid in full. If they cannot provide this, retailers will withhold lump sum amounts and forward them to DSD. For example, retailers will withhold 2.5 percent of the wholesale value of shipments of food, cleaning supplies, and cosmetics from companies without the proper certificate.[10] Moreover, DSD has amended its contracts to allow it to send independent examiners into companies to review their books, and it will impose fines on companies that fail to pay the green dot fees.[11]

The strict enforcement program had immediate impact. For example, one of Germany's largest dairy companies, Molkerei Alois Müller, had been holding its green dot fees in a savings account rather than paying them to DSD. It said it would not pay them until recycling systems for plastics were in place. This company, which has filed a lawsuit claiming the Packaging Ordinance is unconstitutional, has submitted to pressure from retailers and has agreed to pay DSD DM5.4 million ($3.2 million).[12]

The capping of DSD expenditures at DM40 ($24) per person per year through 1994 represents another major change. For the moment, this allays the fears that DSD's costs would increase at a rapid, uncontrolled rate and boost the green dot fees.

Adding to DSD's financial woes are the mounting piles of plastics that cannot be recycled in Germany, and the complaints from European countries to which Germany is exporting plastic packaging waste. The United Kingdom's environment ministry says Germany is stockpiling 250,000 metric tons of plastics.[13] Warehouses are filling up, and there are reports of plastics being stored on military bases and on rafts on a lake in the former East Germany.[14] At a packaging summit Germany hosted in Bonn in late October 1993, Minister Töpfer responded to complaints about shipments of waste and assured the other EC environment ministers that there would be a significant decrease in Germany's exports of packaging waste, particularly plastics.[15] Wolfram Brück, chairman of DSD's board of directors, has said that starting in 1994, DSD will not sign new contracts to recycle plastic packaging waste within the European Community, but it will honor current contracts.[16]

Amending the Packaging Ordinance

Since its passage in 1991, there have been many requests, particularly from industry, to revise the Packaging Ordinance. The Environment Ministry had consistently denied these requests, but in September 1993 it finally relented and agreed to make revising the ordinance a part of the nine-point plan to rescue the Dual System.

The Bundesrat (upper house of Parliament) debated the Ministry's proposed amendments to the Packaging Ordinance in December 1993, but no vote was taken. The principal changes are a slight reduction in the recycling quotas (which are stated, not implied as in the ordinance) and a delay in the time for achieving them as shown in the table on the next page.

A comparison with the ordinance's implied recycling quotas shown in Table 3-3 indicates that the decrease in the highest recycling quotas is small — they are reduced from 64 and 72 percent to 60 and 70 percent, respectively. The time, delay, however is significant. Under the proposed amendments, the maximum quotas do not have to be achieved until January 1998, instead of January 1995. The new quota schedule would significantly impact paper and plastics — the materials that Germany has been accused of dumping abroad. From 1993 to 1996, only 10 percent of paper would have to be recycled, down from the old quotas of 18 percent in 1993 and 64 percent by 1995. Delaying the dates would give the plastics industry much-

Proposed Amended Recycling Quotas

Material	January 1993	January 1996	January 1998
	(percent by weight)		
Glass	40	70	70
Tinplate	30	70	70
Aluminum	20	70	70
Paper/paperboard	10	50˙	60
Plastic	10	50	60
Composite	10	50	60

Source: Provisional draft text of the Amendment to the German Packaging Ordinance.

needed time to develop new recycling capacity.[17]

The proposed amendments specify that the quotas be met with what they call "material" recycling, which is defined to exclude waste-to-energy incineration. For plastics, half of the quota must be met "by mechanical recycling insofar as an appropriate 'high value' recycling is technically possible and economically reasonable."[18] This is a qualified mandate for mechanical recycling and implies that the remainder of the quota can be met by "chemical" recycling. The draft also says that waste-energy incineration can be used for plastics collected in excess of the quota.

Other changes in the proposed amendments would require documentation, confirmed by an auditor, of the number of primary packages a company sells on the German market. The amendments would require that the cost of the green dot for each package be printed on the package for purposes of "informing the consumer." There would also be a requirement that if the Dual System should fail, the take-back provision for retailers would go into effect in one month.[19] This is reduced from the six months specified in the original Packaging Ordinance and addresses the local authorities' concern that they would have to collect the discarded packaging.

As this report goes to press, the proposed amendments to the Packaging Ordinance are under discussion in Germany but no action has been taken by the Parliament. The outcome may be affected by the EC Packaging Directive, as described in the following section.

EC Packaging Directive

After four years of wrangling, the EC Council of Ministers reached a "political agreement" on a Packaging Directive in December 1993, although the agreement will have to be put in writing to make it a "common position." While changes could still be made by the European Parliament, arriving at a "common position" is a highly significant step toward finalizing the directive. As the directive is scheduled to go into effect 18 months after its passage, this could occur as early as 1996.

The EC compromise was difficult to achieve and was accomplished due to the determination of most member states to reach agreement before the term of the Belgian presidency expired at the end of 1993, and before Germany assumes the presidency in the second half of 1994, following Greece. (The Presidency of the EC rotates every six months.) The disagreements with Germany on recycling targets and waste exports provided the impetus for most EC member states to finalize the directive before Germany's term in the presidency.[20] However, the political agreement was not unanimous: Germany, the Netherlands, and Denmark opposed it.[21]

The EC Packaging Directive of December 1993 is very different from the earlier versions. The concern with preventing the generation of waste seems to have been overpowered by the concern about Germany's flooding European Community markets with used packaging materials. In a major change from earlier drafts of the directive, this version sets maximum as well as minimum recovery and recycling targets to which member states must adhere. (Recovery includes all processes that recover value from waste, including waste-to-energy incineration.) Within five years of the directive's effective date, 50 to 65 percent, by weight, of packaging must be recovered and 25 to 45 percent recycled. In other words, no EC country may recycle more than 45 percent of its packaging waste.[22]

These recycling targets differ from those in earlier drafts of the EC directive, which specified minimum recycling of 40 percent in five years, 60 percent in ten years, and did not set any maximum recycling targets. The rates are set for all packaging materials collectively, but at least 15 percent of each packaging material must be recycled. At the end of the five-year period, new targets will be set.[23]

The poorer EC countries Greece, Ireland, and Portugal will have five years longer to comply with the recovery and recycling targets.[24] Countries such as Germany, the Netherlands, and Denmark that want to exceed 45 percent recycling will have to apply to the European Commission for exemptions. These will only be granted if the country can prove it has adequate recycling capacity and that it will not disrupt materials markets in EC member states.[25] This provision is intended to address other EC countries' charges that Germany is flooding the EC markets with used packaging materials. Luxembourg, because it is so small, will be permitted to exceed the limits if it has agreements with waste management facilities in neighboring states. The Dutch have complained that this scenario means that countries operating within the specified recycling limits will be able to export large amounts of packaging waste to other EC countries, whereas those who wish to exceed the limit will be subject to scrutiny.[26]

Considering the lengthy and heated debate that preceded the compromise, EC member states responded as might have been expected. Belgium, which held the presidency, called the agreement "a real step forward." The British said, "common sense has prevailed...and the directive has been transformed...from one driven by green zealots." The Dutch on the other hand claimed "for the single market [i.e., free trade] it's a good proposal, but not for the environment. It has nothing to do with the environment."[27] German Environment Minister Töpfer said the agreement would set back recycling programs in Europe and force Germany to produce more waste. He claimed "it is not supposed to be the EC's job to standardize the environmental tempo in all member states at any price or even to reverse it."[28]

Aspects of the agreement remain unclear. For example, it allows member states to encourage reuse and refilling if this is compatible with the EC treaty and does not create barriers to trade. It is not clear how this will affect Denmark's legislation that bans cans for beer and soft drinks. In a ruling on this legislation, the European Court previously held that barriers to trade could be justified by the need to protect the environment.[29]

Developing a Packaging Directive that will apply to countries as disparate as Germany and Greece is a major challenge. The December 1993 agreement appears to be a step forward for the European Community, although it will pose difficulties for many of its members. If the directive is ultimately approved, all EC member states will have to develop policies for the recovery and recycling of packaging waste and will have to set national targets that conform with the ranges set by the Community. Although the 25 percent minimum target is only slightly higher than the estimated average packaging recycling rate for all EC countries (20 percent), it represents an improvement because all countries will have to meet this minimum. This is likely to increase the average recycling rate in the European Community considerably.

As late as November 1993, only four EC member states — Germany, the Netherlands, Denmark, and Belgium — supported the inclusion of specific recycling targets in the draft directive. Most others argued for setting recovery targets only, and no targets for recycling, so they would be free to use as much waste-to-energy incineration as they chose. The same four member states pushed for recycling targets for each material against strong opposition, particularly from the United Kingdom and France.[30] The compromise resulted in the inclusion of recycling as well as recovery targets, and a minimum 15 percent recycling target for each material. Failure to set targets by material could have led to increased use of heavy packaging materials, such as glass, which is relatively easy to recycle. By using more glass and recycling most of it, the minimum weight-based recycling target could have been met, while all the lighter materials were dumped in landfills. Under the compromise, at least some portion of each packaging material will be recycled.[31]

The EC representatives from Germany, the Netherlands, and Denmark have expressed their disapproval of the maximum targets. However, the EC directive will not go into effect prior to 1996, and the targets become effective five years later — in 2001 at the earliest. This allows time for these countries to develop recycling capacity and thus potentially qualify for exemptions from the maximum limits.

Notes

1. "Collapse of Grüne Punkt Scheme Could Lead to Eco-Tax," *European Report* No. 1882, Europe Information Service, Brussels, September 4, 1993.
2. *Ibid.*
3. Federal Environment Ministry (BMU), "Results of Top-level Discussions on Duales System Deutschland," press release, Bonn, September 3, 1993.
4. DSD, "Board of Managing Directors Extended," press release, Bonn, October 13, 1993; and "Election of New Supervisory Board," press release, October 1993.
5. Jan Bongaerts (Institut für Europäische Umweltpolitik e.V. [Institute for European Environmental Policy]), telephone interview, October 27, 1993.
6. "Widerstand gegen Grünen Punkt" ("Resistance to the Green Dot"), *Frankfurter Rundschau,* September 18, 1993.
7. "Städte drohen DSD mit Gerichtsvollzieher" ("Cities Threatening DSD with Debt Collectors"), *Allgemeine Zeitung Mainz,* September 17, 1993.
8. *Ibid.*
9. Ines Siegler (DSD), telephone interview, November 11, 1993.
10. DSD, "Current Situation: the Reasons for Fee Collection by Retailers," press release, Bonn, October 12, 1993.
11. DSD, "Reorganization Concept for Dual System Produces Results," press release, Bonn, October 12, 1993.
12. "Germany's Packaging Law May Get Court Test," *Modern Plastics,* New York: McGraw Hill, October 1993, p. 12.
13. Bureau of National Affairs, "Germany Briefs EC Environment Ministers on Plans to Cut Packaging Exports," *International Environment Daily,* November 1, 1993.
14. "DSD Drops Contractor as the Waste Piles Up," *Modern Plastics,* New York: McGraw Hill, September 1993, p. 15.
15. Bureau of National Affairs, "Germany Briefs EC Environment Ministers," *op. cit.*
16. *Ibid.*
17. Provisional Draft Text of the Amendment to the German Packaging Ordinance, English version provided by Ursula Schleissner, Brussels, December 16, 1993.

18. *Ibid.*

19. *Ibid.*

20. David Gardner, "Row Over Packaging Waste Divides EU," *Financial Times,* London, December 3, 1993, p. 2.

21. Brian Love, "Environment Council Strikes Deal on Packaging Waste," Reuters News Service, Brussels, December, 16, 1993.

22. *Ibid.*

23. *Ibid.*

24. "Nine-Way Political Agreement on Draft Directive," *European Report,* No. 1911, Europe Information Service, Brussels, December 18, 1993, p. IV-1.

25. *Ibid.*

26. *Ibid.*

27. Love, *op. cit.*

28. "Germans Defend Recycling Scheme," *Financial Times,* London, December 17, 1993, p. 3.

29. William D'Alessandro (Victor House News), written communication, December 15,1993.

30. "EC Member States Head for Showdown over Recycling," *Europe Environment,* No. 420, Europe Information Service, Brussels, November 9, 1993, p. 12.

31. *Ibid.*

Appendix A: The Ordinance on the Avoidance of Packaging Waste

Ordinance on the Avoidance of Packaging Waste
(Packaging Ordinance - Verpackungsverordnung - VerpackVO)
of 12 June 1991

The Federal Government, having heard the parties concerned and pursuant to Art. 14 para. 1 sentence 1 nos. 1 and 4 and para. 2 sentence 3 nos. 1, 2 and 3 of the Waste Avoidance and Waste Management Act (Abfallgesetz) of 27 August 1986 (Federal Law Gazette BGBl. I page 1410), hereby decrees as follows:

Verantwortlich: Bundesumweltministerium
Pressereferat: Marlene Mühe
Postfach 12 06 29, 5300 Bonn 1
Tel. 02 28/305-20 15/20 11

Section I
Waste management objectives
Scope and definition of terms

Art. 1

Waste management objectives

(1) Packaging shall be manufactured from materials which
     are environmentally compatible and do not hamper the
     environmentally compatible reuse or recyling of the
     materials used.

(2) Waste from packaging shall be avoided by ensuring that
     packaging

     1. is restricted in volume and weight to the dimen-
         sions actually required to protect the contents
         and to market the product,

     2. is designed in such a way that it may be refilled
         provided this is technically feasible and reason-
         able as well as compatible with the regulations
         applying to the contents.

     3. is reused or recycled if the conditions for re-
         filling do not obtain.

-3-

Art. 2

Scope of Application

(1) The provisions of this Ordinance shall apply to anyone who, commercially or within the framework of any business undertaking or public body within the area of validity of the Waste Avoidance and Waste Management Act

1. manufactures packaging or products from which packaging is directly manufactured (manufacturer) or

2. brings into circulation packaging, products from which packaging is directly manufactured or packaged products at any commercial level (distributors).

(2) Distributors within the meaning of this Ordinance shall also include mail order firms.

(3) The provisions of this Ordinance shall not apply to packaging

1. with residual substances or preparations or soiled or contaminated by substances or preparations

- that constitute a health risk pursuant to Art. 1 nos. 6 to 15 of the Ordinance on the Hazard Criteria of Substances and Preparations under the Chemicals Act (Verordnung über die Gefährlichkeitsmerkmale von Stoffen und Zubereitungen nach dem Chemikaliengesetz)

- constitute an environmental risk pursuant to Art. 3a para. 2 of the Chemicals Act,

such as plant protection agents, disinfectants, pesticides, solvents, acids, alkalis, mineral oil or mineral oil products; or

2. which must be disposed of in a particular way in compliance with other legal provisions.

Art. 3

Definition of Terms

(1) Packaging within the meaning of this Ordinance shall include

1. Transport packaging

Drums, containers, crates, sacks including pallets, cardboard boxes, foamed packaging materials, shrink wrapping and similar coverings which are component parts of transport packaging and which serve to protect the goods from damage during transport from the manufacturer to the distributor or are used for reasons of transport safety.

2. Sales packaging

Closed or open receptacles and coverings of goods, such as cups, bags, blister packaging, cans, tins, drums, bottles, metal containers, cardboard and cartons, sacks, trays, carrier bags or similar coverings which are used by the consumer to transport the goods or until such time as the goods are consumed. Sales packaging within the meaning of this Ordinance shall also include throw-away dishes and throw-away cutlery.

3. Secondary packaging

    Blister packaging, plastic sheets, cardboard boxes
    or similar packaging which is intended as
    additional packaging around the sales packaging

    a) to allow goods to be sold on a self-service
        basis or

    b) to make more difficult or prevent the
        possibility of theft or

    c) to serve, in the main, advertising purposes.

(2) Drinks packaging within the meaning of this Ordinance
    shall include closed or mainly closed receptacles such
    as bags, cans, bottles, cartons, oblong plastic bags,
    made from any kind of material designed for liquid
    foodstuffs within the meaning of Art. 1 para. 1 of the
    Foodstuffs and Commodities Act (Lebensmittel- und
    Bedarfsgegenständegesetz), intended for consumption as
    drinks, with the exception of yoghurt and kefir.

(3) Return packaging within the meaning of this Ordinance
    shall be receptacles which are returned for repeated
    reuse for the same purpose.

(4) The catchment area of the manufacturer or distributor
    shall be deemed to be the area of the country in which
    the goods are brought into circulation.

(5) The final consumer within the meaning of this Act
    shall be the purchaser who does not further resell the
    goods in the form delivered to him.

Section II

Obligation to accept return
and to recycle and reuse
packaging material

Art. 4

Obligation to accept returned transport packaging

Manufacturer and distributor shall be obliged to accept the
return of used transport packaging and to reuse or recycle
it independently of the public waste disposal system unless
the consumer demands the delivery of the goods <u>in</u> the
transport packaging; in this case the provisions on the
return of sales packaging shall apply accordingly. Packaging which is used as both transport and sales packaging
shall be treated as sales packaging.

Art. 5

Obligation to accept returned secondary packaging

(1) Distributors providing goods in secondary packaging
     shall be obliged to remove such packaging on delivery
     of the goods to the final consumer or to give the
     final consumer the opportunity to remove and return
     the secondary packaging free of charge at the point of
     sale or in the near vicinity of the point of sale
     unless the consumer desires the good to be delivered
     in their secondary packaging; in this case the
     provisions relating to the return of sales packaging
     shall apply accordingly.

(2) If the distributor does not remove the secondary
     packaging himself, he shall be obliged, by means of
     clearly recognisable and legible signs at the cash
     desk, to indicate that the consumer has the oppor-
     tunity, either at the point of sale or in the near
     vicinity of the point of sale, to remove the secondary
     packaging from the acquired goods and to leave it
     there.

(3) The distributor shall be obliged to provide suitable
     collecting containers at the point of sale or in the
     vicinity of the point of sale to accommodate the
     secondary packaging and ensure that these are clearly
     visible and easily accessible to the final consumer.
     Different material groups shall be collected separate-
     ly to the extent this is possible without labelling.
     The distributor shall be obliged to reuse secondary
     packaging or recycle it independently of the public
     waste disposal system.

Art. 6

Obligation to accept returned sales packaging

(1) The distributor shall be obliged to accept sales
     packing used by the final consumer free of charge and
     in or in the near vicinity of the point of sale. This
     obligation shall be limited to packaging of the type,
     form and size of goods supplied by the distributor in
     his own product range and packaging of goods supplied
     by the distributor in his own product range. In the
     case of distributors with sales areas of less than
     200 m^2, the obligation to accept return shall be
     limited to the packaging of brands brought into circu-
     lation by the distributor.

(1a) Mail order firms shall be obliged to accept used
      packaging free of charge from the final consumer, for
      example, by providing suitable return options within
      reasonable distance of the final consumer. Reference
      shall be made to the return option both along with the
      dispatched goods and in the catalogues.

(2)   Manufacturers and distributors shall be obliged to
      accept the packaging returned to distributors pursuant
      to para. 1 and to reuse or recycle it independently of
      the public waste disposal system. This obligation
      shall be limited to packaging of the type, form and
      size of packaging supplied by the manufacturer or
      distributor in question or of goods supplied by the
      said manufacturer and distributor.

(3)   The obligations pursuant to paras. 1, 1a and 2 shall
      not apply to manufacturers and distributors who are
      party to a system which guarantees regular collection
      of used packaging from the final consumer or, to an
      adequate extent, in the vicinity of the final consumer
      throughout the catchment area of distributors subject
      to the provisions of para. 1 and which meets the
      requirements specified in the Annex to this Ordinance.
      This system shall be harmonised with existing
      collection, recycling and reuse systems run by the
      authorities responsible for waste disposal in whose
      area it is set up. This harmonisation shall be a
      prerequisite for the confirmation pursuant to
      sentence 6. Attention shall be given in particular to
      the concerns of the authorities responsible for waste
      disposal. The authorities responsible for waste

disposal may, for a suitable fee, demand the takeover
or joint use of facilities required for collecting and
sorting materials of the type referred to in the Annex
to this Ordinance. The competent upper Land authority
or the authority designated by it, shall, on application, confirm, by means of a general disposition to be
announced publicly, that such a system has been set up
on a comprehensive scale. The exception as defined in
sentence 1 shall be effective from the time of the
public announcement. If the application is filed before 1 January 1993, the proof that a system has been
set up guaranteeing the regular collection of used
sales packaging from the final consumer or in the
vicinity of the final consumer shall suffice for an
exemption up to 1 March 1993.

(4) The competent authorities may revoke their decision
pursuant to para. 3 sentence 6 as soon as and insofar
as they ascertain that the standards set in the Annex
to this Ordinance are not being met. They shall likewise announce the revocation publicly. They may limit
the revocation to certain types of substances provided
that, in respect of these substances only, the collection, sorting and recycling quotas specified in the
Annex to this Ordinance have not been attained. Art. 6
paras. 1, 1a and 2 shall apply on the first day of the
sixth calendar month following the public announcement
of the revocation.

(5) Mail order firms shall be exempt from their obligation
pursuant to para. 1a if they participate in the system
provided under para. 3 sentence 1.

-10-

SECTION III

Obligation to accept return of and charge deposits
on drinks packaging, packaging of washing and
cleansing agents and emulsion paints

Art. 7

Obligation to charge deposits on drinks packaging

Distributors who supply liquid foodstuffs in throw-away
drinks packaging with a net volume of 0.2 l shall be
obliged to charge the purchaser a deposit per drinks
packaging of 0.50 DM including turnover tax. The minimum
deposit for non-reusable packaging shall be 0.50 DM including turnover tax; a deposit of at least 1.00 DM including
turnover tax shall be charged if the net volume equals or
exceeds 1.5 l. The deposit shall be charged by each further
distributor at all commercial levels until delivery to the
final consumer. The deposit shall be repaid on return of
the packaging (Art. 6 paras. 1 and 2).

Art. 8

Obligation to charge deposits on packaging of washing and
cleansing agents and emulsion paints

Art. 7 shall apply mutatis mutandis to packaging of

1. washing and cleansing agents within the meaning of
    Art. 2 para. 1 of the Washing and Cleansing Agents Act
    (Wasch- und Reinigungsmittelgesetz) with a net volume
    of 0.2 l or more, except soft packaging and cardboard-
    reinforced soft packaging in which washing and cleans-
    ing agents are brought into circulation for refill
    purposes,

-11-

2.   emulsion paints with a net weight of 2 kg. In this
      case, the deposit shall be 2.00 DM.

Art. 9

Exemption from the obligation to accept returned packaging
and to charge deposits- protection of return systems

(1)   Arts. 7 and 8 shall not apply if, in the catchment
      area of the final distributor a system in accordance
      with Art. 6 para. 3 has been set up and if the highest
      Land authority responsible for waste disposal or the
      authority designated by it has confirmed this by means
      of a general disposition. Art. 6 para. 4 shall apply
      mutatis mutandis.

(2)   Any exemption pursuant to paragraph 1 shall only apply
      to the packaging of beer, mineral water, spring water,
      table water, drinking water and remedial waters,
      carbonated refreshment drinks, fruit juices, juice
      concentrates, vegetable juices and non-carbonated
      refreshment drinks, wine (except slightly sparkling
      wines, sparkling wines, vermouth and desert wines), if
      the proportion of return packaging in the catchment
      area concerned does not fall below the level register-
      ed in the particular catchment area in 1991 and as a
      whole does not fall below 72% in the area of validity
      of the Waste Avoidance and Waste Management Act; for
      pasteurized milk the corresponding proportion for
      return bottles shall be 17%.

      The Federal Government shall decide, three years after
      this Ordinance comes into force, on any necessary in-
      creases and differentiations of the relevant propor-
      tions of return packaging.

Appendices • 217

(3) The Federal Government shall publish the proportions
     of return packaging pursuant to para. 2 by 30 June
     each year in the Federal Bulletin (Bundesanzeiger). If
     the proportion of return packaging falls below the
     percentages under para. 2, another survey shall be
     carried out on the relevant proportions of return
     packaging as of the first day of the sixth calendar
     month following announcement. This survey shall also
     be published in the Federal Bulletin. If the results
     of this second survey show that the proportion of the
     return packaging is still lower than the percentages
     under para. 2, Art. 7 shall apply from the first day
     of the sixth calendar month following the last public
     announcement.

Art. 10

Restriction on the obligation to accept returned packaging
and to reimburse deposits.

Distributors in a catchment area in which Arts. 7 and 8
apply, may refuse to accept returned packaging and reimburse deposits for packaging originating from catchment
areas in which an exemption has been granted pursuant to
Art. 6 para. 3. They may, for the purposes of differentia-
tion, issue their packaging with deposit stamps or mark it
in another way.

SECTION FOUR

Administrative Offences, Transitional
and Concluding Provisions

Art. 11

Appointment of Third Parties

Manufacturers and distributors may call upon third parties
to fulfill obligations specified in this Ordinance. The
return of packaging and the reimbursement of deposits may
also be carried out using automatic machines.

Art. 12

Administrative Offences

An administrative offence within the meaning of Art. 18,
para. 1 no. 11 of the Waste Management and Waste Avoidance
Act shall be deemed to have been committed by any person
who, deliberately or negligently

1.   in contravention of Art. 4 does not accept returned
     transport packaging or does not reuse or recycle
     transport packaging independently of the public waste
     disposal system,

2.   in contravention of Art. 5 para. 1 does not remove
     secondary packaging and also does not give the final
     consumer the opportunity of removing such packaging,

3.   in contravention of Art. 5 para. 2 does not provide
     the information specified therein,

4. in contravention of Art. 5 para. 3 sentence 1 does not provide clearly visible and easily accessible collection containers,

5. in contravention of Art. 5 para. 3 sentence 2 does not reuse or recycle secondary packaging independently of the public waste disposal system,

6. in contravention of Art. 6 para. 1 sentence 1 or para. 2 sentence 1 does not accept returned sales packaging,

6 a in contravention of Art. 6 para. 1a does not accept return of sales packaging,

7. in contravention of Art. 6 para. 2 sentence 1 does not reuse or recycle returned sales packaging independently of the public waste disposal system, or

8. in contravention of Art. 7, also in conjunction with Art. 8, does not levy or reimburse a deposit.

Art. 13

Entry into Force

With the exception of Arts. 5 to 10 and Art. 12 nos. 2 to 8, this Ordinance shall enter into force on 1 December 1991.

Art. 5 and Art. 12 nos. 2, 3, 4 and 5 shall enter into
force on 1 April 1992; Art. 6 paras. 1, 1a, 2, 4 and 5,
Arts. 7 to 9 and Art. 12 nos. 6, 7 and 8 shall enter into
force on 1 January 1993. Art. 6 para. 3 and the Annex to
Art. 6 para. 3 and Art. 10 shall enter into force on the
day following the promulgation of this Ordinance.

Art. 14

Expiration

The Ordinance on the Return of Packaging Material
and the Levying of Deposits on Plastic Drinks Packaging
(Verordnung über die Rücknahme und Pfanderhebung von
Getränkeverpackungen aus Kunststoffen) shall cease
to be effective on 1 January 1993.

The Bundesrat has given its consent.

Annex to Art. 6 para. 3

The competent authority shall provide the confirmation
pursuant to Art. 6 para. 3 if the following requirements
are met:

I.   **General requirements**

Using appropriate systems, it shall be ensured that
packaging is collected from domestic households
(collection systems), or in the vicinity of domestic
households by means of containers or other suitable
collecting receptacles (so-called "bring systems") or
by a combination of both these systems and subsequent-
ly sorted, reused and recycled. The relevant systems
shall include existing systems operated by municipal
corporations. For the systems under sentence 1

-   the collection quotas specified under II

-   the sorting quotas specified under III and

-   the standards for reuse and recycling specified in
    IV

shall be reached.

II. **Quantitative requirements for collecting systems**

In the catchment area (Art. 3 para. 4) of the applicant, the following minimum mean annual percentages
(in % by weight), referred to the total amount of
packaging material in the catchment area, shall be
achieved for the collected materials:

On 1 January 1993

Material

glass	60%
tinplate	40%
aluminium	30%
cardboard	30%
paper	30%
plastics	30%
compounded matierals	20%

From 1 January 1993 to 30 June 1995, the quotas
specified for each individual packaging material shall
be deemed to be met if at least 50% of the total
packaging material accumulated has in fact been
collected.

From 1 July 1995 proof must be furnished that the
following percentages have been reached:

Material

glass	80%
tinplate	80%
aluminium	80%
cardboard	80%
paper	80%
plastics	80% ·
compounded materials	80%

The Federal Government shall, every three years, beginning on 31 August 1992, based on appropriate surveys, publish in the Federal Bulletin (Bundesanzeiger) the average amount of packaging per inhabitant used in each individual catchment area, classified according to packaging materials and per-capita consumption.

Proof of the actually collected proportion shall be furnished by the applicant by 1 March in 1993 and 1994, based on the population statistics of the catchment area (Art. 3 para. 4) and the per-capita consumption of used packaging published by the Federal Government.

III. Quantitative requirements to be met by sorting facilities:

From the packaging collected in the catchment area (Art. 3 para. 4), at least the following types of materials shall be extracted in an appropriate quality for recycling and reuse and in the following quantities (given in % by weight):

-19-

Material	On 1 January 1993	on 1 July 1995
glass	70%	90%
tin plate	65%	90%
aluminium	60%	90%
cardboard	60%	80%
paper	60%	80%
plastics	30%	80%
compounded materials	30%	80%

Proof of the sorting quotas shall be furnished by the applicant in a verifiable form on the dates specified under II.

Residual material from the sorting process which cannot be recycled or reused shall be transferred as industrial waste to those responsible for public waste disposal.

Residual material from the sorting process which cannot be recycled or reused shall be deemed to be only those materials

- which cannot be broken down by manual or machine sorting into fractions that may be recycled or reused

- which are soiled or contaminated by contents other than that the original contents of the packaging or by soiling or contamination of the packaging material

- which are not parts of packaging.

IV.   Requirements for the recycling of reusable materials

The quantities of reusable materials specified under III shall be recycled or reused. The applicant shall, in a verifiable form and on the dates specified under II, present proof that recycling and reuse of the reusable materials is guaranteed.

Appendix B: Conversion of 1992 and 1993 Green Dot Fees to Dollars

1992 Green Dot Fees

(Conversion of Table 6-2 to ounces and dollars)

Packaging Volume (in ounces)	Dollars per Package
Less than 1.7	$0
1.7 - 6.8	$0.006
6.8 - 101	$0.012
101 - 1014	$0.030
More than 1014 (7.9 gallons)	$0.120

To convert from milliliters to ounces, multiply by 0.0338.

Source: INFORM calculations based on Duales System Deutschland fees.

1993 Green Dot Fees (Effective October 1993)

(Conversion of Table 6-3 to dollars per pound)

Material	Dollars per Material Pound
Plastic	$0.82
Composites	$0.45
Aluminum	$0.27
Tinplate	$0.15
Paper/paperboard	$0.09
Natural materials	$0.05
Glass	$0.04

Source: INFORM calculations based on Duales System Deutschland fees.

Appendix C: Interviews

Bette Fishbein conducted interviews with the following people in Germany. All interviews were held in October 1992 unless otherwise noted.

Olaf Bandt, BUND für Umwelt und Naturschutz Deutschland e.V. (German Federation for the Environment and the Protection of Nature), Bonn.

Jan C. Bongaerts, Institut für Europäische Umweltpolitik e.V. (Institute for European Environmental Policy), Bonn.

Bernd Buckenhofer, Bayerischer Städtetag (Bavarian Council of Cities), Munich.

Bernd Franke, Institut für Energie-und Umweltforschung (IFEU), (Institute for Energy and Environmental Research), Heidelberg.

Rolf Friedel, Stadt Heidelberg, Amt für Abfallwirtschaft und Stadtreinigung (City of Heidelberg Department of Sanitation).

Renate Fries, Presse- und Informationsdienst für Politik, Wirtschaft und Kultur GbR (Information and Press Service for Policy, Economy and Culture), Cologne.

Hubert Gehring, Bundesministerium für Umwelt, Naturschutz und Reaktorsicherheit (BMU) (Federal Environment Ministry), Bonn.

Wigand Kahl, Landeshauptstadt München Umweltschutzreferat (Munich Environment Department).

Sibille Kohler, Schoeller International GmbH & Co., KG, Munich.

Eberhard Kraft, Rudolf Wild International GmbH & Co. KG, Heidelberg.

Petra Löcker, Bundesministerium für Umwelt, Naturschutz und Reaktorsicherheit (BMU) (Federal Environment Ministry), Bonn.

Marlene Mühe, Bundesministerium für Umwelt, Naturschutz und Reaktorsicherheit (BMU), (Federal Environment Ministry), Bonn.

Jürgen Maas, Die Grünen, Fraktion im Rat der Stadt Bonn (Green Party Representative, Bonn City Council).

Hans-Jürgen Oels, Umweltbundesamt (UBA) (Federal Environment Agency), Berlin, May 1991.

Helmut Paschlau, Landeshauptstadt München, Amt für Abfallwirtschaft (Munich Sanitation Department).

Anja Raffalsky, Tengelmann Warenhandelgesellschaft, Mülheim.

Maria Rieping, Die Verbraucher Initiative (DVI) (The Consumer Initiative), Bonn.

Erwin Rothgang, Amtes für Umweltschutz, Stadtverwaltung Wuppertal (Wuppertal Sanitation Department).

Frieder Rubik, Institut für Ökologische Wirtschaftsforschung GmbH (IÖW) (Institute for Environmental Economics), Heidelberg.

Hans-Dieter Schulz, Planungsverband Äusserer Wirtschaftsraum München (Economic Planning Association), Munich.

Rafaella Schuster, Landesverband des Bayerischen Eizelhandels e.V. (Association of Bavarian Retailers), Munich.

Wolfgang Schutt, INTEC, Bonn.

Michael O. E. Scriba, Duales System Deutschland, Bonn.

Cynthia Pollock Shea, Bureau of National Affairs, Bonn.

Karl-Heinz Striegel, Landesamt für Wasser und Abfall Nordrhein-Westfalen (North Rhine-Westphalia Department for Water and Waste), Düsseldorf.

Clemens Stroetmann, Secretary of State for Bundesministerium für Umwelt, Naturschutz und Reaktorsicherheit (BMU) (Federal Environment Ministry), Bonn.

Matthias Wellmer, Die Grünen (Green Party), Wuppertal.

In addition to the personal interviews noted above, Ms. Fishbein conducted extensive telephone interviews and exchanged written communication with many sources in both Germany and the United States, as indicated in the Notes sections of this report.

Appendix D: Bibliography

Ackerman, Frank. "Analyzing the True Costs of Packaging." *Biocycle*. April 1993.

Allenby, Braden (National Academy of Engineering). "Europe Trip Report, Oct. 14-23, 1992." In papers from Massachusetts Institute of Technology: Design and Disposal of Durable Products Conference. Cambridge, MA: March 24-25.

Azar, Jack (Xerox Corporation). "Recycling Initiatives in the American Electronics Industry." Massachusetts Institute of Technology: Design and Disposal of Durable Products Conference. Cambridge, MA: March 24-25, 1993.

Azar, Jack C., James C. MacKenzie, and Richard S. Morabito, "Environmental Life-Cycle Design at Xerox." Draft for *EPA Journal*. June 1993.

Bayerische Motoren Werke A.G. (BMW).
"A Consistent Initiative to Protect the Environment: BMW Car Recycling." July 1992.
"Recycling of Plastics." 1991.

Bayerisches Staatsministerium für Landesentwicklung und Umweltfragen (Bavarian Ministry for Regional Development and the Environment). "Gemeinsame Erklärung von Staatsminister Dr. Gauweiler, der niedersächsischen Ministerin für Umwelt, Monika Griefahn und dem Minister für Umwelt des Landes Baden-Württemberg, Harald Schäfer, zum Dualen System: Derzeit Zulassung nur befristet und mit zusätzlichen Auflagen möglich" (Joint Statement of the Environment Ministers of Bavaria, Lower Saxony, and Baden-Württemberg.) Press release. December 15, 1992.

Boerner, Christopher and Kenneth Chilton (Center for the Study of American Business). "Recycling's Demand Side: Lessons from Germany's 'Green Dot.'" Washington University, St. Louis: 1993.

Bongaerts, Jan C. (Institut für Europäische Umweltpolitik e.V.) (Institute for European Environmental Policy). "The Packaging Ordinance in Germany and its Implementation, First Experiences." Report for European Congress: Packaging and Environmental Strategies. Brussels: November 26-27, 1992.

Bund für Umwelt und Naturschutz Deutschland e.V. (BUND) (German Federation for the Environment and the Protection of Nature). Bonn.

"EEC = European Ecological Collapse?" Response to an EC Commission draft of the packaging directive of September 30, 1991.

"Pet-Mehrweg-(k)eine ökologische Alternative?" ("PET-Refill-(no) Ecological Alternative?"). 1992.

"The Returnables Roundabout – Requirements for an Environmentally Friendly System of Returnable Drink Containers."

Bundesministerium für Umwelt, Naturschutz und Reaktorsicherheit (BMU) (Federal Ministry for the Environment, Protection of Nature and Nuclear Safety [Federal Environment Ministry]). Bonn.

"Environmental Protection in Germany," August 1992.

"The Federal Government Passes New Waste Management Act." Press release. March 31, 1993.

"Germany - The Federal Environment Ministry." August 1992.

Information Sheet on the Packaging Ordinance: "The Distinction between Transport, Secondary, and Sales Packaging."

"Key Point: On the Spot Recycling and Reuse of Transport Packaging."

"Key Point: Where is Used Transport Packaging to be Returned to?"

"Ökobilanz für Gertränkeverpackungen" ("Eco-balance for Beverage Packages"). Press release. September 21, 1993.

"Ordinance on the Avoidance of Packaging Waste" (Packaging Ordinance – *Verpackungsverordnung* – VerpackVO) of June 12, 1991.

"Ordinance on Source Reduction and the Recycling of Used Electrical and Electronic Goods and Appliances" (Draft). July 1991.

"Ordinance on Source Reduction and Recycling of Waste from Automobile Disposal" (Draft). August 1992.

"Packaging Ordinance Approved: Abandoning the Throwaway Society." Press release. November 14, 1990.

"Regulation Regarding the Avoidance, Reduction and Recycling of the Waste of Used Electric and Electronic Equipment - Electronic Scrap Regulation." WA II 3-30 114/7, Working paper as of October 1992.

"Töpfer legt neues Abfallgesetz vor: Kreislaufwirtschaft statt Abfallbeseitigung" ("Töpfer Presents New Waste Legislation: Closed-Loop Economy Instead of Waste Disposal"). Press release. July 17, 1992.

Bundesverband der Deutschen Industrie e.V. (BDI) (Federation of German Industries). Cologne.

"Ein Beitrag zur aktuellen abfallpolitischen Diskussion" ("A Contribution to the Ongoing Waste Discussion"). November 4, 1992.

"Grundsatzstellungnahme" ("Position Paper"). June/July 1992.

"International Environmental Policy — Perspectives 2000." May 1992.

"Making Market Forces Work to Improve the Environment." Paper delivered by Heinrich Weiss, President of BDI, at the Second World Industrial Conference on Environmental Management. Rotterdam, April 10, 1991.

Report 1988-1990: Environmental Policy. October 1, 1990.

"Stellungnahme zum Entwurf einer Verordnung zur Förderung von Getränkemehrwegsystemen" ("Position Paper in Response to the Separate Ordinance on Refillables"). May 1992.

Bureau of National Affairs. Washington, DC.

"Cabinet Approves Amended Waste Law Despite Widespread Industry Objections." *International Environment Daily.* April 2, 1993.

"French Paper Recycling Industry Launches Protests Against German Imports." *International Environment Daily.* April 16, 1993.

"German Cartel Office Will Examine Regulation Scheme for Garbage Collection." *Antitrust and Trade Regulation Report.* January 1, 1993.

"German, EC Packaging Measures Will Hurt U.K. Industry, House of Commons Panel Told." *International Environment Daily.* March 8, 1993.

"Illegal Exports from Germany to France Spur Ministers to Form Interim Trade Plan." *International Environment Daily.* August 25, 1992.

"New Directive Sets Parameters for Incineration, Landfill Disposal." *International Environment Daily.* September 22, 1992.

"Waste Law Proposal Will Require Industry to Recycle All Products." *International Environment Daily.* July 28, 1992.

Cairncross, Frances. "How Europe's Companies Reposition to Recycle." *Harvard Business Review.* March-April 1992.

Case, Clifford. "Eliminating Barriers to Recycling in the 90's: The Work of the National Recycling Coalition and the Recycling Advisory Council." New York State Department of Environmental Conservation: Fifth Annual Recycling Conference. Syracuse: September 28, 1993.

Cavanaugh, Joseph (Joe Cavanagh Associates, Packaging Consultants, Bay Shore, NY). "Non Refillable vs. Refillable Beverage Containers: The United States Experience." Paper presented at Bev-Pak '92 Conference.

Chynoweth, Emma.

"Veba and RWE recycle plastics waste to crude." *Chemical Week.* August 19, 1992.

"Germany's Waste Policy Draws More Complaints." *Chemical Week.* May 12, 1993.

Conradt, David P. (American Institute for Contemporary German Studies, Johns Hopkins University). *Unified Germany at the Polls.* Washington, DC: 1990.

Crossland's European Environmental Bulletin. International Environment Group. August 27 and September 12, 1991.

Cutter Information Corp. "Status of Proposed Takeback Regulation in Sweden and Germany." *Business and the Environment.*, Vol. 4, No. 1. January 1993.

Deveny, Kathleen. "Toothpaste Makers Tout New Packaging." *The Wall Street Journal.* November 10, 1992.

Duales System Deutschland GmbH (DSD). Bonn.
"Agreement with Local Authorities." Press release. July 25, 1993.
"Beverage Cartons." April 1, 1993.
"Business Sector Strengthens Duales System." Press release. May 27, 1993.
"Daten und Fakten zum Grünen Punkt: Ökologische Verpackungsoptimie-rung" ("Data and Facts about the Green Dot: Ecological Packaging Optimization"). March 1992.
"Daten und Fakten zum Grünen Punkt: Der Ökologische Wandel bei Verpackungen" ("Data and Facts about the Green Dot: The Ecological Change in Packaging"). November 1992.
"Daten und Fakten zum Grünen Punkt: Abfallverhalten der Verbraucher im Dualen System" ("Data and Facts about the Green Dot: Waste Behavior of Consumers in the Dual System"). March 1993.
"Don't Let Packaging Go to Waste."
"Drastic Reorganization at Duales System." Press release. June 25, 1993.
"Duales System Finances Assured in the Long Term." Press release. June 20, 1993.
"Informationen zur neuen Gebührenordnung" ("Information about the New Fee Schedule"). April 1993.
"New Sorting Criteria for Plastics: Sorted Material Will Be Recycled." Press release. July 1, 1993.
"Packaging Materials are Raw Materials." August 31, 1992.
"Problems in Rhineland-Palatinate Being Solved." Press release. June 16, 1993.
"Recovery of Raw Materials from Plastic Packaging." Press release. July 7, 1993.
"Recycling Capacities for Plastic 1993." Press release. June 4, 1993.
"Reform Proposals from Five Local Government Bodies are Unimagina-tive." Press release. July 21, 1993."
"Report Regarding Quantity and Reprocessing of Secondary Raw Materi-als Anticipated for 1993."

"Stand der Verwertung" ("State of Recycling"). (Graph). *DSD Business Report 1992.*

"Threats to Revoke Exemption for Plastic Packaging Constitute Totally Wrong Signal." Press release. June 17, 1993.

"Two Years of the Packaging Ordinance." Press release. July 21, 1993.

"Verwertung von Kunststoff-Probemengen in Indonesien ordnungsgemäß" ("Trial Quantities of Plastics Properly Recycled in Indonesia"). Press release. March 29, 1993.

Elkington, John. *The Green Wave: A Report on the 1990 Greenworld Survey.* London: Sustainability. 1990.

Environmental Action Foundation. Solid Waste Action Paper #8, "The Real Wrap on Polyvinyl Chloride Packaging." Washington, DC.

Environmental Data Services Ltd., London.

"Battle Joined Over Packaging Directive." *The ENDS Report* No. 210, July 1992.

"BMW Opens First Car Dismantling Plant." *The ENDS Report No.* 215. December 1992.

"Brussels Makes Concessions in New Draft on Packaging." *The ENDS Report* No. 204. January 1992.

"European Environmentalists Agree on Packaging Agenda." *The ENDs Report* No. 215. December 1992.

"DTI Assessment of EC Packaging Rules." *The ENDs Report* No. 217. February 1993.

"Transfrontier Waste Meeting Focuses on Exports, Liability." *The ENDS Report* No. 215. December 1992.

"U.K. to Oppose EC Targets for Packaging Waste." *The ENDS Report* No. 217. February 1993.

"Uncertainty about Impact of Transfrontier Waste Rules." *The ENDS Report* No. 213. October 1992.

"Environmental Protection in Europe: Abolishing Litter." *The Economist.* August 22, 1993.

Europe Information Service. Brussels.

"ACE Criticizes German Legislation." *Europe Environment* No. 410. May 18, 1993.

"BCME Opposes Discrimination Among Packaging Materials." *Europe Environment* No. 398. November 17, 1992.

"Commission Waves Through Proposal for Directive." *Europe Environment* No. 392. July 8, 1992.

"Communication on Industrial Competitiveness and Environmental Protection." *Europe Environment* No. 399. December 1, 1992.

"Council Adopts Waste Shipments Regulation." *Europe Environment* No. 404. February 16, 1993.

"Court Refuses to Annul Framework Directive." *Europe Environment* No. 407. March 30, 1993.

"Debates on Subsidiarity and Waste Trade." *Europe Environment* No. 403. February 2, 1993.

"EC Court Opines on Waste and Freedom Of Movement." *Europe Environment* No. 391. July 14, 1992.

"EC: Draft Directive on Packaging and Packaging Waste." *Europe Environment* No. 393. September 8, 1992. Supplement.

"EC Experts Want More Flexible Targets." *Europe Environment* No. 399. December 1, 1992.

"Economic Aspects of the Community's Strategy for Limiting CO_2 Emissions." *Europe Environment* No. 397. November 5, 1992. Supplement.

"Environment Ministers Approve Waste Shipments Regulation." *Europe Environment* No. 397. November 5, 1992.

"Environment Ministers Reach Consensus on Waste Prevention." *Europe Environment* No. 413. July 6, 1993.

"ESC Calls for More Preventive Action." *Europe Environment* No. 408. April 15, 1993.

"European Commission Seeks to Consolidate the Links." *Europe Environment* No. 410. May 18, 1993.

"European Parliament Committee Adopts Much Amended Report." *Europe Environment* No. 411. June 8, 1993.

"European Parliament Committee Tables Resolution on Waste." *Europe Environment* No. 396. October 20, 1992.

"European Parliament Mends Draft Directive." *Europe Environment* No. 413. July 6, 1993.

"French Decree and Franco-German Decisions." *Europe Environment* No. 393. September 8, 1992.

"German Forests Continue to Die." *Europe Environment* No. 398. November 17, 1992.

"Germany's Fruit and Vegetable Suppliers in Plastic Crate Scare." *Europe Environment* No. 411. June 8, 1993.

"German System Fights for Survival." *Europe Environment* No. 416. September 14, 1993.

"Green MEP Denounces Suspicious Transport in EC." *Europe Environment* No. 390. June 30, 1992.

"Greenpeace Denounces Decision on Waste Exports." *Europe Environment* No. 397. November 5, 1992.

"Karel Van Miert Unveils Priorities." *Europe Environment* No. 392. July 26, 1992.

"Negotiations Start Up Again on New Foundations." *Europe Environment* No. 414. July 20, 1993.

"No Decision on Transfers before October." *Europe Environment* No. 390. June 30, 1992.

"Packaging Waste: National Experts Call for More Emphasis on Prevention." *Multinational Service: The National and Regional Contexts* Section III, No. 0330. March 12, 1993.

"Progress Toward EC Regulation on Waste Transfers." *Europe Environment* No. 395. October 6, 1992.

"Recovery Loses Out to Eco-Tax Option." *Europe Environment* No. 412. June 22, 1993.

"Regulation of Waste Shipments to go to EC Court of Justice." *Europe Environment* No. 403. February 2, 1993.

"Van Miert Attacks Nigerian Toxic Waste Import Proposal." *Europe Environment* No. 398. November 17, 1992.

"Waste: New German Law for Economic Recycling." *Europe Environment* No. 408. April 15, 1993.

"Waste Shipment Regulation Could End up in the Dock."*European Report* No.1893. February 27, 1993.

"Waste Transfers Top Heavy Agenda for October 20." *Europe Report* No. 396. October 20, 1992.

The European Community. Brussels.

Commission of the European Community. "Amended Proposal for a Council Directive on Packaging and Packaging Waste." September 9, 1993.

Commission of the European Community. "Draft Council Directive on Packaging and Packaging Waste." com (92)278 final-Syn436. July 15, 1992.

Council Regulation #259/93. "Supervision and Control of Shipments of Waste within, into, and out of the European Community." Article 4.3(a). February 1, 1993.

"Discussion Document on Packaging Waste." October 1990.

"Draft Proposal for a Council Directive on Packaging and Packaging Waste, DGXI-A4." Draft No. 2. September 30, 1991.

Fox, Josh and Karen Hurst (Community Environmental Council, Inc.). *A Question of Responsibility: Recycling Market Development* (Review draft). 1993.

Franklin Associates, Ltd., for the US Environmental Protection Agency. *Characterization of Municipal Solid Waste in the United States: 1992 Update.* Prairie Village, KS: 1992.

Fraunhofer-Institut (Fraunhofer Institute). "Ökobilanzen zu Einweg- und Mehrwegverpackungssystemen am Beispiel von Frischmilch und Bier" ("Ecobalances for One-Way and Refillable Packaging Systems Using the Examples of Fresh Milk and Beer.") Press release. Munich: September 8, 1993.

Gardner, David. "Brussels Green Sprouts." *Financial Times.* October 21, 1992.

Gardner, Jonathan.
"Ex-EPA Official Disputes APC, Says Recycling Goal Unrealistic." *Plastics News.* January 18, 1993.
"Feds May Buy More Recyled Products." *Plastics News.* March 22, 1993
"International EPS Groups Ink Recycling Pact." *Plastics News.* November 16, 1992.
"RCRA Plan Would Modify Plastics Recycling Demands." *Plastics News.* July 20, 1993.

Genillard, Ariane.
"Falling Victim to Its Own Success." *Financial Times.* London: January 27, 1993.
"Too Much of a Good Thing." *Financial Times.* London: June 23, 1993.

Gerlinger, Karl H. (BMW). "Market Incentives and the Environment." October 15, 1992.

"German Anti-Rubbish Law Cuts Down on Excess Packaging." *Reuter European Community Report.* January 4, 1993.

"German Efforts Seen as a Threat." *Chemical Week.* February 17, 1993.

German Information Center, New York.
"Cabinet Adopts Recycling Bill, Business Voices Objections." *The Week in Germany.* April 9, 1993.
"The Crude Side of Plastics: They Can be Converted to Oil." *The Week in Germany.* October 2, 1992.
"(Western) Greens and (Eastern) Alliance '90 Vote to Unite." *The Week in Germany.* January 22, 1993.

"German Law May Force Carmakers to Recycle." *Plastics News.* September 7, 1992.

"German Waste Imports Seen Hurting Indonesian Poor." *The Reuter Library Report.* March 5, 1993.

"Germans Heartened by First Test of Chemical Recycling." *Plastics News.* May 18, 1992.

Gesellschaft für Verpackungsmarktforschung (GVM) (Association for Packaging Market Research). *Entwicklung des Verpackungsverbrauchs 1992/1995: Vorausschätzung/Prognose (Development of the Use of Packaging 1992/1995: Estimate / Forecast).* Wiesbaden: July 1993.

Grimm, Ed (IBM). "Update on Safety, Energy and the Environment." 1992.

Hershkowitz, Allen. "How Garbage Could Meet Its Maker." *The Atlantic Monthly.* June 1993.

Hill, Barbara (IBM). "Integrating Environmental Attributes into Product Development." Presented at Faredisfare lo scenario del produttore riproduttore, Politecnico di Milano, Italy: October 23, 1992.

"Indonesia Fights Plastic Waste Invasion." Toxic Trade Update. Greenpeace, Washington, DC.

INFORM (Bette K. Fishbein and Caroline Gelb). *Making Less Garbage: A Planning Guide for Communities.* New York: 1992.

INFORM (David Saphire). *Case Reopened: Reassessing Refillable Bottles.* New York: draft 1993.

International Fruit Container Organization. "A System of the Food Trade." Düsseldorf.

James, Sharpe. "Make Private Industry Responsible for Recycling." Press release, Newark Public Information Office. August 12, 1993.

Kay, Scholer, Fierman, Hays & Handler. *European Community Environmental Law.* April and August 1992.

Kinzer, Stephen. "Green Party Merges with an East German Group." *The New York Times.* January 20, 1993.

"Kippe in Fernost" ("Garbage Dump in Far East"). *Der Spiegel* No. 53. December 28, 1992.

Klepper, Gernot and Peter Michaelis. "Will the Dual System Manage Packaging Waste?" Working Paper No. 503. Kiel Institute of World Economics. Kiel: January 1992.

Koelsch, Claire M. and Hans D. Schulz, "Verpackungverordnung and Duales System Deutschland: Status Report." Draft, 1992. -

Larsson, Gunnar (Volkswagen AG). "Automotive Recycling in Germany Today and in the Future." Massachusetts Institute of Technology: Design and Disposal of Durable Products Conference. Cambridge, MA: March 24-25, 1993.

Latham & Watkins, International Environment Network, *IEN Client Alert*. "German Electronic Waste Regulation." November 20, 1992.

Le Maire, William H. "Germany's Precedent-Setting Dual System, A Model for the Future or a Blueprint for Chaos?" *Packaging Strategies' Green 2000* Vol. 2, No. 7. West Chester, PA: July 1992.

"Lessons in Recycling from Germany." *Plastics News*. November 16, 1992.

Levandoski, Robert C. "Europe Eyes 90% Recovery Rate for All Beverage Packaging." *Beverage Industry*. April 1993.

Lifset, Reid (Yale University Program on Solid Waste Policy). "Extended Producer Responsibility: Rationales and Practices in North America." Massachusetts Institute of Technology: Design and Disposal of Durable Products Conference. Cambridge, MA: March 24-25 1993.

Loepp, Don.
"German Official Rethinks Incineration Stance." *Plastics News*. November 9. 1992.
"German Package Recycling Goals May be Unattainable." *Plastics News*. November 2, 1992.
"Plastics Vulnerable in Green Movement." *Plastics News*. November 2, 1992.

McCarthy, James E.
"Packaging Waste: Can the U.S. Learn from Other Countries?" *Biocycle*. October 1992.
"Waste Reduction and Packaging in Europe." *Resource Recycling*. July 1991.

Michael Peters Brand Development Division and Diagnostics Market Research Ltd., *Green, Greener, Greenest: The Green Consumer in the UK, Netherlands and Germany*. London: September 1989.

Mills, Rowena (RMA Ltd., United Kingdom). "Overview of Approved and Pending Environmental Packaging Legislation within Individual EC Member Countries." Institute of Packaging Professionals Conference: Executive Update on Domestic and International Environmental Packaging Legislation. Alexandria, VA: July, 24, 1992.

Murphy, Mary. "Has Germany Bitten Off More Than It Can Chew?" *Packaging Week*. April 8/15, 1993.

New York City Department of Sanitation, Bureau of Waste Prevention, Reuse and Recycling. "New York City's Waste Prevention Program." July 12, 1993.

Organization for Economic Cooperation and Development. *OECD Environmental Data 1991.* Paris, 1991.

Peel, Quentin. "German Waste Industry Under Fire." *Financial Times.* London, January 18, 1993.

"Plastikbranche macht Druck" ("Plastics Industry Applies Pressure). *Frankfurter Rundschau.* September 21, 1993.

Popoff, Frank. "Life After Rio: Merging Economics and Environmentalism." Chemical Week Conference. Houston: October 15, 1992.

Porritt, Jonathan and David Winner. *The Coming of the Greens.* London: Fontana/ Collins, 1988.

Porter, Winston. "Recycling at the Crossroads." Porter & Associates. Sterling, VA: January 1993.

Powell, Jerry. "Thermal Plastics Processing: Is it recycling?" *Resource Recycling.* May 1993.

Protzman, Ferdinand. "Germany's Push to Expand the Scope of Recycling." *The New York Times.* July 4, 1993.

Purnell, Sonia. "Germany's Waste-Size Problem." *The Daily Telegraph.* March 26, 1993.

"Recycling ist nur der zweitbeste Weg" ("Recycling is the Second Best Choice"). *Der Spiegel.* 25/1993.

Redding, Peter M. "The Development of European Packaging Laws." *Environmental Claims Journal.* Winter 1992/93.

Riding, Alan. "Europeans Try to Revive a Faded Dream of Unity." *The New York Times.* June 20, 1993.

Rose, Michael. "Red Tape for Green Waste?" *Warmer Bulletin* Number 36. February 1993.

Rummler, Thomas and Wolfgang Schutt. *The German Packaging Ordinance: A Practical Guide with Commentary.* Hamburg: B. Behr's Verlag GmbH & Co., 1990.

"Saturn Working Toward Auto Recycling." *Plastics News.* April 5, 1993.

Schoeller International. "Multi-use Returnable Transport Packaging System (MTS)" (Video). Munich.

Scriba, Michael. "Pack Leaders." *Environment Risk.* May 1992.

Shea, Cynthia Pollock.
"Packaging Ordinance Leads Most Firms to Reduce Packaging, Improve Recyclability." *International Environment Reporter.* Washington, DC: Bureau of National Affairs, March 24, 1993.
"Packaging Recycling Laws." *Biocycle.* June 1992.

Short, Herb. "Germans Heartened by the First Test of Chemical Recycling." *Plastics News.* May 18, 1992.

Short, Herb and Gardner, Jonathan. "Global Firms Must Struggle with German Recycling Law." *Plastics News.* March 30, 1992.

Sims, Jonathan (RMA, Ltd., United Kingdom). "Current Status of European Community Environmental Legislation." Institute of Packaging Professionals Conference: Executive Update on Domestic and International Environmental Packaging Legislation. Alexandria, VA: July 24, 1992.

Skumatz, Lisa A. and Philip A. Zach. "Community Adoption of Variable Rates: an Update." *Resource Recycling.* June 1993.

Spangenberg, Joachim H. "The German Waste Policy." Wuppertal Institute. September 27, 1993.

"Stadt drohen DSD mit Gerichtsvollzieher" ("Cities Threatening DSD with Debt Collectors"). *Allgemeine Zeitung Mainz.* September 17, 1993.

Stroetmann, Clemens (German Secretary of State for the Environment). Speech on the Federal Government's Environment Policy as a Framework for Entreprenuerial Actions, given at the meeting of the DOW Corporate Environmental Advisory Council. July 19, 1992.

Swiss, Samantha. "Pack up your Troubles." *Environment Risk.* April 1992.

Talley, Audrey (USDA). "The EC's Directive on Packaging and Solid Waste and Germany's Ordinance on Avoidance of Packaging Waste: Current Status and Likely Impact on the American Packaging Community." Institute of Packaging Professionals Conference: Executive Update on Domestic and International Environment Packaging Legislation. Alexandria, VA: July 24, 1992.

Teasley, Harry (Coca-Cola Company). "Presentation to Implementation Subcommittee/Packaging Standards Committee." Source Reduction Council of the Coalition of Northeastern Governors. Boston, MA: April 24, 1990.

Technische Fachhochschule Berlin (Berlin Technical College), (Professors Dieter Berndt, Marcus Thiele, Karsten Klappert, Thomas Reiner, and Andreas Riedel). *Abschätzung der gegenwärtigen und zukünftigen Kosten für das Sammeln und Sortieren von Verkaufsverpackungen im dualen System (Transparente Modellrechnung) (Estimate of Present and Future Costs for Collection and Sorting of Sales Packaging in the Dual System).* Berlin: August 1992.

Tengelmann. Unternehmensgruppe Tengelmann.
"ÖKO-Logistische Verpackungsanforderungen" ("Environmental Packaging Requirements 1990").
"Overview of activities for environmental protection in the Tengelmann group since 1984."

Tengelmann and Schoeller International. "MTS Returnable Transport Packaging System." Munich.

Umweltbundesamt (UBA) (Federal Environmental Agency). *Facts and Figures on the Environment of Germany: 1988/89.* Berlin.

United States Department of Commerce. "Germany's New Packaging Laws – The Green Dot Arrives." Washington, DC: January 16, 1992.

US Congress, Office of Technology Assessment. *Green Products by Design: Choices for a Cleaner Environment.* OTA-E-541. Washington, DC: October 1992.

Volkswagen. "Recycling at Volkswagen." 1991.

Von Hettler, Jorg. "Probleme tonnenweise" *("Tons of Problems"). Die Zeit.* No. 2. January 8, 1993.

The Warmer Group. Tunbridge Wells, Kent, United Kingdom.
"Over-Packaging, or Over-Consumption?" *The Warmer Bulletin.* No. 37. May 1993.
"A Red Light for the Rule of Reason?" *The Warmer Bulletin.* No. 38. August 1993.
"World News: Germany." *The Warmer Bulletin.* No. 36. February 1993.

"Welche Computer Strom sparen und leise arbeiten" ("Computers that Save Electricity and Run Quietly"). *Impulse.* March 1993.

"Widerstand gegen Grünen Punkt, Großstädte wollen bei Sanierung der DSD nicht mitziehen" ("Resistance to the Green Dot: Large Cities Do Not Want to Cooperate on Plan to Restructure DSD"). *Frankfurter Rundschau.* September 18, 1993.

Zentralverband Elektrotechnik- und Elektronikindustrie e.V. (ZVEI) (Association of Electrotechnical and Electronic Industries). "Elektronik-Schrott-Verordnung: ZVEI diskutiert offene Probleme mit BMU-Staatssekretär Stroetmann" ("Scrap Electronics Ordinance: ZVEI Discusses Open Problems with Environmental Secretary of State Stroetmann"). April 29, 1993.

Ziwica, Karl-Heinz (BMW of North America). "Lessons from the German Experience with Vehicle Recycling." Massachusetts Institute of Technology: Design and Disposal of Durable Products Conference. Cambridge, MA: March 24-25, 1993.

Index

A

Abfall (waste), 2, 133
Advanced Disposal Fees (ADFs),
   189-190
Alliance '90/Greens, 16
Alter, Harvey, 126
Annighofer, Frank, 120
Apple Computer, 67, 143, 147
Arthur D. Little, Inc., 120, 127, 189-
   190
Association of Bavarian Retailers, 46,
   143
Association of European Plastics
   Manufacturers, 121
Association of German Chambers of
   Industry and Commerce (DIHT),
   51
Association of Local Authorities, 103
Association of the Electronics Indus-
   try (ZVEI), 142, 143
Association of Tool Makers (VDMA),
   142
Australia, PVC packaging phase out
   in, 107
Austria
   legislation for reduction and recy-
      cling of auto waste, 140
   "polluter pays" principle, 10, 127
Automobiles, proposed ordinance on
   the reduction and recycling of
   waste from, 135-140, 178-179
Automotive Dismantlers and Recyclers Association (ADRA), 139
Azar, Jack, 146

B

Baden-Württemberg, Germany, 156
   Dual System exemption (primary
      packaging), 50, 102
Barnier, Michel, 124
BASF, 99, 100
Baucus, Sen. Max, 7, 175, 190, 192
Bavaria, Germany
   Dual System exemption, 50
Bavarian Retailers Association, 46,
   143
Bayerische Moteren Werke A. G.
   (BMW), 137, 139-140
Belgium
   and the European Community (EC)
      packaging directive, 204
   "FOST PLUS," 127
   German exports of packaging ma-
      terials to, 123
   MTS in, 39
   "polluter pays" principle, 10
Berlin Technical College (TFB), 59,
   64, 100, 105
Beverage cartons, recycling, 57
Beverage container system, maintain-
   ing the refillable, 82-98
Beverage containers
   disposable, ban on, 153
   environmental debate of one-way
      vs. refillable, 84-85
   US policy and refillable, 186-188
Bins
   per-bin charges, 176, 177

D

DEKUR-Kunststoff Recycling GmbH (DKR), 54, 105-106
Dell Computer Corp., 143
Denmark
  German exports of packaging materials to, 123
  on European Community (EC) packaging directive, 166, 202, 204
Deposits on refillable bottles, 89-92
Deutscher Industrie- und Handlestag (DIHT). See Association of German Chambers of Industry and Commerce (DIHT)
Disposables
  at events held on public property, banning, 153
  taxing, 153
Dow Chemical Co., 193
Drop-off and curbside collection, 51
Dual System, 22
  criticisms of the, 113-130
  establishing the, 49-51
  exemption negotiations and DSD, 49-50
  financing the, 58-68
  primary packaging and the, 48-81
  recycling and the, 51-58
  and refillables, 115-116
  revenue for municipalities and shifting financial responsibility, 68-70
Duales System Deutschland GmbH (DSD), 22
  contracts with the, 68-69, 119, 155
  criticisms of the, 113-130
  drop-off and curbside collection, 51

Duales System Deutschland GmbH (continued)
  Dual System exemption negotiations and, 49-50
  exports of used packaging materials, 165
  financial crisis of 1993, 59-60, 197-200
  and Germany's antitrust laws, 120-121
  and localities, 68-70, 119
  membership in, 50-51
  packaging reduction surveys, 74-75
  and the plastics industry, 99-110
  recyclables dumped abroad, 122
  refill rates for beverages and, 25
  revenues and costs, 58-59
  and secondary packaging, 43, 44-45
  stockpiling recyclables, 116-117
  the waste management system and harmonization of, 68-70

E

"Eco-balance" (life-cycle analysis) of packaging, 84
"Eco-Emballage" system, 127
Electric and electronic equipment, proposed ordinance on the reduction and recycling of used, 141-147, 178-179
EMMAUS, 154
Energiewerke Schwarze Pumpe (ESPAG) gasification plant, 104
Environmental impact assessment (EIA), 145
European Commission, 20, 121, 193

N

O

P

Tetra Pak, 87, 89

Thermal recycling. See Waste-to-energy incineration

Töpfer, Klaus
  on Closed-Loop Economy and Waste Management Act, 132, 134
  and DSD, 103, 121, 194, 197-198, 200
  and the European Community (EC) packaging directive, 203
  and the Green Party, 16
  on life-cycle analysis, 84
  and Packaging Ordinance, 18, 20, 31, 115
  on results of GVM study, 71, 74
  and secondary packaging, 43

Transboundary shipment of waste, European Community regulation of the, 163-164

Transport packaging
  Heidelberg ban on, 158
  Packaging Ordinance's rules for, 21, 33-35
  reusable transport containers, 35-41

Trippage rates, 85, 93

TÜVs. See Technical Inspection Agencies (TÜVs)

U

Ullman, Al, 184

Ulm, Germany, export of waste for disposal, 4

Umweltbundesamt (UBA). See Federal Environmental Agency

"Umweltzentrum West" (Environment Center West) pilot project, 154

United Kingdom
  BMW recycling centers in the, 139
  on European Community (EC) packaging directive, 166, 169, 204
  German exports of
    packaging materals to the, 123
    paper to the, 58
    plastics to the, 200
    recyclable packaging to the, 123
  legislation for the reduction and recycling of auto waste, 140
  MTS in the, 39
  view of packaging industry, 125

United States
  BMW recycling project in the, 139-140
  computer industry, 143-147
  EC packaging legislation and the, 161-162, 164
  Gross Domestic Product (GDP) in the, 13
  implications of the German approach for US waste policy, 172-196
  incineration, 4
  landfills in the, 4
  municipal solid waste in the, 2
  municipal solid waste management structure in the, 15
  municipal solid waste problems in the, 4
  plastics to Indonesian recycling plants, 124
  "polluter pays" principle and hazardous waste management, 194
  population density in the, 11, 12
  PVC packaging phase out in the, 107, 109

Wuppertal, Germany (continued)
  Municipal Solid Waste Depart-
    ment, 154
  University of Wuppertal, 159
Wuppertal Institute, 119

X

Xerox Corp., 145-147, 193

Z

Zenith Electronics Corp., 143
Zentralverband Elektrotechnik-und
  Elektronikindustrie e.V. (ZVEI).
  See Association of the Electronics
  Industry (ZVEI)

About the Author

Bette K. Fishbein

Bette Fishbein joined INFORM in March 1990 and is Senior Fellow in the Municipal Solid Waste Program. For INFORM, Ms. Fishbein has directed research projects that include solid waste planning for states and municipalities, development of source reduction initiatives in the business sector, and development of a methodology for evaluating recycling programs. Her speeches and testimony on solid waste have focused on source redution. She is the principal author of *Making Less Garbage: A Planning Guide for Communities*, published in January 1993. She is also the co-author of *Reducing Office Paper Waste* (December 1991).

Previously, Ms. Fishbein was an economist and public policy analyst for the Institute for Socioeconomic Studies in White Plains, New York, directing research on social welfare policy. She is the author of *Social Welfare Abroad* and articles on social welfare, the consumer price index, and the food stamp program. Ms. Fishbein has also been a research analyst with the National Bureau of Economic Research and Resources for the Future and an intern with the Joint Economic Committee. She received a B.A. from Wellesley College and graduated Phi Beta Kappa, with honors in economics.

INFORM Publications and Membership

Publications

Municipal Solid Waste
Selected Publications

Case Reopened: Reassessing Refillable Bottles (David Saphire), Spring 1994, ca. 150 pp., $25.

Making Less Garbage: A Planning Guide for Communities (Bette K. Fishbein and Caroline Gelb), 1993, 192 pp., $30.

Business Recycling Manual (copublished with Recourse Systems, Inc.), 1991, 202 pp., $85.

Burning Garbage in the US: Practice vs. State of the Art (Marjorie J. Clarke, Maarten de Kadt, Ph.D., and David Saphire), 1991, 288 pp., $47.

Reducing Office Paper Waste (Robert Graff and Bette Fishbein), 1991, 28 pp., $15.

Garbage Management in Japan: Leading the Way (Allen Hershkowitz, Ph.D., and Eugene Salerni, Ph.D.), 1987, 152 pp., $15.

Garbage Burning: Lessons from Europe: Consensus and Controversy in Four European States (Allen Hershkowitz, Ph.D.), 1986, 64 pp., $9.95.

Chemical Hazards
Prevention
Selected Publications

Preventing Industrial Toxic Hazards: A Guide for Communities (Marian Wise and Lauren Kenworthy), 1993, 208 pp., $25.

Environmental Dividends: Cutting More Chemical Wastes (Mark H. Dorfman, Warren R. Muir, Ph.D., and Catherine G. Miller, Ph.D.), 1992, 288 pp., $75.

Tackling Toxics in Everyday Products: A Directory of Organizations (Nancy Lilienthal, Michèle Ascione, and Adam Flint), 1992, 192 pp., $19.95.

259

Toward a More Informed Public: Recommendations for Improving the Toxics Release Inventory (Jacqueline B. Courteau and Nancy Lilienthal), 1991, 26 pp., $10.

Preventing Pollution Through Technical Assistance: One State's Experience (Mark H. Dorfman and John Riggio), 1990, 72 pp., $15.

Cutting Chemical Wastes: What 29 Organic Chemical Plants Are Doing to Reduce Hazardous Wastes (David J. Sarokin, Warren R. Muir, Ph.D., Catherine G. Miller, Ph.D., and Sebastian R. Sperber), 1986, 548 pp., $47.50.

Energy and Air Quality

Paving the Way to Natural Gas Vehicles (James S. Cannon), 1993, 192 pp., $25.

Other INFORM Publications

For a complete publications list, including materials on land and water conservation and a quarterly newsletter, or for more information, call or write to INFORM.

Sales Information

Payment

Payment, including shipping and handling charges, must be made in US funds drawn on a US bank and must accompany all orders. Please make checks payable to INFORM and mail to:

INFORM, Inc.
381 Park Avenue South
New York, NY 10016-8806

Please include a street address; UPS cannot deliver to a box number.

Shipping Fees

United States:	add $3 for first book + $1 for each additional book. (4th class delivery; allow 4-6 weeks)
Canada:	add $5 for first book + $3 each additional book.
Foreign/surface:	add $8 for first book +$4 each additional book.
Foreign/airmail:	add $20 for first book + $10 each additional book.
Outside the US:	allow additional shipping time.

Priority shipping is higher; please call for charges.

Discount Policy

Booksellers: 20% on 1-4 copies of same title; 30% on 5 or more copies of same title

General bulk: 20% on 5 or more copies of same title

Public interest and community groups providing tax-exempt certificate:

	Price:
Books under $10:	No discount
Books $10-$25:	$10
Books $25 and up:	$15

Government, upon request: Books $45 and under – No discount; Books over $45 – $45

Returns

Booksellers may return books, in saleable condition, for full credit or cash refund up to 6 months from date of invoice. Books must be returned prepaid and include a copy of the invoice or packing list showing invoice number, date, list price, and original discount.

Membership

Individuals provide an important source of support to INFORM and receive the following benefits:

Member ($25): A one-year subscription to *INFORM Reports*, INFORM's quarterly newsletter.

Friend ($50): A one-year subscription to *INFORM Reports* and advance notice of new publications.

Contributor ($100): Friend's benefits, plus a 10% discount on new INFORM studies.

Supporter ($250): Friend's benefits, plus a 20% discount on new INFORM studies.

Donor ($500): Friend's benefits, plus a 30% discount on new INFORM studies.

Associate ($1000): Friend's benefits, plus a complimentary copy of new INFORM studies.

Benefactor ($5000): Friend's benefits, plus a complimentary copy of new INFORM studies.

All contributions are tax-deductible.

INFORM Board of Directors